Beginning with Deep Learning Using TensorFlow

A Beginners Guide to TensorFlow and Keras for Practicing Deep Learning Principles and Applications

Mohan Kumar Silaparasetty

www.bpbonline.com

FIRST EDITION 2022
Copyright © BPB Publications, India
ISBN: 978-93-55510-471

All Rights Reserved. No part of this publication may be reproduced, distributed or transmitted in any form or by any means or stored in a database or retrieval system, without the prior written permission of the publisher with the exception to the program listings which may be entered, stored and executed in a computer system, but they can not be reproduced by the means of publication, photocopy, recording, or by any electronic and mechanical means.

LIMITS OF LIABILITY AND DISCLAIMER OF WARRANTY

The information contained in this book is true to correct and the best of author's and publisher's knowledge. The author has made every effort to ensure the accuracy of these publications, but publisher cannot be held responsible for any loss or damage arising from any information in this book.

All trademarks referred to in the book are acknowledged as properties of their respective owners but BPB Publications cannot guarantee the accuracy of this information.

To View Complete
BPB Publications Catalogue
Scan the QR Code:

www.bpbonline.com

Dedicated to

Shanthi
my wife and my best friend.

Vinita and **Nikita**
Our lovely daughters

About the Author

Mohan Kumar Silaparasetty is a recognized thought leader in AI and emerging technologies. He is a graduate from IIT Kharagpur with more than 30 years of experience in the IT industry in a variety of roles. He is an author, keynote speaker, trainer and entrepreneur.

He worked for global MNC's like SAP and IBM in a variety of leadership roles. He has also gained international exposure during this stint with SAP America in the USA.

About the Reviewer

Dr Vinita Jindal is an Associate Professor in the Department of Computer Science, Keshav Mahavidyalaya, the University of Delhi having more than 20 years of experience. She did her Doctorate in Computer Science from the University of Delhi. She is mainly working in the area of Artificial Intelligence and Networks. Her areas of interest include Network Protocols, Cybersecurity, Intrusion Detection Systems, Dark Web, Deep Learning, Recommender Systems and Vehicular Adhoc Networks to name a few.

Acknowledgement

There are a few people I want to thank for the continued and ongoing support they have given me during the writing of this book. First and foremost, I would like to thank my wife and my daughters, Vinita and Nikita for their encouragement and support throughout the process.

I would like to thank BPB Publications for giving me this opportunity to write my first book for them.

Preface

With VDI deployments, IT teams would need to build and manage several gold images such that they can be used as templates for these virtual desktop machines so that the right applications can be delivered to the correct end users. It also meant that they would potentially need to rebuild a gold image just so that they could update a single application. This would mean spending a large proportion of their time building and configuring desktop images, taking time, and even worse, introducing end user downtime should anything go wrong.

To address this issue of having several different gold builds to manage applications and operating systems as one, admins needed a solution whereby they could manage the applications independently. A way that is very familiar today in how virtualization works is by abstracting the operating systems from the hardware. However, this time you are one level up, with abstracting the applications from the operating system. This approach would allow admins to deliver apps independently.

One of the ways how applications can be abstracted from the underlying operating system, and be able to deliver them back independently, is via application layering. With application layering, admins can create that layer of abstraction, separate the applications from the underlying OS and deliver them back to the end users on demand. Equally, they can also be removed. As the applications are now independent of the operating system, they can be easily patched and updated without having to touch the operating system image.

VMware added an application layering solution to its end user computing portfolio in August 2014, when they acquired a start-up company called CloudVolumes. CloudVolumes provided a virtualized, real-time application-delivery engine for virtual desktop infrastructures as well as physical desktops.

In December 2014, CloudVolumes was rebranded and renamed as App Volumes.

What does App Volumes deliver? At a high level, App Volumes provides a real-time application-delivery and application life cycle management solution, which can be used as a delivery system for your virtual desktop machine and remote app session servers.

viii

The primary goal of this book is to provide information and skills that are necessary to deploy VMware App Volumes in your own environment. This book contains real-life examples that will show you how to install, configure, and manage VMware App Volumes, as well as how to integrate it into other VMware and third-party solutions.

Over the 7 chapters in this book, you will learn the following:

Chapter 1 Introduces the high level concepts of Artificial Intelligence, Machine Learning and Deep Learning.

Chapter 2 Basic Machine Learning concepts required for Deep Learning. Steps to set up the Python environment to develop ML models.

Chapter 3 Programming with TensorFlow 1.x. This chapter covers the concepts of computational graphs and sessions of TensorFlow 1.x. Provides a lot of code examples.

Chapter 4 The concepts of Neural networks are covered in a systematic step by step manner using TensorFlow 1.x. Starting a an implementation of single neuron (Perceptron), all the way to a deep multilayer neural network. The MNIST case study is used as an example.

Chapter 5 this chapter introduces TensorFlow 2.x and Keras. It covers how to develop and train deep neural networks with several code examples.

Chapter 6 Convolution Neural Networks are introduced in this chapter with practical examples of how to build binary and multiclass image classifiers with TensorFlow and Keras. This chapter also covers how to build object detection applications using pretrained models.

Chapter 7 The last chapter covers Speech Recognition and Natural language processing (NLP). It covers the traditional Recurrent Neural Networks (RNN) and the latest Transformers. Provides code examples to develop NLP tasks like sentiment analysis and Question and Answer systems with pretrained language models. Readily usable code examples are provided to get you up and running quickly.

Code Bundle and Coloured Images

Please follow the link to download the
Code Bundle and the *Coloured Images* of the book:

https://rebrand.ly/lkqr41a

The code bundle for the book is also hosted on GitHub at **https://github.com/bpbpublications/Beginning-with-Deep-Learning-Using-TensorFlow**. In case there's an update to the code, it will be updated on the existing GitHub repository.

We have code bundles from our rich catalogue of books and videos available at **https://github.com/bpbpublications**. Check them out!

Errata

We take immense pride in our work at BPB Publications and follow best practices to ensure the accuracy of our content to provide with an indulging reading experience to our subscribers. Our readers are our mirrors, and we use their inputs to reflect and improve upon human errors, if any, that may have occurred during the publishing processes involved. To let us maintain the quality and help us reach out to any readers who might be having difficulties due to any unforeseen errors, please write to us at :

errata@bpbonline.com

Your support, suggestions and feedbacks are highly appreciated by the BPB Publications' Family.

Did you know that BPB offers eBook versions of every book published, with PDF and ePub files available? You can upgrade to the eBook version at www.bpbonline.com and as a print book customer, you are entitled to a discount on the eBook copy. Get in touch with us at :

business@bpbonline.com for more details.

At **www.bpbonline.com**, you can also read a collection of free technical articles, sign up for a range of free newsletters, and receive exclusive discounts and offers on BPB books and eBooks.

Piracy

If you come across any illegal copies of our works in any form on the internet, we would be grateful if you would provide us with the location address or website name. Please contact us at **business@bpbonline.com** with a link to the material.

If you are interested in becoming an author

If there is a topic that you have expertise in, and you are interested in either writing or contributing to a book, please visit **www.bpbonline.com**. We have worked with thousands of developers and tech professionals, just like you, to help them share their insights with the global tech community. You can make a general application, apply for a specific hot topic that we are recruiting an author for, or submit your own idea.

Reviews

Please leave a review. Once you have read and used this book, why not leave a review on the site that you purchased it from? Potential readers can then see and use your unbiased opinion to make purchase decisions. We at BPB can understand what you think about our products, and our authors can see your feedback on their book. Thank you!

For more information about BPB, please visit **www.bpbonline.com**.

Table of Contents

1. Introduction to Artificial Intelligence 1
Structure 1
Objective 1
Brief history of artificial intelligence 2
    Classification of AI 7
    How did we reach here? 9
AI adoption by industries 12
Conclusion 17
Points to remember 17

2. Machine Learning 19
Introduction 19
Structure 19
Objectives 20
Defining machine learning 20
    Supervised learning 22
Setting up the environment 24
    Using Google Colab 24
    Setting up local environment in Python 26
        Prerequisite 26
    Regression algorithms 34
        Code demo 37
    Multilinear regression 41
    Logistic regression 44
    Decision tree 46
    Support vector machine (SVM) 48
        Unsupervised learning 48
Conclusion 51
Questions 52

3. TensorFlow Programming 53
Introduction 53
Structure 53
Objective 54
TensorFlow development environment 54
Introducing TensorFlow 59
    Elements of TensorFlow program 62
        Constant 63
        Variable 63
        Placeholder 63
        Session 64
Constants, variables, and placeholders 65
    Linear algebra with TensorFlow 78
    Optimizer 86
        Applying optimizer to solve simple mathematical problems 92
Conclusion 93
Questions 94

4. Neural Networks 95
Introduction 95
Structure 96
Objective 96
About Neural Networks 96
    Inputs 99
    Weights 99
    Bias 100
    Net input function (F) 100
    Activation function (G) 100
    MNIST 119
MNIST—single layer multi-neuron model 126
    Multilayer Neural Network 130
    Multilayer binary classifier 131
ReLu activation function 135
Multilayer multiclass neural network 135

Conclusion	138
Questions	138

5. TensorFlow 2 139
Introduction 139
Structure 139
Objective 140
Installing TensorFlow 2 140
    Using Anaconda Navigator *140*
    From Anaconda command prompt *145*
        Google Colab *148*
    What is new in TensorFlow 2? *149*
    Kera API *151*
Classification with Iris data set 158
Conclusion 162
Points to remember 162

6. Image Recognition 163
Introduction 163
Structure 163
Objective 164
Introducing Convolutional Neural Networks (CNN) 164
    Convolution layer *166*
    MNIST with CNN *173*
    Binary image classification with Keras *181*
Multiclass image classification 189
Load from data frame—binary 197
Load from data frame—multiclass 203
    Save and restore models *208*
Pre-trained models 212
    Transfer learning *215*
Inference with Webcam images 224
Object detection 228
Conclusion 231
Points to remember 231

7. Speech Recognition 233
Introduction 233
Structure 233
Objective 234
What is speech recognition?—Historical perspective 234
    Application of speech recognition 235
Natural Language Processing (NLP) 239
    Word Embedding 240
        Language model 245
Recurrent Neural Networks (RNN) 245
Text classification 247
    Transformers 250
        Pre-trained transformer models 253
    BERT 256
Machine language translation 261
Q&A—SQUAD 263
Conclusion 266
Further reading 266

Index 267-271

CHAPTER 1
Introduction to Artificial Intelligence

In this first chapter, we will introduce artificial intelligence, deep learning, and TensorFlow. Although, it is expected that the people buying this book already have this knowledge and experience, it is a good way to lay the ground for a smooth transition in the upcoming chapters. This also helps in making sure the reader and the author are on the same page, especially with respect to terminology and method of coding and so on.

Structure

This chapter will cover the following topics:

- Brief history of AI
- Why now?
- Applications of AI
- Industry examples of AI applications

Objective

At the end of this chapter, you will be able to learn about artificial intelligence and its applications in various industries. You will get an understanding of the evolution of AI and the relation between **artificial intelligence (AI)**, **machine learning (ML)**, and **deep learning (DL)**.

Brief history of artificial intelligence

Today, we are on the verge of a huge technological revolution. Before we talk about AI, let us take a look at the multitude of emerging technologies (*Figure 1.1*). The convergence of these technologies along with AI will completely change the world in the next few decades.

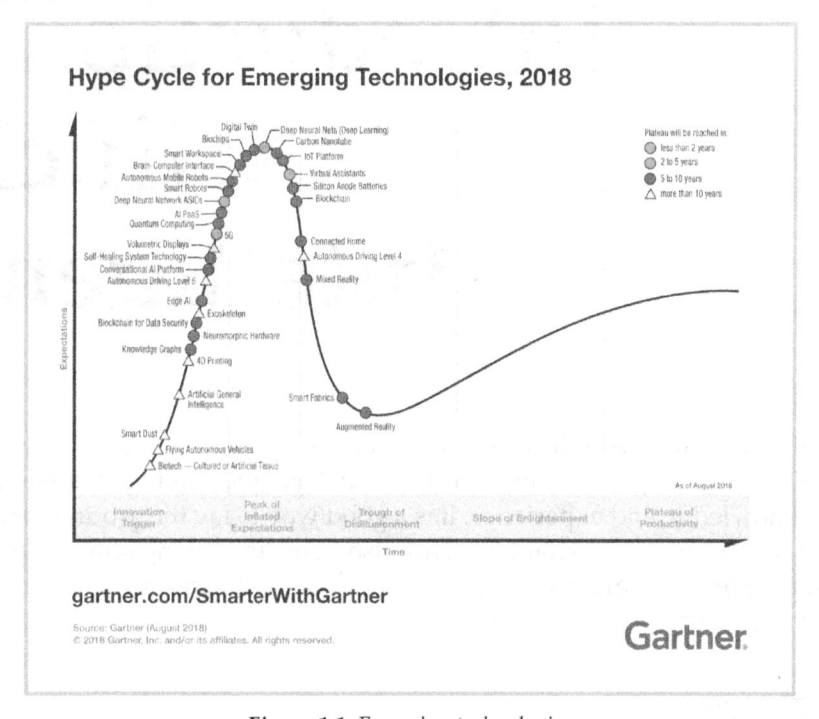

Figure 1.1: Emerging technologies

According to leading analysts, the following technologies will mature over the next 5–10 years:

- 5G
- BlockChain
- 3D printing
- IoT

These technologies, along with AI, are bound to have an immense impact on humankind. The way we work, live, and fight! Yes, Warfare will also be completely different and unimaginable. AI will, of course, play the biggest role in all of it.

So, what is AI, and how is it going to change our life. AI is the intelligence demonstrated by machines. A formal definition of AI as per Wikipedia:

In computer science, AI, sometimes called machine intelligence, is intelligence demonstrated by machines, in contrast to the natural intelligence displayed by humans.

Like it or not, AI is already here, although at a very basic level. We are all using AI, knowingly or unknowingly. Here are some examples as follows:

- Chatbots
- Robots
- Smart speakers (Alexa)
- Virtual assistants
- Recommendation engines
- Drones
- Self-driving cars or autonomous vehicles.

Figure 1.2*: AI is here (source: Google)*

For all the buzz around AI over the past few years, this is not a new concept. The term Artificial Intelligence was first coined by *Prof. John McCarthy* at a conference at Dartmouth College in 1956.

And even before that, there was a semblance of a humanoid robot in Greek Mythology. *Talos* was a giant automaton made of bronze to protect the mythological character Europa – after whom Europe was named. Talos circled the island's shores thrice daily to protect Europa from pirates and invaders.

And then, there was the *Turing* test developed by *Alan Turing* in 1950.

According to Wikipedia, *"Turing Test is a test of a machine's ability to exhibit intelligent behavior equivalent to, or indistinguishable from, that of a human."*

This is a test of model Natural Language Processing as this considers just conversations and in text-only mode.

In 1966, *Joseph Weizenbaum*, a professor at MIT, created a program called ELIZA, which can be considered to be the first Chatbot. ELIZA appeared to pass the Turing test. The program worked by identifying keywords. If a keyword is found, a rule that transforms the user's comments is applied, and the resulting sentence is returned.

A few years later in 1972, another program named *Parry* was created by *Kenneth Colby* – a pioneer in cognitive functions. It was like an enhanced version of ELIZA. It could simulate a paranoid schizophrenic.

Back to the Dartmouth conference, there was a lot of excitement after the conference, and the USA government even granted funds to conduct research on AI, but it could not take off. After a couple of years of research, the project was put on the back burner – this is referred to as the winter of AI.

One of the reasons was the lack of computing power. Subsequently, the interest in AI was renewed in the 90s. With the advent of cloud computing and cheap hardware, the availability of computing power tremendously increased. In addition to that, the availability of a large amount of data and the ability to handle large amounts of data with technologies like Hadoop has further strengthened AI research. It is like all the pieces of the puzzle falling in place.

One of the highly publicized events of the resurrection of AI was IBM Watson. In 2011, IBM Watson was pitted against the reigning human champions of the game show called Jeopardy, and it won. However, the term AI has not yet regained the popularity as it has today, and hence, Watson was just called a supercomputer. But the Natural Language Processing technique that was used is a significant component of Artificial Intelligence. And today, Watson is, of course, called AI.

It has to be noted that it was not the first time that such an event has occurred where a machine beat a human being. Way back in 1997, a supercomputer named Deep Blue defeated the reigning world champion of Chess – Gary Kasparov. And Deep Blue was also developed by IBM.

Figure 1.3: IBM Deep Blue (source: www.stream-live-tvchannel.top/ProductDetail. aspx?iid=88929267&pr=40.88)

However, the difference is that Deep Blue was actually just a supercomputer with the ability to evaluate 200 million positions per second. So, it was brute force rather than any learning. Hence, it was not AI.

Then, in March 2016, AlphaGo an AI developed by a startup Deep Mind defeated the reigning world champion of Go named *Lee Sedol* 4 games to 1. This was truly a watershed moment in AI, and even the AI experts were shocked. Not because they did not believe AI could achieve this feat but because it has done it so fast.

Deep Mind was set up in 2013 with the idea of developing an AI to play the game of Go, and the experts believed it would take a good decade, if not more, to achieve this feat. And they were shocked when the AI achieved this in less than four years. Subsequently, of course, Google acquired Deep Mind:

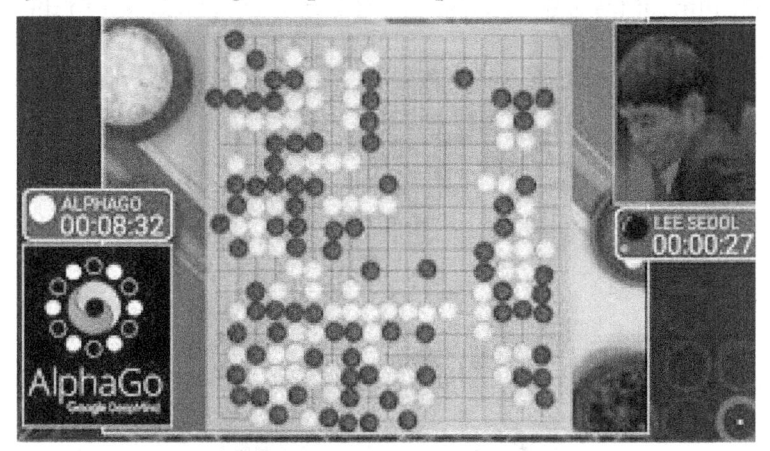

Figure 1.4: DeepMind's AlphaGo (source: https://247newsupdate.com/2016/03/12/computer-program-beats-human-master-in-go-game/)

This was a significant achievement at multiple levels. For one, Go, unlike Chess, is a game of intuition rather than rules. And there are these many legal positions as shown in *Figure 1.5*:

208,168,199,381,979,984,699,478,633,344,862,770,286,522,

453,884,530,548,425,639,456,820,927,419,612,738,015,378,

525,648,451,698,519,643,907,259,916,015,628,128,546,089,

888,314,427, 129,715,319,317,557,736,620,397,247,064,840,

935.

Figure 1.5: Number of legal positions in Go

And to put this in context, this is more than the number of atoms in the whole of the universe – yes, the universe, not just earth.

So, there is no way anyone can write a program for this. Then, how did Deep Mind achieve it? They used a technique called *reinforcement learning* which is a form of deep learning. In this technique, the system learns by playing the game over and over, perhaps several tens of million times and each time learning from its mistakes and improving itself.

This was probably the first time a machine has, in a way, shown signs of intuition!

Another significant incident in the world of AI took place on November 4, 2017. Saudi Arabia conferred citizenship on a humanoid robot called *Sophia*, which was developed by *Hansen Robotics*. Experts are divided over the capabilities of Sophia – some even calling it fake; this just shows the amount of interest in the field of AI.

Figure 1.6: Sophia (https://simple.wikipedia.org/wiki/Sophia_(robot))

Classification of AI

AI is classified into three categories, as shown in *Figure 1.7*.

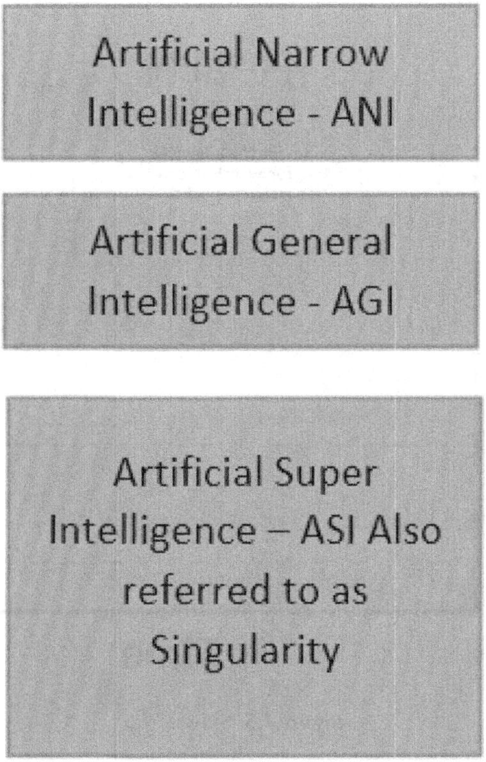

```
Artificial Narrow
Intelligence - ANI

Artificial General
Intelligence - AGI

Artificial Super
Intelligence – ASI Also
referred to as
Singularity
```

Figure 1.7: Types of AI

Artificial Narrow Intelligence (ANI), also referred to as an expert system, is a system that can perform one task but can perform much better than human beings. Today's AI like AlphaGo and autonomous vehicles fall in this category.

Artificial Super Intelligence (ASI), also referred to as singularity, on the other hand, is a system that can perform multiple tasks and all of them significantly better than human beings. This is like the holy grail of AI and would take at least 30–40 years from now, if not more.

Artificial General Intelligence (AGI) is an intermediate stage where the AI will perform multiple tasks, and in one or two of them, it will be better than humans. In spite of all the buzz today around AI, we are still at the ANI stage. We barely scratched the surface.

However, the move toward ASI or singularity will be relatively faster. Even if it takes 50 years from now, that is too fast when viewed within the context of the time frame of human civilization. This is often depicted in the form of the following diagram:

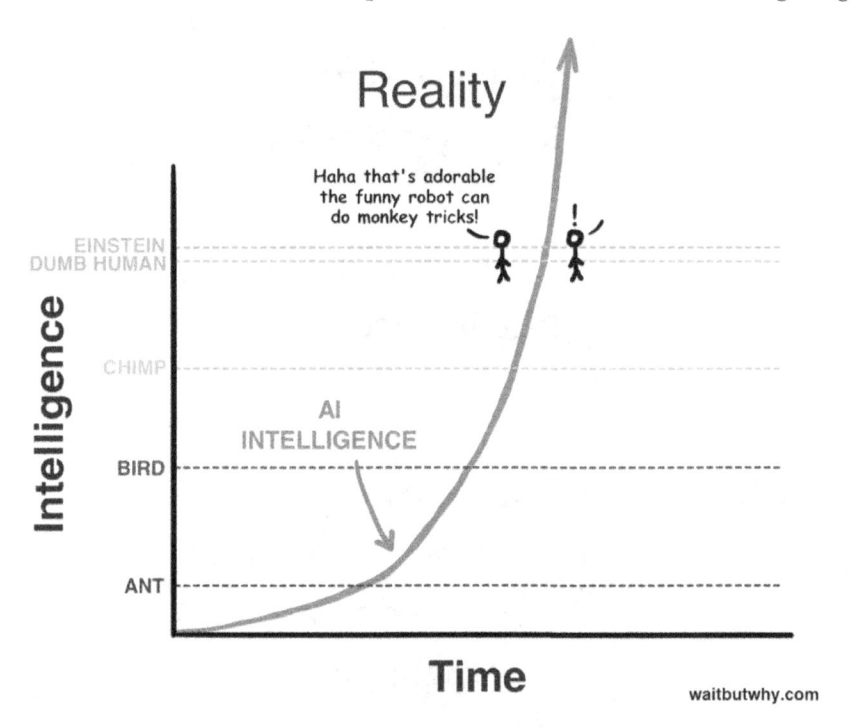

Figure 1.8: Singularity

This concept is explained brilliantly by *Tim Urban* in his blog post titled:

The AI Revolution: The Road to Superintelligence.

This is available on the following link:

https://waitbutwhy.com/2015/01/artificial-intelligence-revolution-1.html

Let us take a closer look at AI. AI is aimed at developing intelligence in machines along with the lines of the human brain. Human intelligence, in a simplified manner, can be explained as decisions taken based on the inputs received from our five senses – sight, hearing, touch, smell, and taste.

The actions taken are in the form of speech or movement. Today's AI is capable of sight, hearing, and speech. The two main branches of AI today are Image recognition that corresponds to sight, and speech recognition that corresponds to speech and hearing.

These will be discussed in great detail in the upcoming chapters. AI is a broad concept and the underlying techniques used are known as *machine learning* and *deep learning*.

That is the reason very often these terms are used interchangeably or together like AI-ML or AI-DL.

The following figure depicts the relation between AI, ML, and DL:

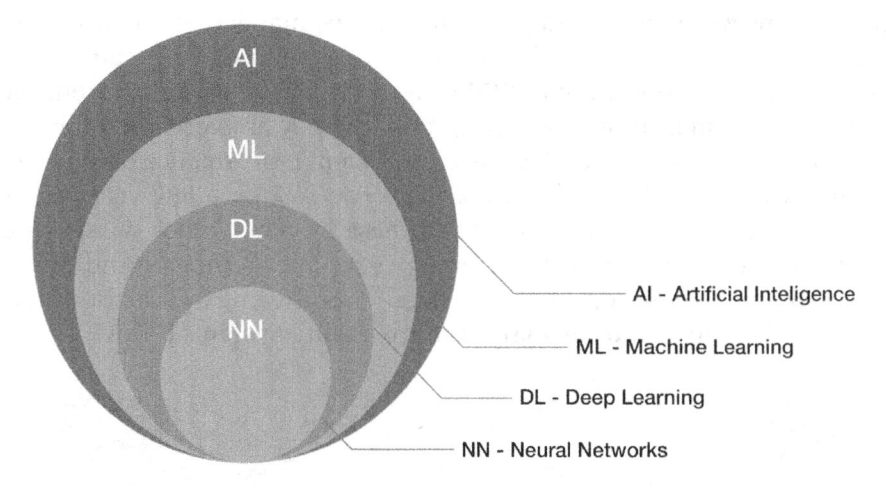

Figure 1.9: AI, ML and DL

The secret sauce to AI is neural networks which are used in deep learning. And deep learning is a subset of machine learning.

We will take a look at machine learning in the next chapter.

How did we reach here?

Today, AI is a part of the field called data science. Data science involves the process of data capture all the way to taking action based on the data.

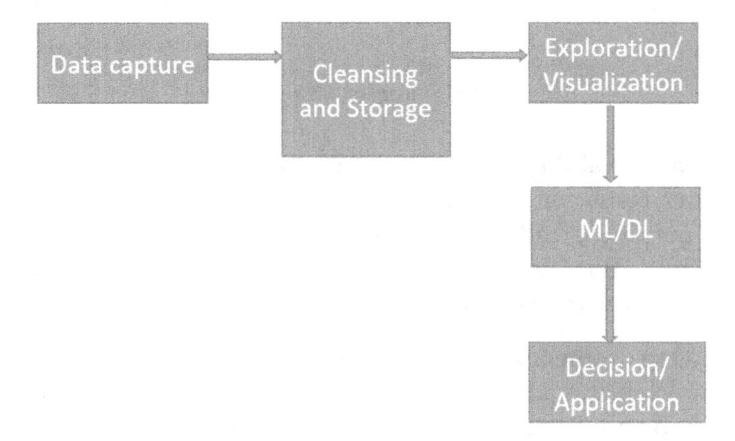

Figure 1.10: Data Science

It all began with the information technology revolution with started in the 1990s when we started creating and storing data. Initially, software was used for office automation – such as word processing, spreadsheets, and so on where the data was stored in the form of files. Then, came the enterprise automation era, where ERP applications were developed to capture orders, manage production, sales, and distribution, and so on. This was the beginning of generating larger amount of data. Around this time, the concept of RDBMS was born. These are transactional systems known as **online transaction processing (OLTP)**. They are very good for capturing the data. However, when the data grows, the system performance deteriorates, and that is what was happening with most OLTP systems after a few years. In order to maintain the high level of performance of these systems, older data was backed up from the live databases and stored on tapes for later retrieval. And this made it difficult to run an analysis on the entire data. This gave birth to data warehouses, which are also known as **online analytical processing systems (OLAP)**.

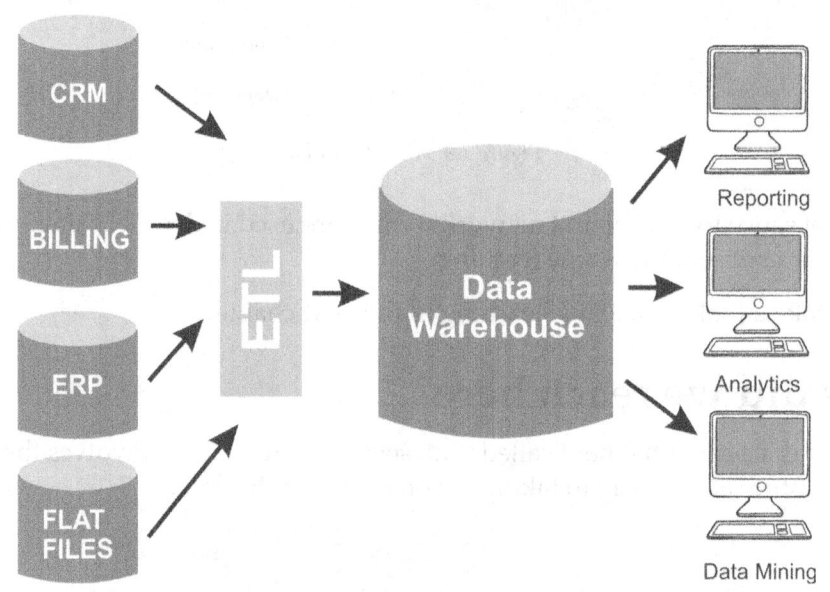

Figure 1.11: Business Intelligence (BI)

These systems had the ability to store large amounts of data from different systems, and they are much faster for querying. Data is transferred from the OLTP systems to the OLAP systems periodically – typically at the end of the day. This kept the OLTP systems lean while allowing you to repot and analyze the historical data on the OLAP system. This was the beginning of *business analytics*.

Data kept growing tremendously over the next few years. This was primarily structured data. With the advent of social media in the late 90s, including search engines like Yahoo and Google, there was an explosion in unstructured data – text, video, and audio.

Introduction to Artificial Intelligence ■ 11

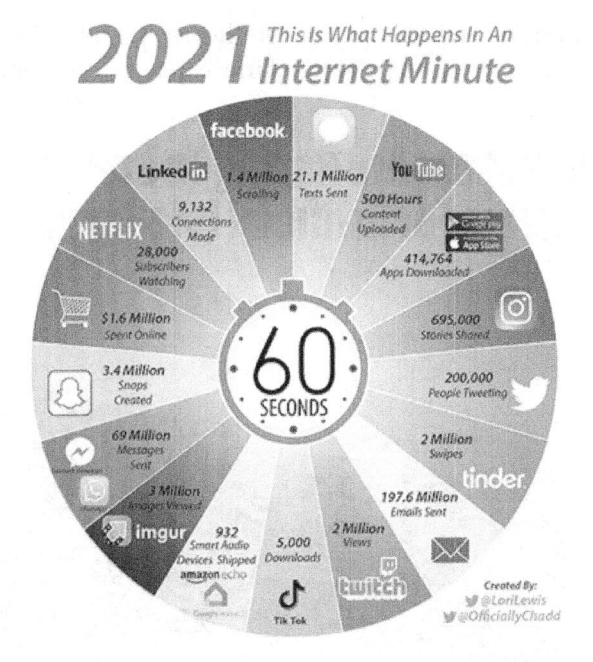

Figure 1.12: Internet minute

This was the advent of Big Data. Traditional databases and warehouses were unable to handle Big Data. That led to the Big Data technology – Hadoop.

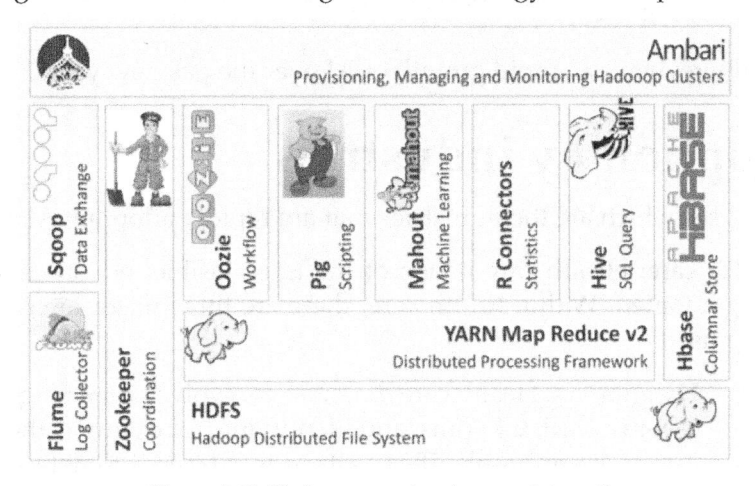

Figure 1.13: Hadoop ecosystem (source: Internet)

Hadoop was developed in the early 2000s and has matured over the years enabling us to handle large amounts of data at a terabyte-scale with ease, including unstructured data. In the meanwhile, data started growing at an exponential rate. And the availability of large amounts of data helped in the revival of machine learning, deep learning, and AI.

This is like the falling of all the pieces of the AI puzzle. Availability of cheap hardware – including GPU's, huge computing capacity on-demand on cloud and large amounts of data.

Figure 1.14: Hardware (source: www.fastcompany.com/3065843/ artificial-intelligence-chips-race-nvidia-intel)

This led to the revival and rapid growth of AI over the past few years.

AI adoption by industries

Now we will see which are the industries that are rapidly adopting AI as follows:

- **Health care**: Health care is one of the most visible industries where AI is being adopted. Within health care, there are three major areas where AI is being used:
    - **Diagnostics**: Health care diagnostics involves analyzing images such as x-ray, MRI, CT scans, and identifying, for example, the presence of cancer. For example, IBM Watson was trained to detect and predict lung cancer. In these scenarios, deep learning models are trained to classify images into cancerous and non-cancerous. Once trained, these models can then predict the presence of cancer in new images. There is still a lot of research is going on in this space to improve the accuracy of the prediction. Doctors are using these as productivity tools to prioritize and speed up the diagnostic process. As of date, these cannot replace doctors.

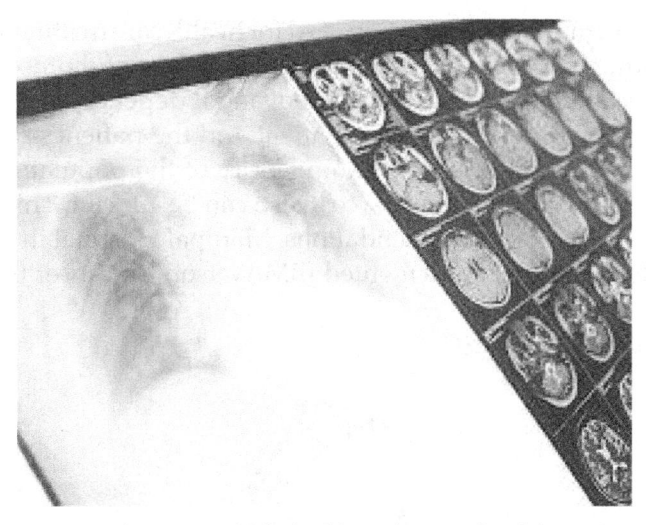

Figure 1.15: AI for healthcare (source: Google)

Blindness is another major problem facing the world. Accordingly to **World Health Organization (WHO)** – 1.3 billion people have some form of vision impairment, out of which 36 million are blind. While some forms of blindness are congenital and cannot be prevented, many forms of blindness are avoidable if detected in time. For example: Diabetic Retinopathy. And this is where companies like Microsoft and Google are conducting a lot of research.

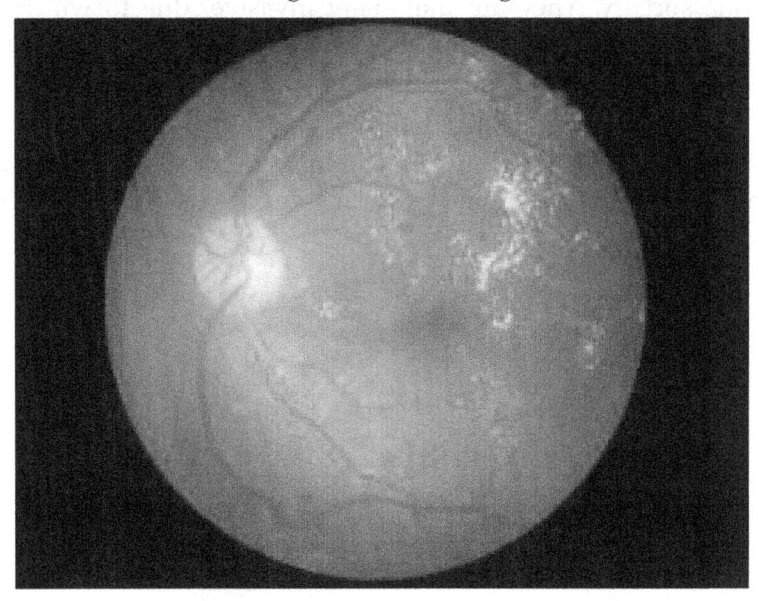

Figure 1.16: Diabetic retinopathy (source: www.clinicaladvisor.com/home/topics/diabetes-information-center/fda-approves-ai-device-to-detect-diabetic-retinopathy/)

o **Treatment**: The adoption of AI for health care treatment is not very well known. Cancer treatment is a long and painful process. The course of treatment needs to be planned, and it depends on several factors like the health history of the patient and the patient's immediate family. And in countries where a majority of the population is not covered by medical insurance – cost also can be a factor. This is where AI can be used for recommendations. Manipal Hospital in Bangalore, India, for example, implemented IBM Watson for cancer treatment.

Figure 1.17: IBM Watson (source: www.giannibarbacetto.it/wp-content/uploads/2017/03/ibmwatson_logo-1)

- **Robotic surgery:** Robotic surgery or AI-assisted robotic surgery involves performing surgeries using robotic arms. There are several advantages of Robotic surgery. They are minimally invasive, due to which the patient recover faster and the hospital time is minimal. There is less blood loss and minimum risk of infection.

  The robotic arms can be operated remotely, which means the surgeon need not be physically present and can conduct the surgery remotely that, in turn, means an expert surgeon can perform surgeries at multiple locations, sitting in one place.

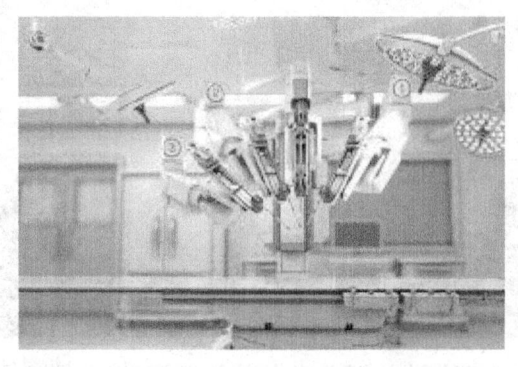

Figure 1.18: Robotic surgery (source: https://www.fontanaheraldnews.com/news/inland_empire_news/local-boys-suffering-ends-thanks-to-robotic-assisted-surgery-at-loma-linda-university-childrens-hospital)

- **Automotive**: Autonomous vehicles or driverless cars have now been tested successfully for millions of miles by several companies, including Google and Tesla. They are still not commercially deployed on a large scale but are being made available on an experimental basis in many locations. Let us take a look at the functioning of an autonomous vehicle.

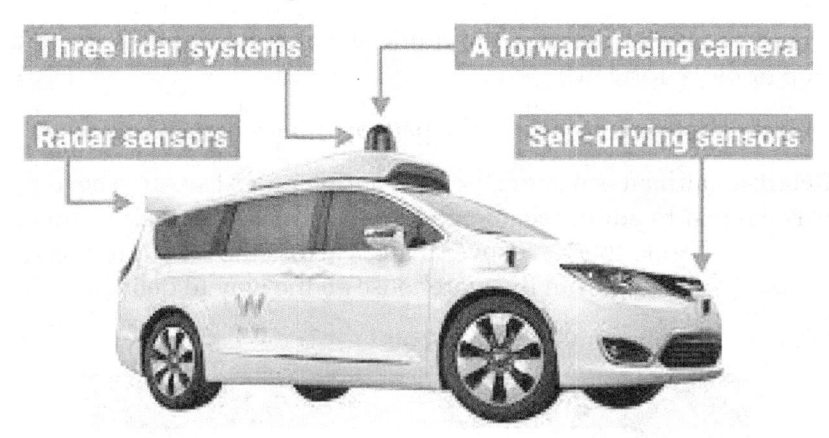

Figure 1.19: Wymo autonomous car (source: http://globalstudieshonorstopics.blogspot.com/2017/10/self-driving-cars_27.html)

Autonomous vehicles have a whole set of paraphernalia attached to them. There is a Lidar that is mounted on the top, which provides a 360 degree perspective of obstacles around the car. A Lidar functions similar to Radar, but it uses a laser instead of radio waves.

Figure 1.20: Lidar (source: www.powerelectronicsnews.com/digital-power-combined-with-gan-heads-towards-99-efficiency/)

In addition, there are other regular radars in the front and back to detect any immediate obstacles. There are multiple cameras providing streaming video, which is analyzed in real-time by the onboard AI system.

It has a GPS system to provide location information and also maps to determine the route. The onboard AI that is a trained Neural Network model takes all the inputs from various sensors to process and take decisions such as applying the brakes, accelerating, or turning left or right.

For example, from the video feed from the front cameras, the onboard AI would be able to detect if the traffic signal is Red or Green and according stop or move forward.

Or if it detects an obstacle in the path, it applies brakes, and so on.

- **Retail**: Retail has been one of the early adopters of AI ad ML. The retail industry was the first to adopt recommendation engines – on their e-commerce sites and apps. Today there are several areas across the retail process where AI is adopted – starting from the warehouse all the way to delivery using drones.

  Warehouse management with robots.

Figure 1.21: Warehouse robots (source: www.istockphoto.com/photos/warehouse-robot)

Retail organizations have to maintain huge warehouses for quick and efficient fulfilment. And managing these warehouses is a highly complicated task. In the past, there was Warehouse management software developed by companies like SAP, but even implementing such software is extremely cumbersome.

Today AI is being adopted in the form of robots in these warehouses, especially for fulfilling orders. This drastically reduces the time for packaging. Earlier the warehouse employees had to manually move from bin to bin in order to put together the items of the order and package them. Now with these robots, the employee stays in one place and summons the bins that contain the items of the order. The robots carry the bins. They are autonomous and move around in the warehouse without colliding with each other or other obstacles in their way.

In addition to the warehouse, the retail industry is adopting AI in the brick and mortar model as well. Amazon introduced unmanned physical retail stores called AmazonGo. Customers can just walk in, pick what they want and walk out. The items will be automatically detected, and the customer gets billed accordingly online. They used computer vision, sensor technology and deep learning to achieve this.

The retail industry is also adopting drone delivery to reduce the delivery time. Today the average delivery time for products ordered online (other than food delivery) is 24 hours, as the delivery is mainly done by the shipping company. This is where companies like Amazon are exploring the use of drones for delivery. This could potentially bring down the delivery time to a few hours, if not minutes.

- **Manufacturing**: Manufacturing was one of the early adopters of robots in the assembly line. However, these were electromechanical programmable robots with no AI. Today AI-enabled robots are available for use on the shop floor. These robots can see and move autonomously. In addition, they can also work as teams. This tremendously increases the efficiency.

Conclusion

There are many other industries such as financial services, real estate, and energy where AI is being rapidly adopted. In a decade, a lot of these applications will become commonplace and will be commoditized.

This brings us to the end of this introductory chapter. In the next chapter, we will get into the technical aspects of artificial intelligence, starting with machine learning.

Points to remember

- AI is one of the leading emerging technologies.
- AI, along with other emerging technologies such as 5G, IoT, and BlockChain, will change our lives over the next 5–10 years.
- AI is already here, and we see rapid adoption of AI in every industry.

CHAPTER 2
Machine Learning

Introduction

Machine learning is a vast topic, and detailed coverage is out of the scope of this book. However, an understanding of the basic tenets of machine learning is essential for deep learning, and hence, that is what is covered in this chapter. If you would like to do a deep dive into machine learning, it may be a good idea to get hold of one of the several books available on machine learning.

In this chapter, we will take a practical approach. We will cover the basics of machine learning that are essential to understanding deep learning. And we will take a hands-on approach with code examples rather than going into theory in detail.

If you are already familiar with and have done some work in machine learning using Python and scikit-learn, you may choose to skip this chapter.

Structure

In this chapter, the following topics will be covered:

- Machine learning
- Types of ML:
    - Supervised learning

- Unsupervised learning
- Reinforcement learning
- Introducing scikit-learn
- Machine learning algorithms: linear regression, logistic regression, support vector machines, and others
- Training and testing the models
- Code demos

Objectives

After studying this chapter, you will be able to:
- Understand what is machine learning?
- Set up a development environment.
- Learn the different types of learning.
- Use scikit-learn to train and test models.
- Get hands-on with coding.

Defining machine learning

Machine learning is the technique to teach a machine to perform a task without explicitly coding. There are, of course, several definitions for machine mearning. Here is the Wikipedia definition:

Machine learning (ML) is the scientific study of algorithms and statistical models that computer systems use in order to perform a specific task effectively without using explicit instructions, relying on patterns and inference instead. It is seen as a subset of artificial intelligence.

The definition of machine learning can sometimes be confusing. As it says, there is no explicit programming, but we have to write a program in Python or Java to achieve ML. The key here is the term *explicit*. This is very important to understand.

In general, ML has the following three major components:
- Algorithms
- Data
- Programming/code

Let us take a simple example to illustrate the point. If you need to teach your system to recognize an Apple, the traditional way of doing it is by explicit coding, i.e., You have to write several `if -then-else` conditions to make sure all the conditions of the features of an apple-like color, shape, and size are met. This is almost impossible because no two apples are exactly the same in all aspects.

This is where *learning* comes in. Instead of writing explicit code to determine the features of apples – the system is fed with data in the form of several images of different apples and an algorithm to identify the patterns of an apple. And this is done in the form of a code or program usually written in Python. So, we write a program, but that is just to inform the system, what algorithm/algorithms to use, what data to use, where it is located and what action to take once an apple is correctly recognized. The program does everything except telling the system how to recognize an apple.

And the system takes time to learn – very similar to human beings. And it is an iterative process. This is known as the training process. It makes mistakes a lot of mistakes at the beginning of the training process, and then it corrects itself over a period of time.

Machine learning is broadly categorized into two types – **supervised learning** and unsupervised learning.

When labeled data is used for training, it is known as supervised learning. On the other hand, if the data is not labeled, it is known as unsupervised learning. So now, what is labeled data?

In the case of structured data, features are nothing but the columns of the table. And one of the columns that designate the class of the item is known as the label or target. In the following table, species is the label or the *target*. All other columns are features. This data belongs to three classes: *rose, tulip, jasmine*:

Sepal.Length	Sepal.Width	Petal.Length	sss	Species (Label)
5.1	3.5	1.4	0.2	Rose
4.9	3	1.4	0.2	Tulip
4.7	3.2	1.3	0.2	Rose
4.6	3.1	1.5	0.2	Rose
5	3.6	1.4	0.2	Jasmine
5.4	3.9	1.7	0.4	Tulip
4.6	3.4	1.4	0.3	Tulip
5	3.4	1.5	0.2	Rose
4.6	3.4	1.4	0.3	Tulip
5	3.4	1.5	0.2	Rose
4.4	2.9	1.4	0.2	Jasmine

Table 2.1: Labeled data

Unlabeled data

This is an example of unlabeled data – there is no label or target column in this:

Sepal.Length	Sepal.Width	Petal.Length	Petal.Width
5.1	3.5	1.4	0.2
4.9	3	1.4	0.2
4.7	3.2	1.3	0.2
4.6	3.1	1.5	0.2
5	3.6	1.4	0.2
5.4	3.9	1.7	0.4
4.6	3.4	1.4	0.3
5	3.4	1.5	0.2
4.4	2.9	1.4	0.2
4.9	3.1	1.5	0.1
5.4	3.7	1.5	0.2

Table 2.2: Unlabeled data

Supervised learning

Based on the type of the target, supervised learning uses two techniques – classification and regression. If the target is continuous, for example, price, temperature, height, weight, then the regression is used, and if the target is discrete (cat, dog, rose, tulip) then classification is used.

One easy way to figure out whether a target is continuous or discrete is: discrete values can be counted and not measured, whereas continuous values can be measured.

This is an example of label data with a continuous value. Hence, we cannot apply classification for this, but we can apply regression to build a predictive model to predict the price of the property:

Rooms	Bedrooms	Population	Households	Income	Price/target
880	129	322	126	8.3252	452,600
7099	1106	2401	1138	8.3014	358,500
1467	190	496	177	7.2574	352,100
1274	235	558	219	5.6431	341,300
1627	280	565	259	3.8462	342,200
919	213	413	193	4.0368	269,700
2535	489	1094	514	3.6591	299,200
3104	687	1157	647	3.12	241,400
2555	665	1206	595	2.0804	226,700
3549	707	1551	714	3.6912	261,100
2202	434	910	402	3.2031	281,500

Table 2.3: Labels with continuous values

And if the target is discrete, for example, yes/no, spam, not spam or cats, dogs, and so on, then classification is used, like in the following example:

Glucose	Diastolic	Insulin	BMI	Age (years)	Diabetes/target
148	72	0	33.6	50	Yes
85	66	0	26.6	31	No
183	64	0	23.3	32	Yes
89	66	94	28.1	21	No
137	40	168	43.1	33	Yes
116	74	0	25.6	30	No
78	50	88	31	26	Yes
115	0	0	35.3	29	No
197	70	543	30.5	53	Yes
125	96	0	0	54	Yes
110	92	0	37.6	30	No
168	74	0	38	34	Yes
139	80	0	27.1	57	No

Table 2.4: Labels with discrete values

In the case of unsupervised learning, the technique used is known as clustering, which we will see later on in the chapter.

All this is summarized in the following figure:

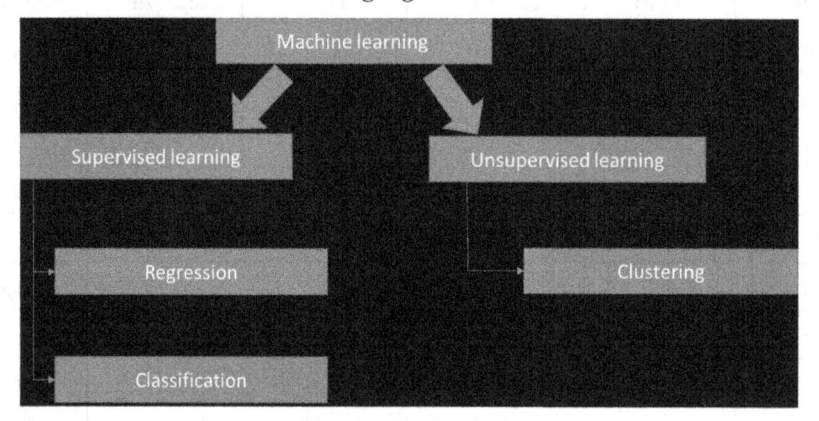

Figure 2.1: Types of learning

Before getting into the details of the algorithms, it is a good idea to set up the environment, as the algorithms will be explained with hands-on examples.

Setting up the environment

You can get started with the coding part in two ways – set up your own local environment or use a cloud environment like Google Colab. It is advisable to set up your own local environment so that you can continue to work and learn without being tethered to the internet. We mention both the methods here.

Using Google Colab

Make sure you have a Google account (like Gmail), and make sure you login to the account before you start.

Access Google Colab using the following URL or simply by searching for Google Colab:

https://colab.research.google.com/

You might get a screen as follows; you can click **Cancel**:

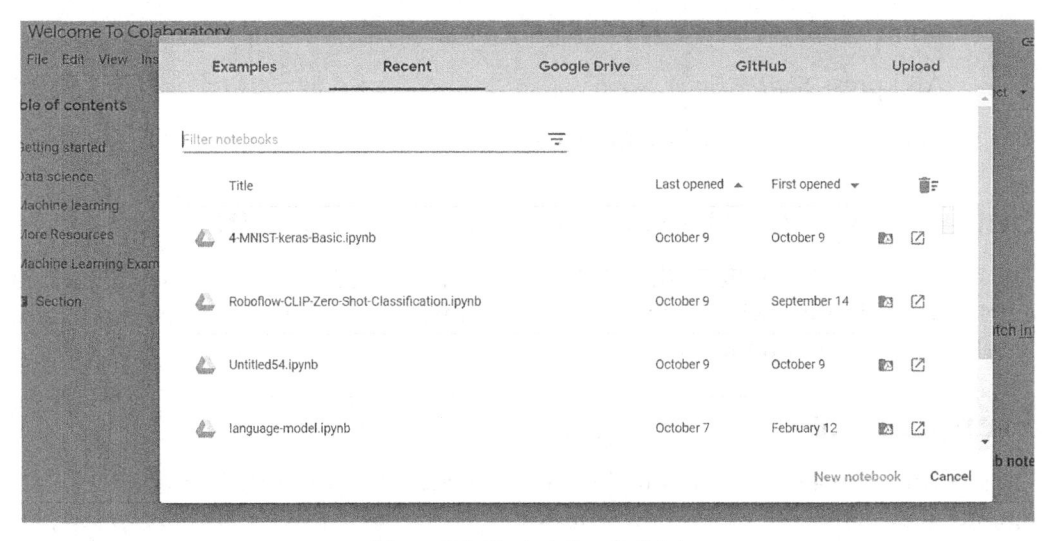

Figure 2.2: To start Google Colab

You can see the welcome screen:

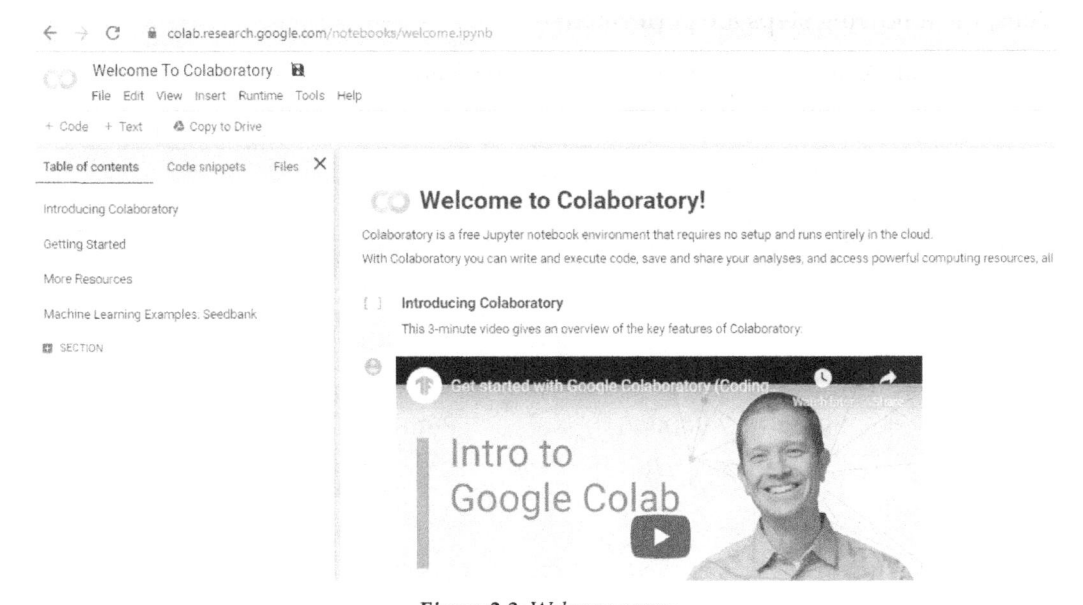

Figure 2.3: Welcome screen

Now, perform the following steps:

1. From the menu, select: **File | New Python 3 notebook**.

2. That's it! You are ready to start coding.

3. Just type in:

print("Hello world")

And press *Shift + Enter*.

This should print `Hello world` in the next line.

Setting up local environment in Python

The best way to set up the Python ML environment locally is to use Anaconda. It is a Python distribution with an easy-to-use user interface. Follow the steps given here to set up the environment.

Prerequisite

Laptop with min 4 GB RAM, Intel i5 or equivalent with Windows 7 or above. Other operating systems like MacOS, Ubuntu can also be used, but for simplicity, we just give the instructions here for Windows.

Internet connection – min 2 MBPS.

Thus, the following steps are performed:

1. Install Anaconda from the Anaconda website:

    https://www.anaconda.com/distribution/

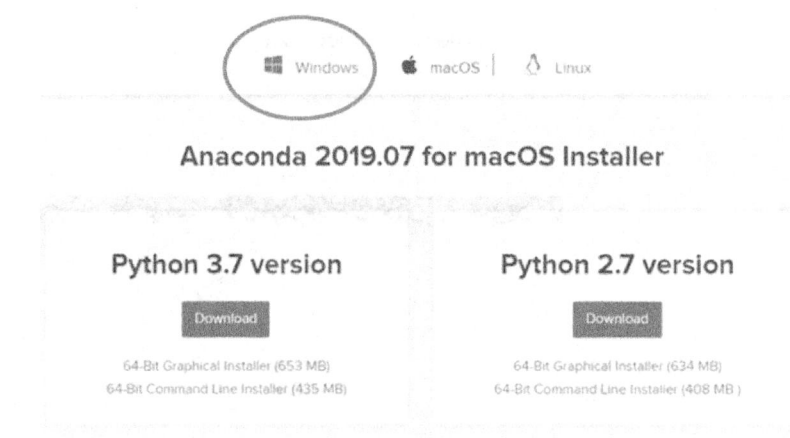

![Anaconda download page showing Windows selected, macOS and Linux tabs, with Python 3.7 and Python 2.7 version download buttons]

Anaconda 2019.07 for macOS Installer

Python 3.7 version — Download — 64-Bit Graphical Installer (653 MB) / 64-Bit Command Line Installer (435 MB)

Python 2.7 version — Download — 64-Bit Graphical Installer (634 MB) / 64-Bit Command Line Installer (408 MB)

Figure 2.4: Select Python 3.7

2. Select the Python 3.7 version.

    This will start the download of the install file. Once it is downloaded, double click on this file to start the installation. This may take a while, depending on your internet connection.

Machine Learning ■ 27

3. Once the installation is done, you will be able to see Anaconda Navigator from the windows start. Open **Anaconda Navigator** and select **Environments**. By default, a base environment will be created that contains Python:

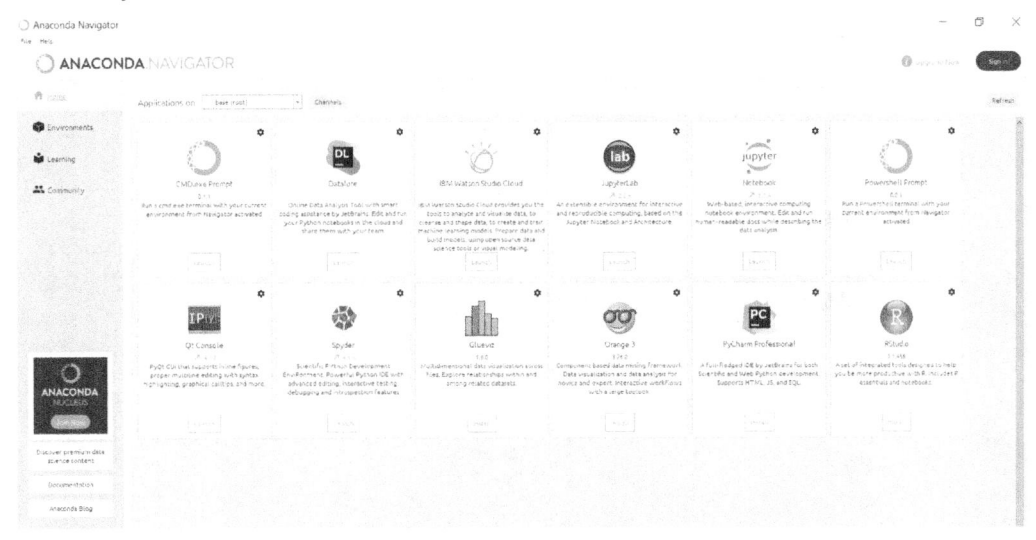

Figure 2.5: Anaconda Navigator home page

4. It is a good idea to create a new environment for your learning or projects.
5. Create a new environment using the create button on the bottom left. Choose **Python 3.7** version and give a meaningful name like TensorFlow. This will take a while, depending on your internet connection.

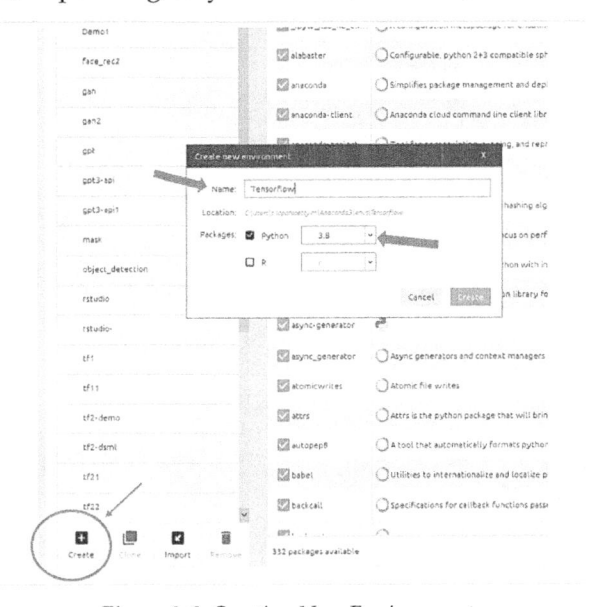

Figure 2.6: Creating New Environment

28 ■ *Beginning with Deep Learning Using TensorFlow*

6. Once it is done, select this environment, as shown in *figure 2.7*. Install additional libraries like NumPy, pandas, scikit-learn, and Matplotlib using the button on the right as shown in the following diagrams:

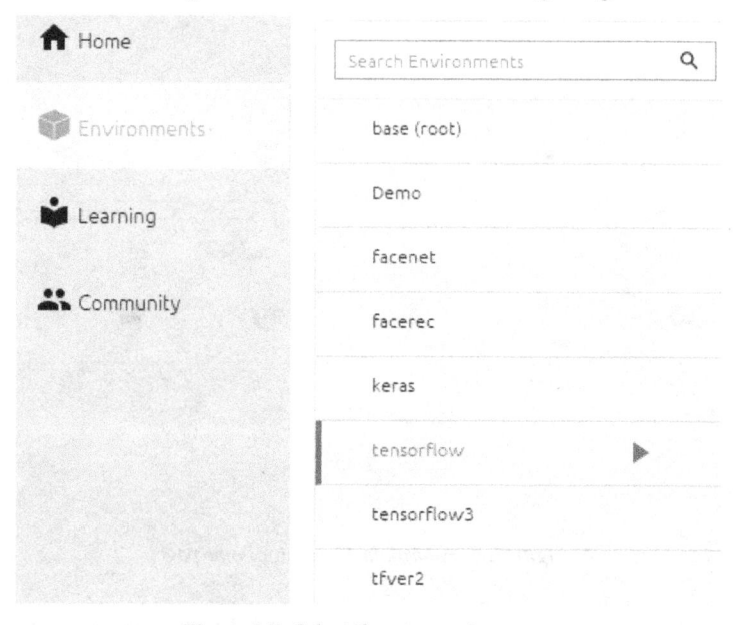

Figure 2.7: *Select the new environment*

7. Install additional library like NumPy:

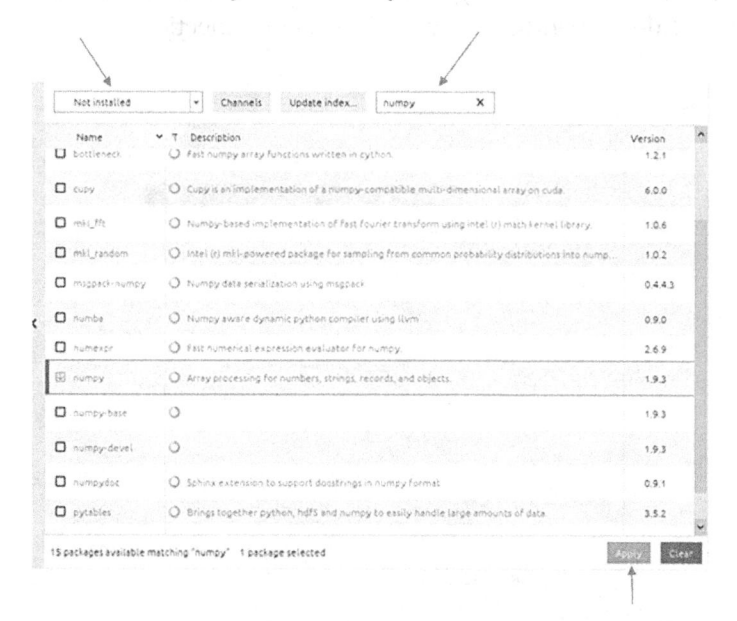

Figure 2.8: *Installing NumPy*

8. Now one more library to install like pandas:

Figure 2.9: Installing pandas

9. Next to install **scikit-learn**:

Figure 2.10: Installing scikit

10. Use the same process to install Matplotlib.

11. Go to the home page by selecting **Home** on the navigation bar on the left. Install Jupyter Notebook by clicking on **Install** (refer to *figure 2.11*). Take care not to install Jupyter Lab.

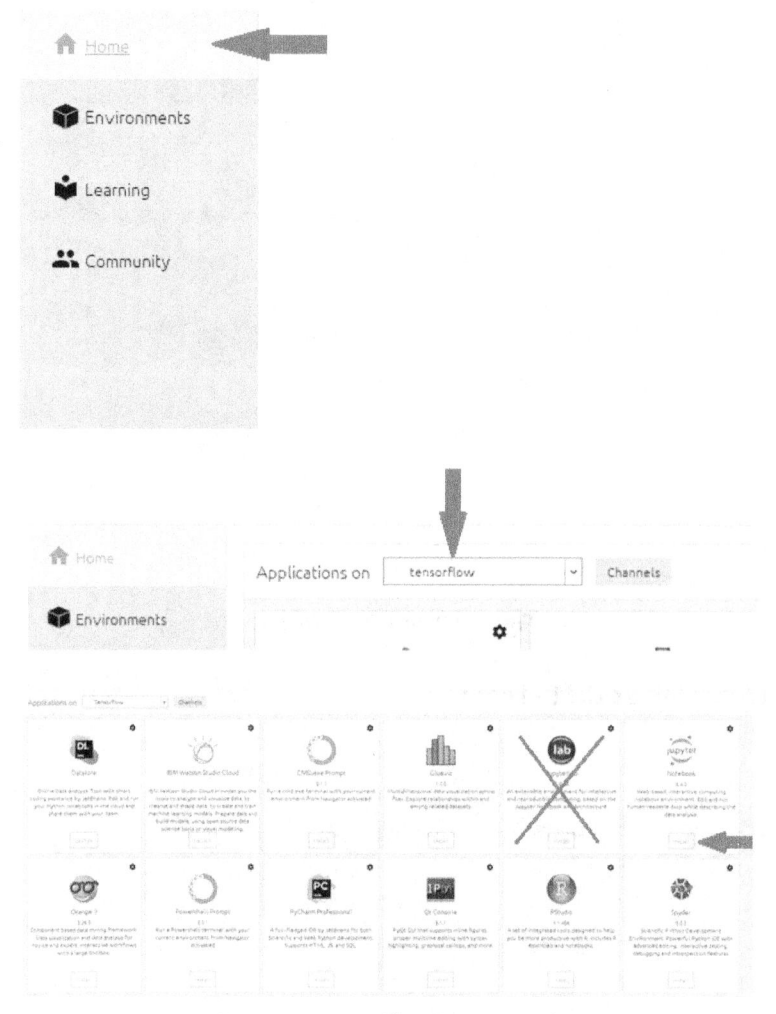

Figure 2.11: Installing Jupyter notebook

12. This completes the installation process. TensorFlow installation steps will be provided in the corresponding chapter.

13. Open Jupyter notebook to check the installation is successful and the libraries are installed properly.

14. Open Anaconda prompt from Windows start menu:

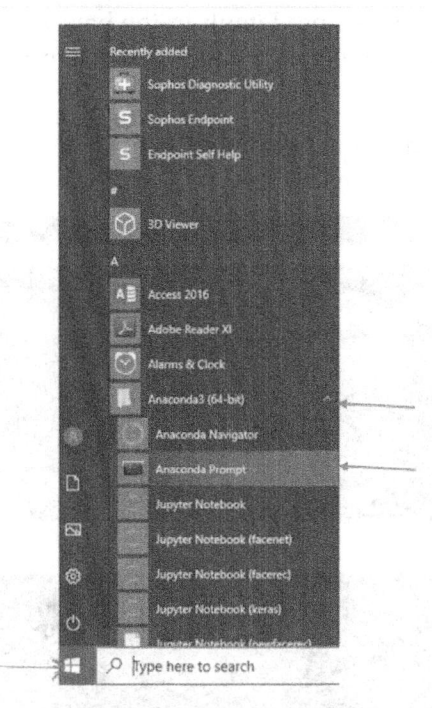

Figure 2.12: Anaconda prompt

Or by typing cmd in the search at the bottom:

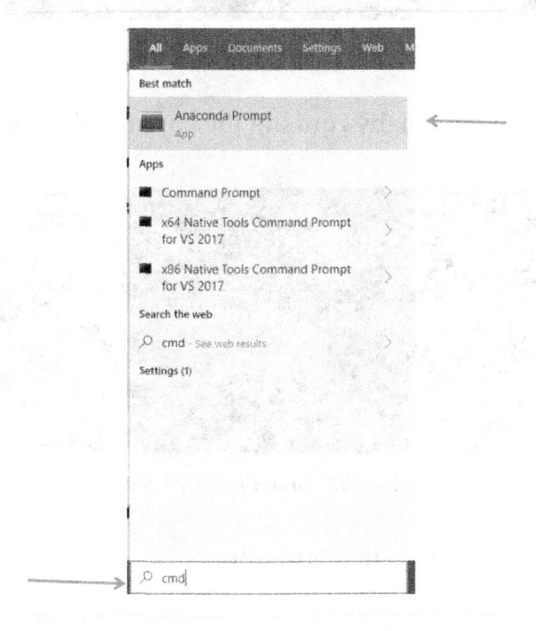

Figure 2.13: To open Anaconda prompt by cmd

15. Anaconda prompt opens by default in the base environment. Switch to the newly created environment by using the command – activate TensorFlow (as shown in *figure 2.14*).

16. Note the change in the environment name that is displayed on the left. It changes from base to TensorFlow.

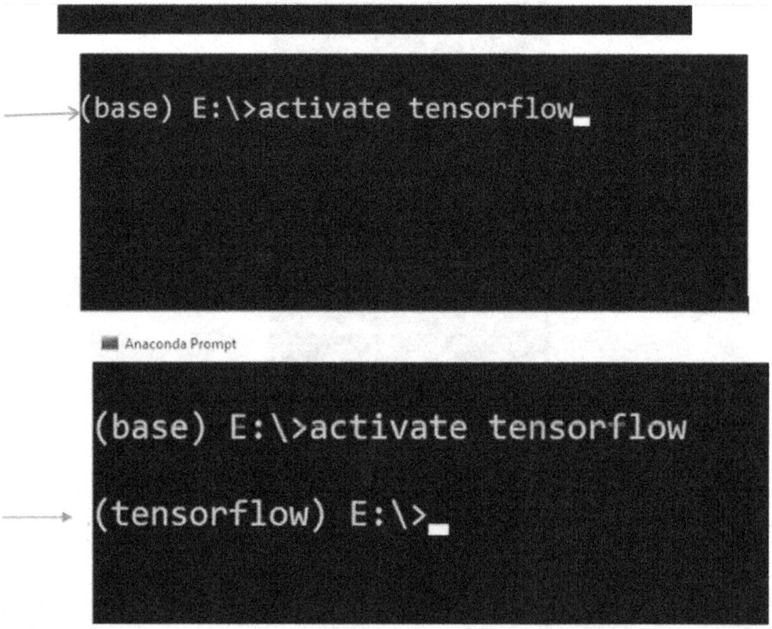

Figure 2.14: *Changes from base to TensorFlow environment*

17. Open Jupyter notebook by running the command – **jupyter notebook**:

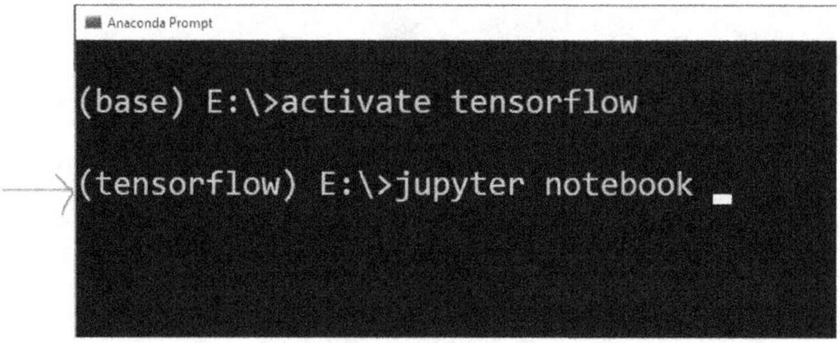

Figure 2.15: *To run Jupyter notebook*

18. Jupyter notebook opens in a browser:

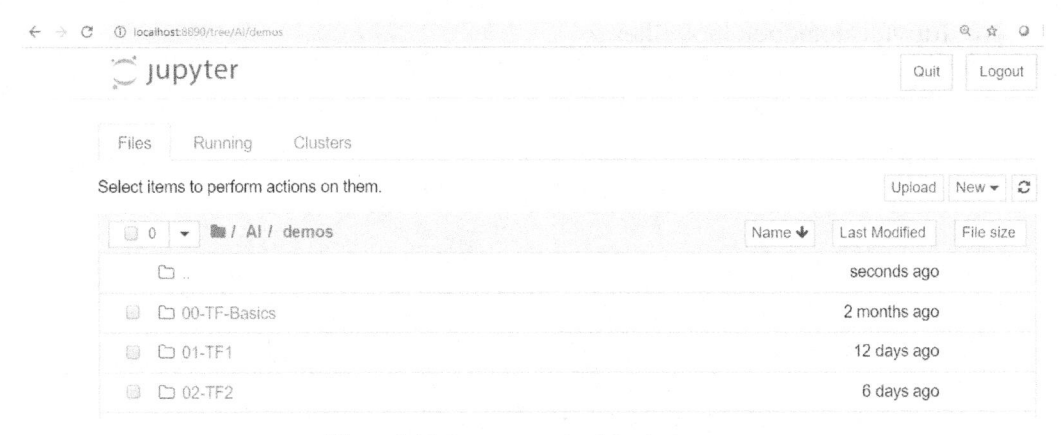

Figure 2.16: Jupyter notebook in the browser

19. Open a Jupyter notebook file by clicking on the **New** button:

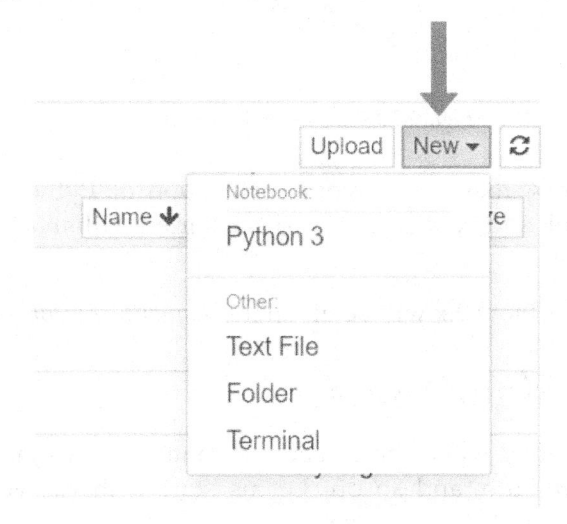

Figure 2.17: Click "New" to open Jupyter

20. Type in the following commands in each cell and execute to check if there are any errors:

```
from platform import python_version
python_version()
import pandas as pd
import numpy as np
import matplotlib.pyplot as plt
```

Jupyter notebook look like:

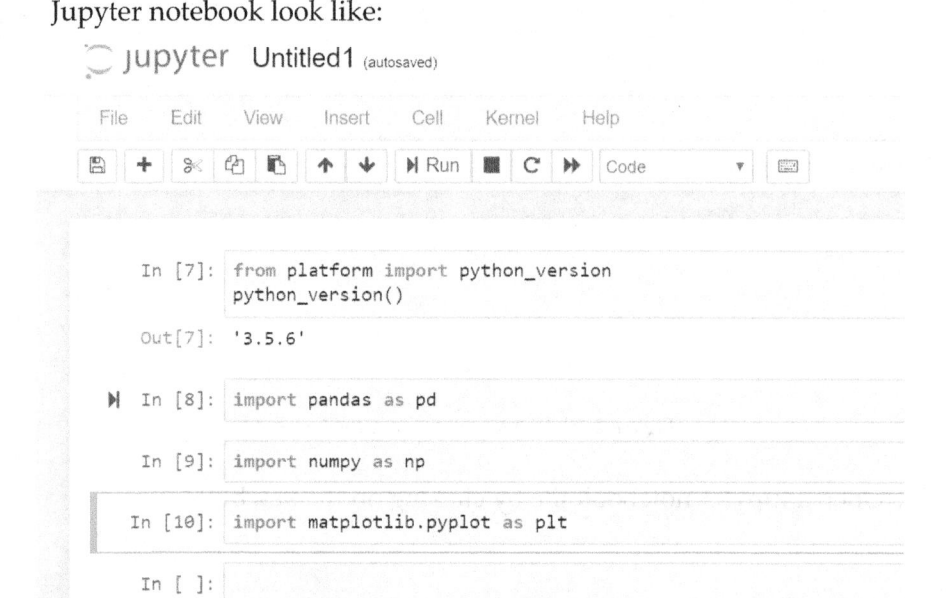

Figure 2.18: Jupyter notebook window

If there are no errors, that means your installation of Python and the required libraries is successful, and you are ready to get started with machine learning using scikit-learn.

Steps to install TensorFlow 2.x will be given in *Chapter 5: TensorFlow 2*.

Regression algorithms

Regression is performed when the target is a continuous variable such as height, weight, volume, pressure, and so on. Let us start with the very basic machine learning algorithm: simple linear regression.

Simple linear regression is the simplest machine learning algorithm. As the name suggests, it is a linear function – the model is the equation of a straight line:

$Y = mx + c$

where m and c are the parameters of the model. Y is known as the dependent variable, and X is known as the **independent variable**. In simple linear regression, there is only one independent variable or feature. If there is more than one feature or independent variable, it is known as multilinear regression.

After training, this model is used for predicting the value of Y for a given value of x. Let us take an example. Given below is training data for total cost and number of items. Let us assume that a seller offers a random discount on the items being sold, and in general, the discount is higher if the number of items is higher – but the amount of the discount is not fixed or consistent. The problem on hand is to develop a linear regression model so that, given the number of items (x), it should predict the total cost:

No. of items (x)	Total cost (Y)
40	300
20	170
10	90
50	450
100	800
35	320
24	210
20	190
20	180
30	270
40	360
50	400
30	100
45	400
30	270
10	95
20	180
30	280
25	230
49	460
57	470
67	570

Table 2.5: Data

If a basic scatter plot is drawn, it will look like *figure 2.19*. It can be visually seen that there is a linear correlation between the number of items and the total cost, but at the same time, the data is not collinear, that is, on the same straight line. Hence, there can be multiple straight lines possible. And that is the challenge of simple linear regression to find the line that gives minimum error while predicting:

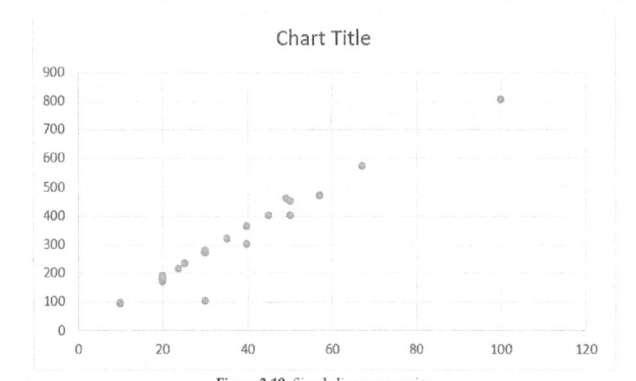

Figure 2.19: Simple linear regression

The training process of simple linear regression can be depicted by the following diagram:

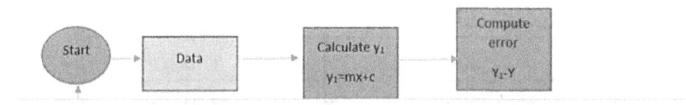

Figure 2.19: *Simple linear regression*

The training process of simple linear regression can be depicted by the following diagram:

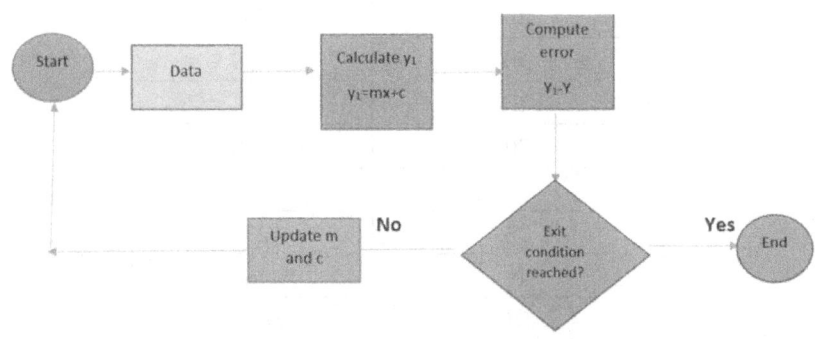

Figure 2.20: *Training process*

During the model training process, the parameters of the model – m and c are initialized to some random values. With the given values of x the output ($y1$)is calculated (*predicted*). The output is then compared with the known values/labels (y), and the error is calculated. The parameter values are updated, and the process is repeated. This is performed iteratively to reduce the error. In other words, the training process tries to fit a straight line in each iteration and calculates the error. Although the aim is to minimize the error to zero, it is not always possible to achieve this. Hence, an exit condition is defined in terms of the number of iterations or percentage accuracy or the amount of error.

At the end of the training process, the *best fit line* is determined, and the values of *m* and *c* at this point are known as the **model parameters**.

Code demo

In this demo, we will see how to train a simple linear regression model on a data set using Python and scikit-learn. The code is available on GitHub link.

Machine learning code, by and large, has the following three sections:

1. Load and prepare the data.
2. Train the model with training data set.
3. Evaluate the model.

A quick walkthrough of the following code:

1. To import the libraries:

```
from sklearn import linear_model
```

```
In [1]: import matplotlib.pyplot as plt
        import numpy as np
        import pandas as pd

In [2]: %matplotlib inline
        %pylab inline
```

Figure 2.21: Importing libraries

2. Load the data which is in the CSV file using pandas. The data is loaded into the data frame named data.

```
In [1]: import matplotlib.pyplot as plt
        import numpy as np
        import pandas as pd

In [2]: %matplotlib inline
        %pylab inline
        Populating the interactive namespace from numpy and matplotlib

In [3]: data = pd.read_csv("data.csv")

In [4]: data.head()
Out[4]:
           number  Target
        0    40     300
        1    20     170
```

Figure 2.22: load data

38 ■ *Beginning with Deep Learning Using TensorFlow*

3. Visualize the data using a scatter plot. As seen from the following plot, there is a linear correlation between **x** and **y** values:

```
plt.scatter(data.number, data.Target , color='red')
```

```
<matplotlib.collections.PathCollection at 0x263836288d0>
```

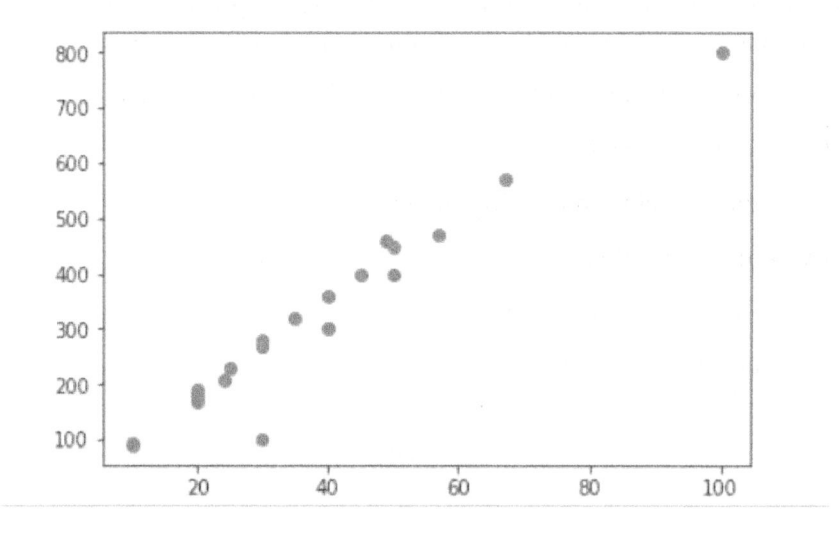

Figure 2.23: Scatter plot

4. Prepare the data for feeding to the model for training. This is done by splitting the data frame into **x**, the independent variable and **y**, the dependent variable as shown here:

```
In [7]: X = data.values[:,0].reshape(-1,1)
        y = data.values[:,1]
```

```
In [8]: # Create linear regression object
        from sklearn import linear_model

        regr = linear_model.LinearRegression()
```

```
In [9]: # Train the model using the training sets
        regr.fit(X, y)
```

```
Out[9]: LinearRegression(copy_X=True, fit_intercept=True, n_jobs=1, normalize=False)
```

```
In [10]: # The coefficients
         from sklearn.metrics import mean_squared_error, r2_score

         print('Coefficients: \n', regr.coef_)
         #Intercept
         print('Intercept: \n', regr.intercept_)
```

Figure 2.24: Feeding to the model

5. Instantiate a linear regression model from sklearn. The **fit** method is used to train the model by passing the feature (**x**) and the label (**y**):

```
In [7]: X = data.values[:,0].reshape(-1,1)
        y = data.values[:,1]
```

```
In [8]: # Create linear regression object
        from sklearn import linear_model

        regr = linear_model.LinearRegression()
```

```
In [9]: # Train the model using the training sets
        regr.fit(X, y)
```

```
Out[9]: LinearRegression(copy_X=True, fit_intercept=True, n_jobs=1, normalize=False)
```

```
In [10]: # The coefficients
         from sklearn.metrics import mean_squared_error, r2_score

         print('Coefficients: \n', regr.coef_)
         #Intercept
         print('Intercept: \n', regr.intercept_)
```

Figure 2.25: Fit method

Now the model is trained, and the coefficients **m** and **c** for the best fit line are computed, which can be viewed by printing them.

```
In [10]: # The coefficients
         from sklearn.metrics import mean_squared_error, r2_score

         print('Coefficients: \n', regr.coef_)
         #Intercept
         print('Intercept: \n', regr.intercept_)

         Coefficients:
          [8.10316993]
         Intercept:
          13.46625984891557
```

```
In [11]: newdata = pd.read_csv("new-data.csv")
```

Figure 2.26: Print coefficient

Now that we have the trained model, we can use this to predict the output when the new set of independent variables are provided.

6. Read the new data that has only **X** values into a dataframe newdata.

7. The **predict** function of our trained model **regr** is used to predict the new values:

```
In [12]: newdata.head()
Out[12]:
            number
         0    40
         1    20
         2    10
         3    50
         4   100
```

```
In [13]: # Make predictions using the testing set
         y_pred = regr.predict(newdata)
```

```
In [14]: y_pred
Out[14]: array([337.59305702, 175.52965844,  94.49795914, 418.62475632,
                823.78325278])
```

Figure 2.27: Predict method

The new values can be plotted along with the best fit line:

```
In [15]: # Plot outputs
         plt.scatter(X, y,  color='red')
         plt.scatter(newdata, y_pred, color='blue')
         plt.plot(newdata, y_pred, color='blue', linewidth=3)

         plt.show()
```

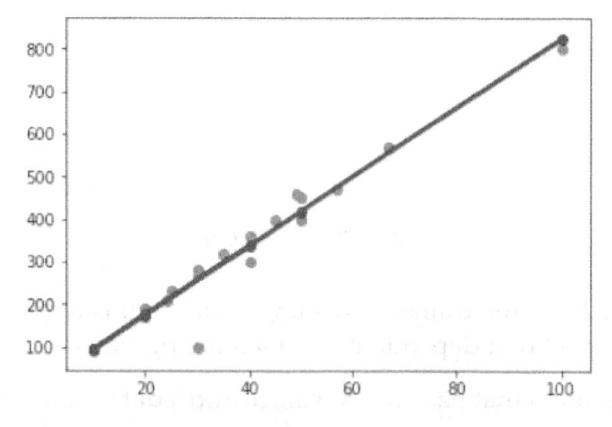

Figure 2.28: To plot the line.

Multilinear regression

Multilinear regression is, in a way, an extension of simple linear regression. In simple linear regression, there is only one feature. When there are more than one feature, we use multilinear regression.

In this example, we take real estate data to build a predictive model. We build a multilinear regression model and find its accuracy:

```
In [5]: import pandas as pd
        import numpy as np

        import seaborn as sns
        import matplotlib.pyplot as plt

In [6]: data= pd.read_csv("house_price_data.csv")
        data.head()
```

Out[6]:

	id	date	bedrooms	bathrooms	sqft_living	sqft_above	grade	price
0	7129300520	20141013T000000	3	1.00	1180	1180	7	221900.0
1	6414100192	20141209T000000	3	2.25	2570	2170	7	538000.0
2	5631500400	20150225T000000	2	1.00	770	770	6	180000.0
3	2487200875	20141209T000000	4	3.00	1960	1050	7	604000.0
4	1954400510	20150218T000000	3	2.00	1680	1680	8	510000.0

Figure 2.29: multilinear regression model

Import the required libraries – NumPy, pandas, and seaborn. Load the data using pandas:

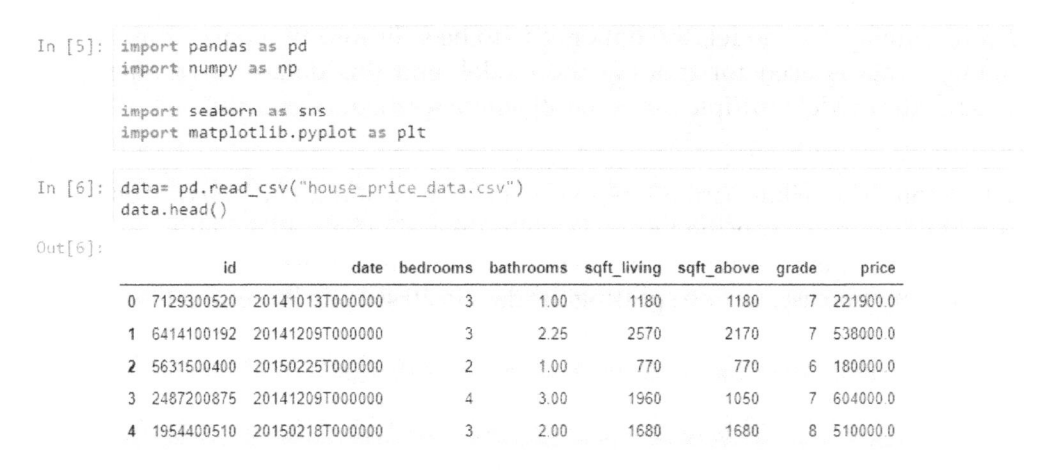

```
In [5]: import pandas as pd
        import numpy as np

        import seaborn as sns
        import matplotlib.pyplot as plt

In [6]: data= pd.read_csv("house_price_data.csv")
        data.head()
```

Out[6]:

	id	date	bedrooms	bathrooms	sqft_living	sqft_above	grade	price
0	7129300520	20141013T000000	3	1.00	1180	1180	7	221900.0
1	6414100192	20141209T000000	3	2.25	2570	2170	7	538000.0
2	5631500400	20150225T000000	2	1.00	770	770	6	180000.0
3	2487200875	20141209T000000	4	3.00	1960	1050	7	604000.0
4	1954400510	20150218T000000	3	2.00	1680	1680	8	510000.0

Figure 2.30: Loading data using panda

This has eight columns consisting of 7 features and 1 target. Price is the target. This will be used for training our model to predict the price of the property based on the given features. Obviously, not all the columns can be considered as features. For example, **id** is just a unique identifier of the records and will not have any impact on the price of the property. As a data scientist, you decide which of the features should be considered to build your model. This is known as **feature selection**. Very often, this is done out of experience and domain knowledge. In this particular example, we consider the following columns as features:

Bedrooms, bathrooms, sqft_living, sqft_above, grade

We split the dataframe into two parts, the features (**x**) and the target (**y**):

```
In [7]: X = data[['bedrooms','bathrooms','sqft_living','sqft_above','grade']]

In [8]: y = data['price']

In [9]: from sklearn.model_selection import train_test_split
        X_train,X_test,y_train,y_test=train_test_split(X,y,test_size=0.4,random_state=42)

In [10]: from sklearn.linear_model import LinearRegression
         reg=LinearRegression()
         reg.fit(X_train,y_train)

Out[10]: LinearRegression(copy_X=True, fit_intercept=True, n_jobs=1, normalize=False)

In [11]: print('Coefficients: \n', reg.coef_)
         Coefficients:
          [-4.45962172e+04 -1.93752352e+04  2.73018557e+02 -8.52670724e+01
           1.08112961e+05]
```

Figure 2.31: Dataframe

Before training the model, the data needs to be split into two parts: train and test. Training data is used for training the model, and this data is very often passed through the model multiple times iteratively to let the model learn.

Then, the model tested for accuracy using the test data, which the model had never seen before. The scikit-learn offers a very useful function called **train_test_split** to split the data in a specified ratio. Usually, the train test split is in the ratio of 60:40 or 70:30, and this is provided as a parameter to the function in decimal form. For example, in this case, we are splitting the data in 60:40 ratio by setting the parameter **test_size = 0.4**:

```
In [7]: X = data[['bedrooms','bathrooms','sqft_living','sqft_above','grade']]

In [8]: y = data['price']

In [9]: from sklearn.model_selection import train_test_split
        X_train,X_test,y_train,y_test=train_test_split(X,y,test_size=0.4,random_state=42)

In [10]: from sklearn.linear_model import LinearRegression
         reg=LinearRegression()
         reg.fit(X_train,y_train)
Out[10]: LinearRegression(copy_X=True, fit_intercept=True, n_jobs=1, normalize=False)

In [11]: print('Coefficients: \n', reg.coef_)
         Coefficients:
         [-4.45962172e+04 -1.93752352e+04  2.73018557e+02 -8.52670724e+01
           1.08112961e+05]
```

Figure 2.32: *Data split*

Now the data preparation is done, and we are ready to create and train the model. The scikit-learn offers an implementation of the linear regression algorithm in the package **LinearRegression**. We use this package and create an instance of a linear regressor by the name **reg**:

```
In [9]: from sklearn.model_selection import train_test_split
        X_train,X_test,y_train,y_test=train_test_split(X,y,test_size=0.4,random_state=42)
```

Figure 2.33: *fit function*

The function call **fit** trains the model using the training data set, which is passed as parameters:

```
In [10]: from sklearn.linear_model import LinearRegression
         reg=LinearRegression()
         reg.fit(X_train,y_train)
```

Figure 2.34: *Training the model*

Now that the model is trained, we measure the accuracy of the model using the test data set:

```
In [13]: reg.score(X_test,y_test)
Out[13]: 0.5426321179276173
```

Figure 2.35: *Model evaluation*

The accuracy can be measured by calling the method **score**, which takes test data as its parameters. In the next section, we will take an example of classification and try to apply the various classification algorithms.

Logistic regression

Logistic regression is primarily a binary classification algorithm, i.e., it is used for classifying data into two classes. Of course, with a slight tweak, it can be used for multiclass classification as well.

In this example, we will look at building a classifier that can predict whether a student will get admission into a college or not. This is based on training data that has the features – GRE score, TOEFL score, university rating, and so on. Admit is the Target that has a binary value – 0 or 1.

1 means the student got admission and 0 means he did not. Logistic regression has a sigmoid function to perform the classification. The mathematical expression of the sigmoid function is as follows:

$$F(z) = \frac{1}{1+e^{-z}}$$

where $z = a_1 * x_1 + a_2 * x_2 + a_3 * x_3 + \cdots + b$

$a1, a2, \ldots,$ and b are the trainable coefficients that the model will continue to readjust during the training process. Let us walk through the code:

```
In [1]: #import pandas
        import pandas as pd
        import numpy as np

In [2]: diabetes = pd.read_csv("Admissions.csv")

In [3]: diabetes.head()
Out[3]:
```

	Serial No.	GRE Score	TOEFL Score	University Rating	SOP	LOR	CGPA	Research	Admit
0	1	337	118	4	4.5	4.5	9.65	1	1
1	2	324	107	4	4.0	4.5	8.87	1	1
2	3	316	104	3	3.0	3.5	8.00	1	1
3	4	322	110	3	3.5	2.5	8.67	1	1
4	5	314	103	2	2.0	3.0	8.21	0	1

Figure 2.36: Import data

Read the data into a data frame using pandas:

```
In [5]: #Extracting the feature into X, reshaping into 2d
        X = diabetes.values[:,1:-1]
        #Extracting the target into y
        y=diabetes.values[:,-1]
```

Figure 2.37: Data preparation

Split the data frame into features (**x**) and target (**y**). Split the data into the train (75%) and test (25%):

```
In [6]: from sklearn.model_selection  import train_test_split
        X_train,X_test,y_train,y_test=train_test_split(X,y,test_size=0.25,random_state=4)
```

Figure 2.38: Splitting data

Like in the case of linear regression, there is an implementation of the logistic regression available in scikit-learn. An instance of the logistic regression is created, and the model is trained using the fit method by passing the training data:

```
In [6]: from sklearn.model_selection  import train_test_split
        X_train,X_test,y_train,y_test=train_test_split(X,y,test_size=0.25,random_state=4)

In [7]: # import the class
        from sklearn.linear_model import LogisticRegression

In [8]: # instantiate the model (using the default parameters)
        logreg = LogisticRegression()

In [9]: # fit the model with data
        logreg.fit(X_train,y_train)

Out[9]: LogisticRegression(C=1.0, class_weight=None, dual=False, fit_intercept=True,
                  intercept_scaling=1, max_iter=100, multi_class='ovr', n_jobs=1,
                  penalty='l2', random_state=None, solver='liblinear', tol=0.0001,
                  verbose=0, warm_start=False)
```

Figure 2.39: Logistic Regression

Once trained, the model is tested using the predict method with the test data.

In the case of classification, the confusion matrix is a good visual tool to understand the accuracy of the model. The scikit-learn provides a readily available function to create and confusion matrix. It takes the labels (**y_test**) of the test data and the predicted values (**y_pred**).

The sum of all the numbers in the confusion matrix is equal to the number of observations in the test data. For example, in our case, there are a total of 125 observations.

The sum of the diagonal values is the correctly predicted values. In this case, it is 119, which means 6 (5+1) observations are misclassified. So, the accuracy is 119/125 = 0.952 or 95.2%:

```
In [11]: #Predict on the test Dataset
         y_pred=logreg.predict(X_test)
```

```
In [12]: from sklearn import metrics
         cnf_matrix = metrics.confusion_matrix(y_test, y_pred)
         cnf_matrix
```

```
Out[12]: array([[  0,   5],
                [  1, 119]])
```

```
In [13]: accuracy = metrics.accuracy_score(y_test,y_pred)
         print(accuracy)

         0.952
```

Figure 2.40: Model performance

A detailed discussion on the confusion matrix is out of scope, but it suffices to say that it is a powerful visual tool in classification, and we will be using it when we perform classification later with neural networks as well.

Accuracy can also be calculated using the method **metrics.accuracy_score** and passing the test labels and the predicted values as the parameters. And the output is the same as earlier: 95.2%.

This will also be used with neural networks.

Decision tree

The decision tree is a very popular ML algorithm that can be used for both classification and regression, but it is mainly used for classification. It is popular because it is easy to understand and it has powerful visualization capabilities.

Let us take an example and walk through the code. In this demo, we will use a decision tree algorithm to build and train a model to classify the leads:

```
In [2]: from sklearn import model_selection
        import pandas as pd
        import numpy as np
        from sklearn.tree import DecisionTreeClassifier
        import matplotlib.pyplot as plt
        import seaborn as sns

In [4]: lead = pd.read_csv('LEAD.csv')
        lead.head()
```

Out[4]:

	OWN_HOUSE	OWN_CAR	HOUSE_LOAN	CAR_LOAN	SMOKER	HEART_DISEASE	DIABETES	MARITAL_STATUS	CHILDREI
0	1	0	0	0	0	0	1	1
1	0	0	0	0	0	0	1	1
2	0	0	0	0	0	0	1	1
3	0	0	0	0	0	0	0	1
4	1	0	0	0	1	0	0	0

Figure 2.41: Decision Tree algorithm

After importing the required libraries, we load the data (**LEAD.csv**) into a pandas data frame. A quick visual inspection shows the various columns in the data frame. We will do a feature selection by identifying the columns that we feel are applicable and create a new data frame (**x**) with just these features.

The column **PURCHASE** is the target, and hence, we separate that into a new data frame (**y**):

```
In [9]: X = np.array(lead[['OWN_HOUSE', 'OWN_CAR', 'HOUSE_LOAN', 'CAR_LOAN',
                           'SMOKER', 'HEART_DISEASE', 'DIABETES', 'MARITAL_STATUS', 'CHILDREN', 'OTHER_INSURANCE
        Y = np.array(lead[['PURCHASE']])
```

Figure 2.42: To train model

Then the next step is to split the data into train and test sets:

```
In [10]: X_train, X_test, Y_train, Y_test = \
         model_selection.train_test_split(X, Y, test_size=0.2, random_state=25)
```

Figure 2.43: Splitting the data into train and test sets

An implementation of the decision tree algorithm is available in scikit-learn. We create an instance by calling **DecisionTreeClassifier** by passing the parameter **criterion="entropy"**.

The other option for the parameter is `gini` which is also the default value. These are the two possible ways of measuring the impurity during training:

```
Now we will be fitting the Decision Tree model on the training dataset.

In [13]: #Decision Tree Model
         #Training Model
         DecisionTree = DecisionTreeClassifier(criterion='entropy')
         DecisionTree.fit(X_train, Y_train)

Out[13]: DecisionTreeClassifier(class_weight=None, criterion='entropy', max_depth=None,
             max_features=None, max_leaf_nodes=None,
             min_impurity_decrease=0.0, min_impurity_split=None,
             min_samples_leaf=1, min_samples_split=2,
             min_weight_fraction_leaf=0.0, presort=False, random_state=None,
             splitter='best')
```

Figure 2.44: How to use DecisionTreeClassifier

Then we call the **fit** method to train the model using the training data. Accuracy of the model is measured using **DecisionTree.Score** and pass the test data:

```
In [14]: print("Decision Tree Score=",DecisionTree.score(X_test,Y_test)*100)
         Decision Tree Score= 91.99807182453603
```

Figure 2.45: Model evaluation

In this case, the accuracy is 91.99%.

Support vector machine (SVM)

Support vector machine (SVM) can be used for classification and regression. In this demo, we will use it for classification. The data set is plants data set, and we use this:

Unsupervised learning

Clustering is the technique used for unsupervised learning. There are two common types of clustering:

- K-means clustering
- Hierarchical clustering

In this demo, we will use k-means clustering to understand how it works. As mentioned in the earlier section, unsupervised learning is used when the data is not labelled. In this demo, we have data on the height and weight of several individuals, but there are no predefined classes and hence no labels.

Using K-means clustering, we can group the individuals into K clusters. The K in K-means clustering stands for the number of clusters, and this has to be defined by us. Technically, K can have a value as low as 1 and as high as the number of observations. But to get some meaningful insights, the number of clusters is usually small, say 3 or 5. Once the number is defined, the algorithm finds similarities between each data point using all its features and creates clusters of similar data together.

Now let us do the code walkthrough of the demo. As always, load the data from the file into a data frame. Unlike in supervised learning, there is no need to separate the features and the labels because there are no labels here. And there is also no need to split the data into test and train. The only data preparation step needed would be to scale the data using **StandardScaler**. This will ensure all the features have a uniform range:

```
In [1]: #Importing the libraries
        import numpy as np
        import matplotlib.pyplot as plt
        import pandas as pd
        from sklearn.cluster import KMeans
```

Figure 2.46: Importing data set

Let us import the data set and look at the top few records on the data set:

```
In [2]: dataset = pd.read_csv('Height_Weight.csv')

In [3]: dataset.head()
```

Out[3]:

	Height	Weight
0	174	96
1	189	87
2	185	110
3	195	104
4	149	61

Figure 2.47: load data

```
In [18]: #X = dataset.values[1:]
         X = dataset.values

In [21]: from sklearn.preprocessing import StandardScaler
         sc = StandardScaler()
         X = sc.fit_transform(X)
```

Figure 2.48: Data set values

We run the K-means algorithm by calling the function **KMeans** and passing the value for K, which is the number of clusters:

```
kmeans = KMeans(n_clusters=4)
cluster = kmeans.fit_predict(X)
```

Figure 2.49: KMeans function

The **fit_predict** performs the actual clustering of the data. This method returns a list of cluster numbers (in this case – 0, 1, 2, 3) for each record depending on which cluster the record belongs to. This is stored in the variable cluster:

```
cluster
array([1, 1, 2, 2, 3, 2, 3, 0, 1, 3, 1, 3, 1, 3, 1, 3, 0, 0, 0, 2, 0, 0,
       3, 2, 1, 3, 1, 1, 0, 2, 0, 1, 1, 0, 0, 2, 2, 3, 0, 1, 2, 3, 3, 0,
       2, 1, 2, 2, 3, 0, 0, 1, 0, 2, 2, 1, 1, 2, 3, 3, 1, 0, 1, 1, 2, 2,
       1, 3, 3, 2, 3, 2, 3, 1, 1, 2, 3, 3, 2, 1, 3, 0, 2, 2, 0, 1, 2, 0,
       3, 2, 2, 1, 2, 1, 2, 0, 3, 0, 1, 1, 2, 3, 0, 2, 2, 2, 0, 0, 2, 3,
       3, 0, 2, 1, 1, 3, 3, 3, 3, 2, 3, 2, 2, 2, 0, 3, 2, 3, 2, 3, 0, 1,
       0, 0, 0, 2, 2, 2, 0, 0, 1, 3, 2, 0, 3, 2, 2, 0, 1, 0, 1, 3, 3, 0,
```

Figure 2.50: cluster number

It may be noted that in the case of unsupervised learning, there is no need to split the data into training and test, as there are no labels available for training and testing. Hence, there is no concept of the accuracy of the model. There are, of course, other ways of measuring the goodness of the model.

Now the question is how to determine the value of **k** (that is, the number of clusters). This should not be confused with classification. In the case of classification, the number of classes is known because we have the labels for the classes. But in the case of clustering, we do not know what should be the right number of clusters. Technically, the data can be split into any number of clusters (that is, **K** can have any value). But practically, that will not make sense.

There is a technique called the elbow technique that is used for determining the optimum value of **k**. The name comes from the shape of the plot of the **wcss** and the number of clusters.

One of the ways of measuring the performance of the model is **wcss** – short form for a within-cluster sum of squares. This is the sum of the square of the distance of each point in a cluster from its centroid. The smaller the value of this number, the better. A smaller value means the items in a cluster are very similar. The value of **wcss** varies with the value of **k**. when these values are plotted; the graph takes the shape of a bent elbow:

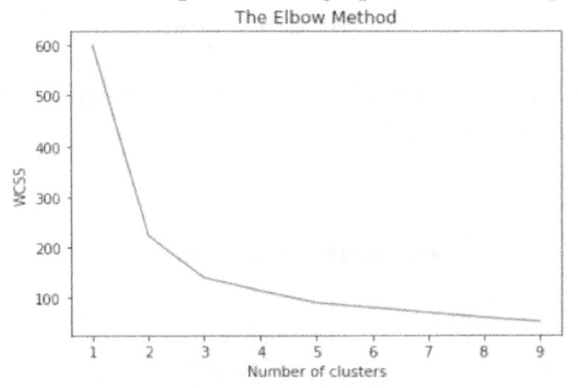

Figure 2.51: Elbow method

For a certain value of **k**, the **wcss** value tapers off. This is the optimum value of **k**. In order to achieve this, we create a **for** loop for **k** starting from 1 to 10 or 15 and calculate the value of **wcss** and plot it:

```
In [75]:  wcss = []
          for i in range(1,10):
              kmeans = KMeans(n_clusters=i )
              kmeans.fit(X)
              wcss.append(kmeans.inertia_) #the value of within sum of squares
          plt.plot(range(1,10),wcss)
          plt.title('The Elbow Method')
          plt.xlabel('Number of clusters')
          plt.ylabel('WCSS')
          plt.show()
```

Figure 2.52: wcss plot

From the plot, the optimum value of **k =4**:

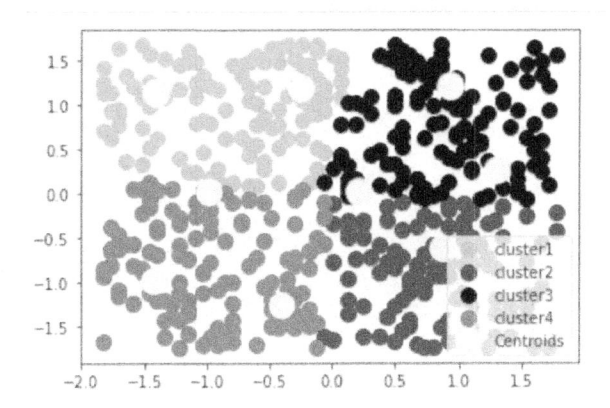

Figure 2.53: Cluster plot, k=4

The code for this is available on GitHub.

For now, this is all you need to know about machine learning and scikit-learn. Many of these concepts will be reused when we talk about deep learning. We will also reuse some of the code, especially the methods **accuracy_score**, **train_test_split**, and **confusion_matrix**.

Conclusion

This brings us to the end of this chapter about machine learning. With these fundamentals of machine learning, you will be able to understand the concepts of deep learning in the upcoming chapters. For deep learning, we will be using the

TensorFlow library. In the next chapter, you will learn how to install and set up the TensorFlow environment for deep learning.

Questions

1. What is machine learning?
2. What are the two main types of learning?
3. What is the difference between regression and classification?
4. Name two common classification algorithms.

CHAPTER 3
TensorFlow Programming

Introduction

TensorFlow is today the most popular deep learning library. Although it is very powerful and provides a lot of flexibility for developing deep learning models, it is not very easy to learn. In this chapter, we will take you through a simple step-by-step process to get a good understanding of how to write TensorFlow programs. We take very simple mathematical examples, which have nothing to do with machine learning or deep learning, to help you understand the concepts of the TensorFlow programming model. There will be a lot of simple small code examples to make the whole learning process easy.

We start with TensorFlow 1.x, which is the mature and stable version and widely used in the industry, and then move to TensorFlow 2.x, which is a newer version recently released.

Structure

In this chapter, the following topics will be covered:

- TensorFlow development environment
- Introduction to TensorFlow 1.x

- TensorFlow programming structure and its elements
- Linear algebra with TensorFlow
- Concept of optimizer
- Applying optimizer to solve simple mathematical problems

Objective

At the end of this chapter, you will learn how to install and set up the TensorFlow 1.x environment, and you will also understand the intricacies of writing Python code using TensorFlow library, which works in lazy execution mode.

TensorFlow development environment

As a first step, let us set up the development environment for TensorFlow. There are two ways of having the TensorFlow environment: one is online, and the other is offline on your local system. Starting the online environment using Google Colab. Here, we will describe the steps to install TensorFlow on your local system using Anaconda. TensorFlow needs Python as a pre-requisite. You must follow the steps mentioned in *Chapter 2: Machine Learning* for setting up the local Python development environment using Anaconda if you have not done so already. Here are the additional steps required to install TensorFlow.

Assuming you have already installed Python, and created the virtual environment by the name TensorFlow when you open anaconda navigator, you should see a screen like in *figure 3.1* when you click on **Environments**. TensorFlow is listed here:

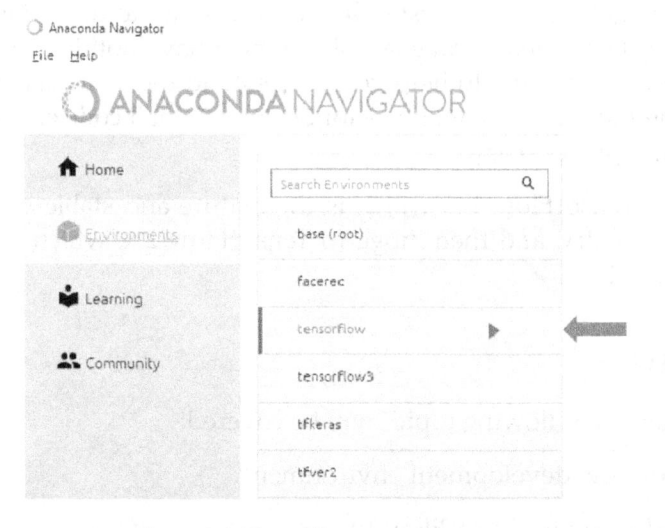

Figure 3.1: TensorFlow environment

TensorFlow Programming ■ 55

If you do not see TensorFlow, please make sure you carefully follow all the steps shown in *Chapter 2: Machine Learning* before you proceed to the next steps.

If you see **TensorFlow**, it means the python installation is successful. Following are the steps to install TensorFlow:

1. From the list of environments, select **TensorFlow,** and you will see all the installed packages on the right-hand side:

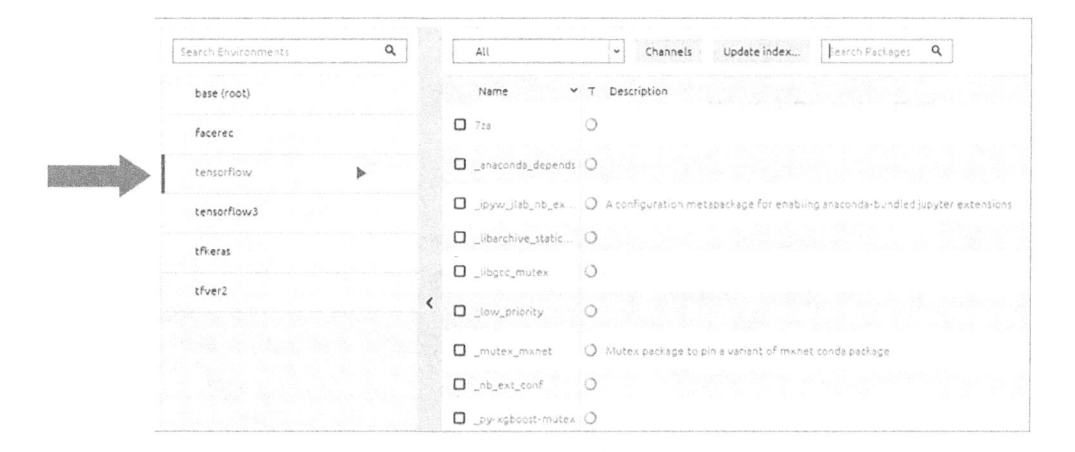

Figure 3.2: *Installed packages in environments*

2. From the dropdown (where it shows **All**) select **not installed** and enter **TensorFlow** in the search box:

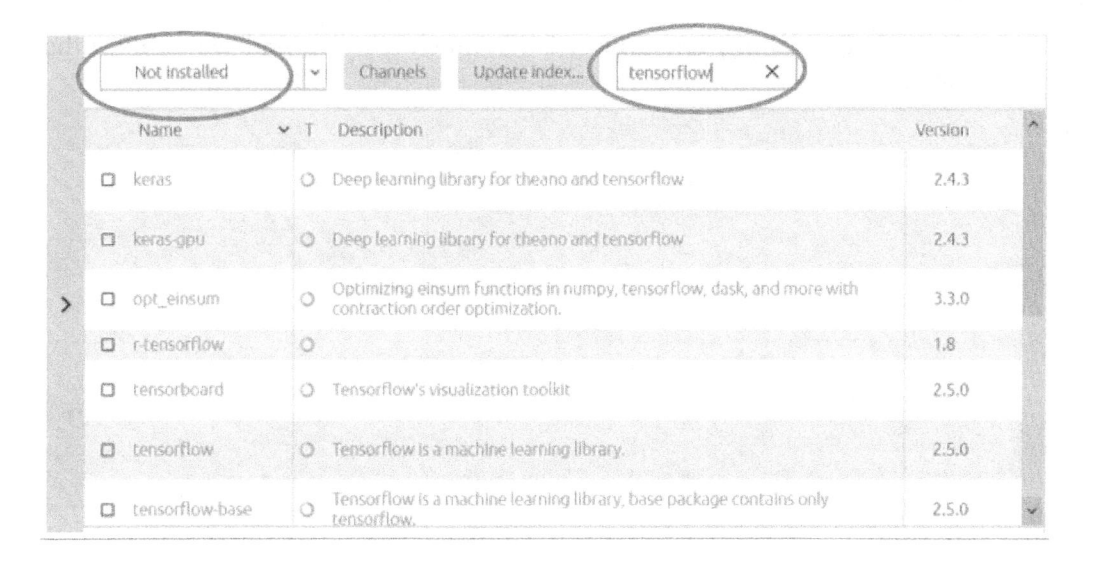

Figure 3.3: *Changing "all" to "not installed"*

3. Then **TensorFlow** will be highlighted:

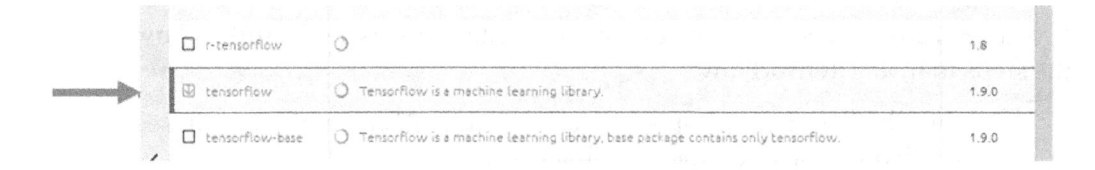

Figure 3.4: Searching TensorFlow

4. Then click on **Apply**:

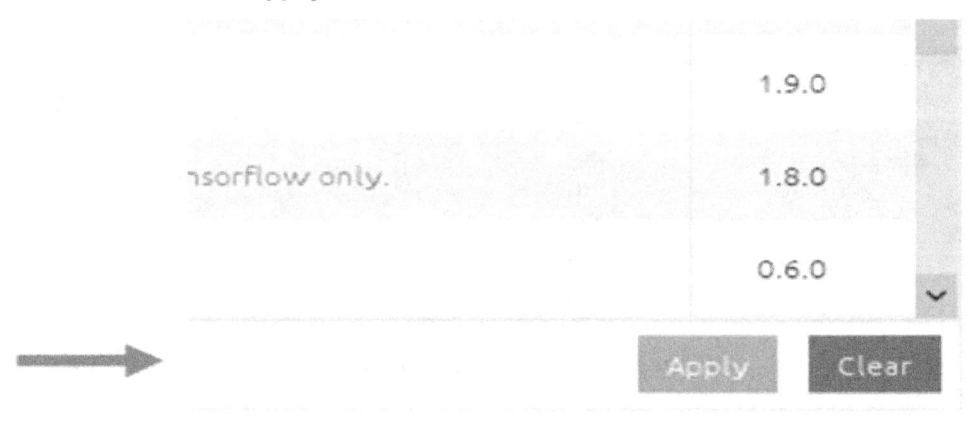

Figure 3.5: Clicking "Apply"

5. Note that installing TensorFlow 2.x is much simpler, and we will see that later.

6. In order to test the installation is complete and working fine, open Jupyter notebook from the command prompt using these steps:

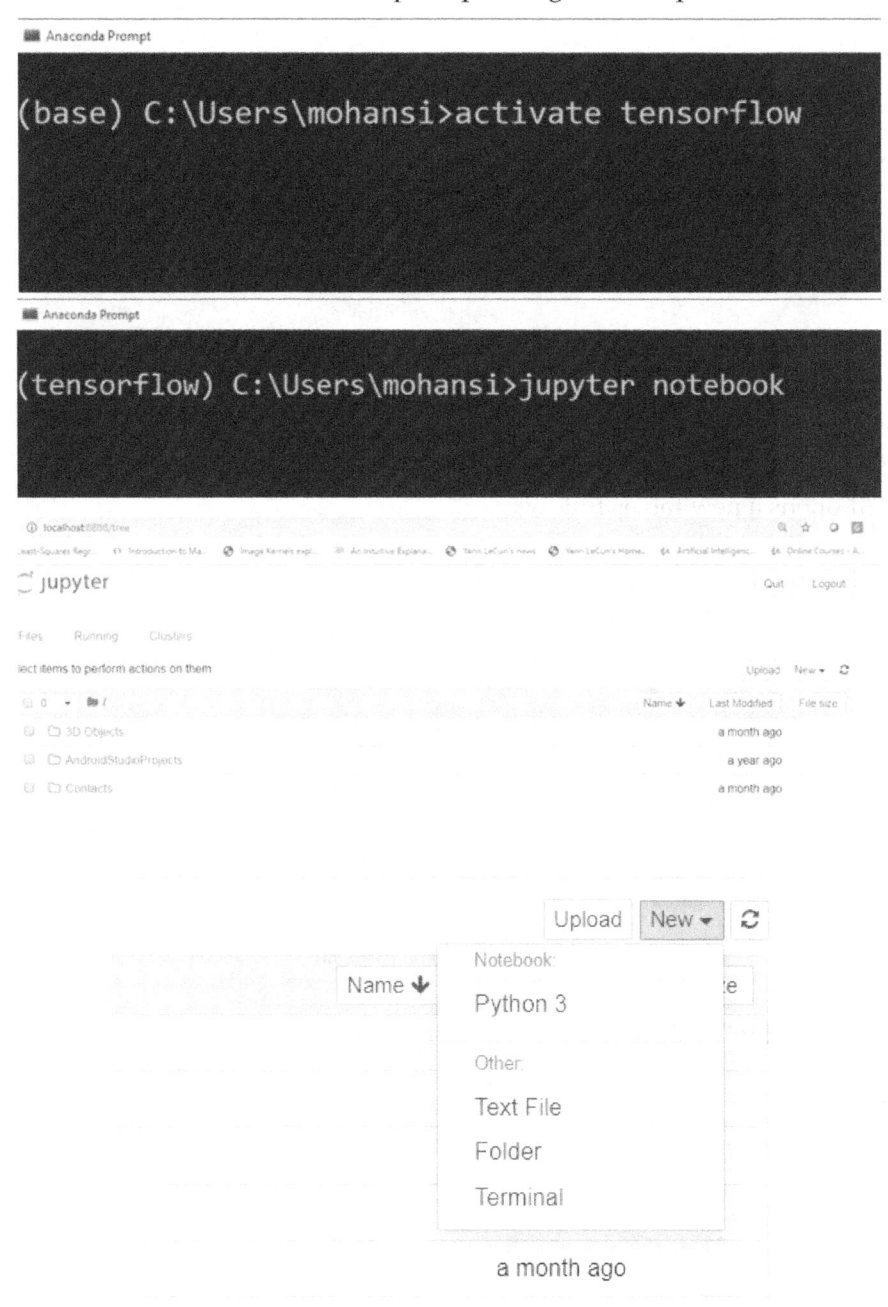

Figure 3.6: Jupyter notebook from the command prompt

58 ■ *Beginning with Deep Learning Using TensorFlow*

7. To create a notebook, click on **New**:

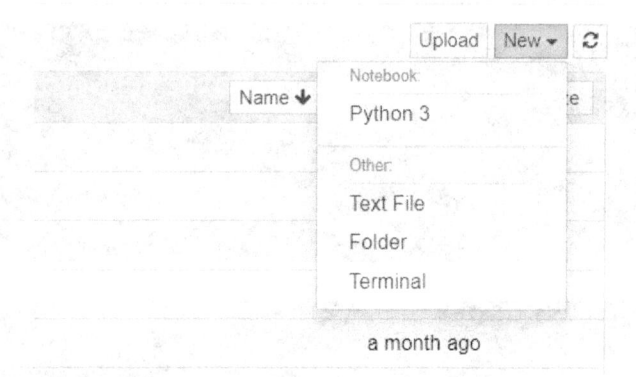

Figure 3.7: *Creating a new notebook*

It opens a new tab as follows:

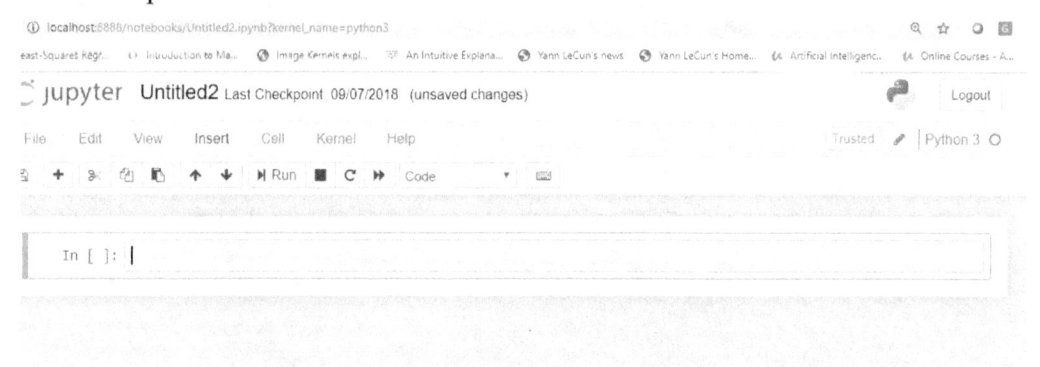

Figure 3.8: *New notebook tab*

8. Type `import tensorflow as tf` and execute.

Figure 3.9: *Executing TensorFlow*

If it runs successfully without any error; then, the TensorFlow installation is successful.

9. To check the TensorFlow version, type in **tf.__version__** and execute. It will print the version of the TensorFlow installed:

```
]:  tf.__version__
]:  '1.10.0'
```

Figure 3.10: Checking TensorFlow version

In this case, its version is 1.10.0, but in your case, it would show the version you have installed.

That is it! Now you are ready to code.

Introducing TensorFlow

TensorFlow is not a programming language. It is a deep learning library. As of writing this book, TensorFlow is by far the most popular deep learning library, as seen in *figure 3.11*. This was originally developed by a team within Google called Google Brain for their internal use and was subsequently open-sourced. Google Brain team is responsible for the development of some of the cool Google apps such as Google Photos and Google Cloud Speech. TensorFlow 1.0 was released in 2017, and within a short period of time, it became the most popular deep learning library ahead of other existing libraries such as Caffe, Theano, and PyTorch. It is considered as the industry standard, and almost every organization that is doing something in AI and deep learning space has adopted it. The following are some of the key features of TensorFlow include:

- It can be used with all common programming languages such as Python, Java, and R.
- It can be deployed on multiple platforms, including Android and Raspberry Pi.

- It can run in a highly distributed mode and hence highly scalable.

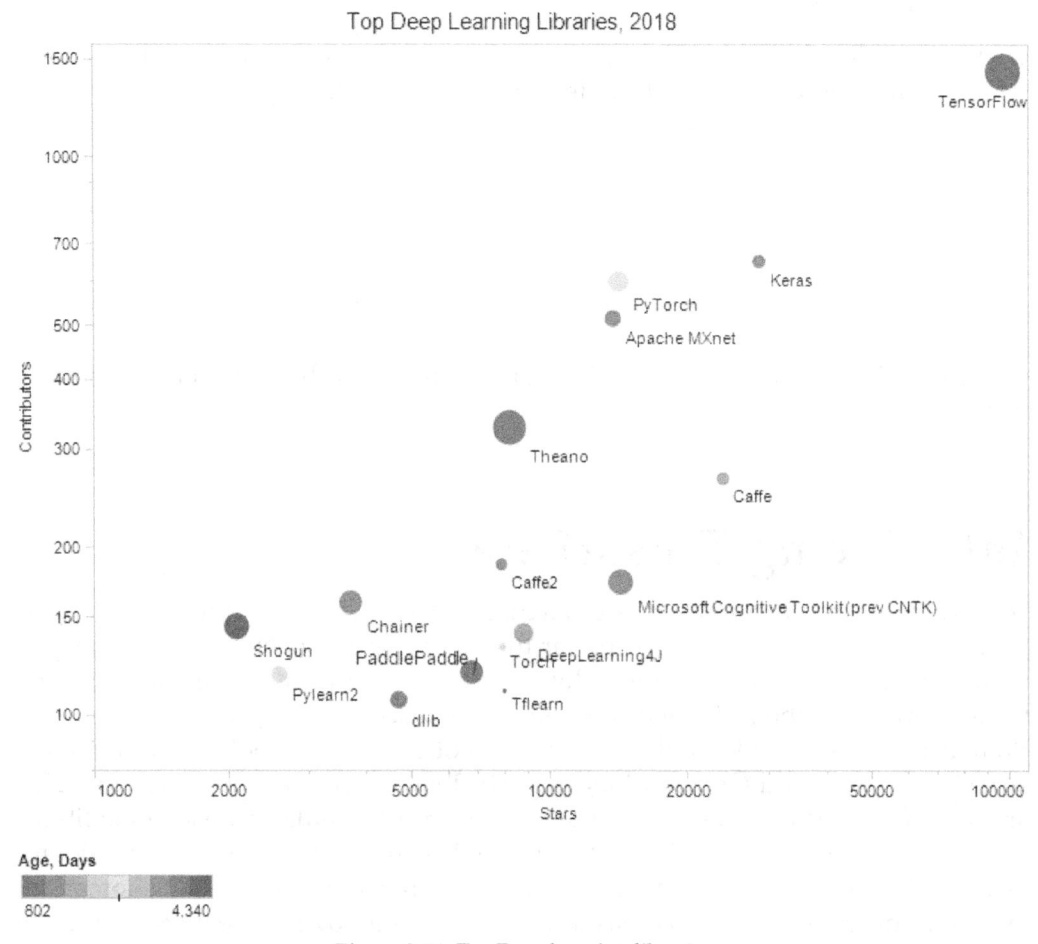

Figure 3.11: *Top Deep learning libraries*
(*Source: https://www.kdnuggets.com/2018/04/top-16-open-source-deep-learning-libraries.html*)

However, there are also some challenges with TensorFlow. It is not very easy to learn because of its execution model (TF 1.x) that uses lazy execution mode and graphs and sessions. You can write the programs in any common programming language such as Java, Python, or R, although the combination of Python and TensorFlow is considered to be formidable and most popular. Even if you are very good at Python programming, writing TensorFlow code can be an altogether different ball game. And in this chapter, we will slowly introduce you to this new programming paradigm and help you gain expertise in writing TensorFlow programs. At the time of writing the book, TensorFlow 2 was just released, but we will begin with TF1.x, which is a stable and mature version and widely used in the industry, and then we will move to TF2.0.

It may be noted that things will be fuzzy at the beginning and a bit difficult to understand, which is quite natural, and it happens with everyone. Do not get discouraged. Many of the sections are interdependent. So, it may be a good idea to go through all the sections once, even if you do understand fully, and then read it through once again. At the end of it, a combination of the concepts along with the code examples will help get a good handle on TensorFlow programming.

So let us get started.

TensorFlow has following two major components:

- Tensors
- Computational graphs (Flow)

And this is why it gets its name as TensorFlow.

Tensors are multidimensional arrays where data is stored at runtime:

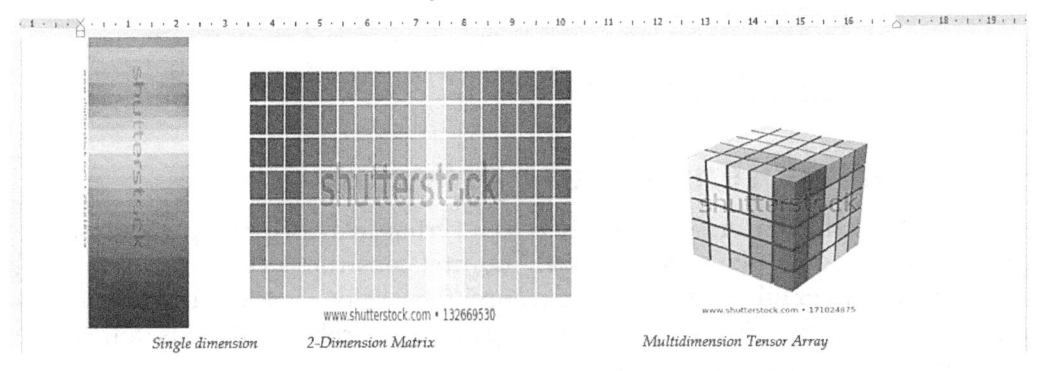

Figure 3.12: Tensors (source: www.shutterstock.com)

Inside the TensorFlow program, every data element is called a **Tensor**. A tensor has rank and shape. The rank of a tensor is a number, and it denotes how many dimensions the tensor has. For example, a tensor of 4 dimensions has a rank of 4.

The shape of a tensor is represented by an array, and it indicates the number of elements in each dimension. For example, if the shape of the tensor is [2,3,5], it means the tensor has 3 dimensions, and the number of elements in the first dimension is 2, the second dimension is 3, and the third dimension is 5. We can also get the rank from the shape. In this particular example, the rank of the tensor is 3 because there are 3 dimensions. This is further illustrated in the following diagram:

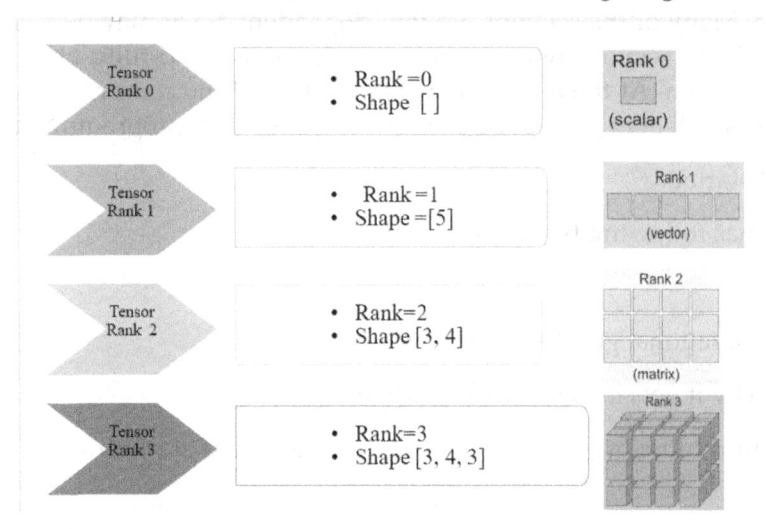

Figure 3.13: Examples of Tensor rank and shape

Elements of TensorFlow program

We will start with TensorFlow 1.x. There is a certain way of writing a TensorFlow program that may not be very intuitive. You first construct a computational graph and execute the graph in a session. Because TensorFlow is a library, we need to import it into the Python code before adding any TensorFlow code. It is done by the following line of code:

import TensorFlow as tf

From there on, all the library elements are accessed using the **TensorFlow** instance **tf**.

The main elements of TensorFlow program are as follows:

- Constant
- Variable
- Placeholder
- Session

Constants, variables, and placeholders can be considered as different types of tensors used to store data in a program at runtime. The creation of each of these elements results in adding a node to a computational graph. There is a default computational graph, that is, created in the background and need not be explicitly created as part of the code.

Constant

Constant is used to store values that are not changed or modified during the course of the program. There are multiple ways in which a constant is created, but the simplest way to create a constant is as follows:

    a = tf.constant (10)

This creates a tensor initialized to 10. And this cannot be updated or modified by reassigning a new value.

Variable

A variable is used to store data that can be updated and modified during the course of the program. Variables are one of the critical elements of the TensorFlow program as they are used for training neural networks. We will see this in the Neural Networks chapter. There are multiple ways of creating a **Variable**, but the simplest way is as follows:

b=tf.Variable(20)

This is initialized to **20** but can be reassigned to any different value during the course of the program. You can also create multidimensional arrays.

tf. Variable([[1,2,3],[4,5,6],[7,8,9]])

This is a **Variable** initialized to a 3×3 matrix as follows:

1	2	3
4	5	6
7	8	9

Table 3.1: 3×3 matrix

Note the upper case in **Variable**. Unlike constant and placeholder **Variable** starts with uppercase **V**.

Placeholder

A placeholder is a special type of storage that cannot be initialized during creation but can be populated only at runtime. While creating a placeholder, you just specify the data type or the shape of the tensor that it will be populated with at runtime. The simplest way to create a placeholder is as follows:

p= tf.placeholder(tf.float32)

This will create a placeholder that can be populated at runtime with a tensor of data type **float32,** and the shape can be anything. We will see how it is populated at runtime in a code example later.

Session

Every time you create a constant, **Variable,** or placeholder, a node gets added to a default graph in the background. The program does not get executed. In order to actually execute the program, you need to create a session and execute the graph in the session. This is how the session is created:

```
sess = tf.Session()
```

A particular node of a graph can be executed using the run function of the session and passing the node as a parameter. For example,

```
 myconst = sess.run(a)
```

The **myconst** will have a value of 10 since **a** was initialized to 10.

```
myvar=sess.run(b)
```

Now **myvar** will have value of 20 because we initiated **b** to 20.

There is a different way of dealing with placeholders which we will see later.

So, a TensorFlow program has two major parts – the creation of the computational graph and execution of the graph in a session.

Now, let us put all of this together and write our first complete **Hello World** program in TensorFlow as a part of our first code demo.

Open Jupyter notebook and type the following lines of code. Type one line in each cell so that you can check if there is any syntax error:

```
#creation of the graph
import tensorflow as tf
hello =tf.constant('Hello World')


#execution of the graph in a session
sess=tf.Session()
sess.run(hello)
```

The code in Jupyter notebook looks like:

```
[1]: #creation of the graph
[2]: import tensorflow as tf
[4]: hello =tf.constant('Hello World')
[5]: #execution of the graph in a session
[6]: sess=tf.Session()
[7]: sess.run(hello)
t[7]: b'Hello World'
```

Figure 3.14: Typing code in Jupyter notebook

Congratulations! You have written your first TensorFlow program!!

Constants, variables, and placeholders

In this section, we will see how to work with constants, variables, and placeholders in TensorFlow. We will use a code demo to demonstrate the difference between these three storage types.

The notebooks for these code demos are available on GitHub, link:

Let us start by creating a constant and a variable:

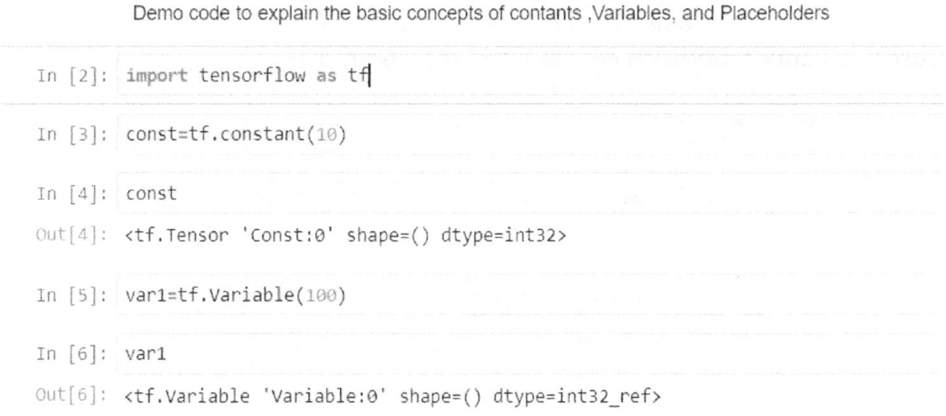

Demo code to explain the basic concepts of contants, Variables, and Placeholders

```
In [2]: import tensorflow as tf
In [3]: const=tf.constant(10)
In [4]: const
Out[4]: <tf.Tensor 'Const:0' shape=() dtype=int32>
In [5]: var1=tf.Variable(100)
In [6]: var1
Out[6]: <tf.Variable 'Variable:0' shape=() dtype=int32_ref>
```

Figure 3.15: A demo code

66 ■ Beginning with Deep Learning Using TensorFlow

The constant const is initialized to 10. And when you try to display the value, it just shows the data type as **int32** but not the actual value. This is the concept of lazy execution. When you run this line of code in the Jupyter notebook, it is not actually executing the code but just does a syntax check. The actual execution happens inside the session; we will see this shortly.

The same happens with the variable. The variable **var1** is initialized to 100, but when we try to display the value, it just shows the data type as **int32** but not the value 100.

In order to display the values, we have executed these nodes in a session, which we will see shortly.

What we have done so far is to build the computational graph. Let' us continue to build it by adding a few more computations:

```
In [6]: #tensorflow offers mathematical methods like add
        #there is also operator overloading..so you can also use zero+one
        sum=tf.add(const,var1)
```

```
In [7]: #assign method is the equivalent of "=" ...so this is same as zero=sum
        var2=tf.assign(var1,sum)
```

Figure 3.16: Building a computational graph

In Cell 6, we are creating a node by the name sum, which performs the **sum** of **const** and **var1** using the add method offered by TensorFlow. In Cell 7, we create another node that assigns the value in **sum** to **var1**.

In Cell 8, when we try to assign the **sum** to **const,** it throws an error. Why? That is because you cannot modify a constant (refer to *figure 3.17*):

```
In [8]: var3=tf.assign(const,sum)
------------------------------------------------------------
AttributeError                          Traceback (most recent call last)
<ipython-input-8-802b70563a1c> in <module>()
----> 1 var3=tf.assign(const,sum)

E:\Continuum\anaconda3\envs\tensorflow\lib\site-packages\tensorflow\python\ops\state_ops.py in assign
(ref, value, validate_shape, use_locking, name)
    215         ref, value, use_locking=use_locking, name=name,
    216         validate_shape=validate_shape)
--> 217     return ref.assign(value, name=name)
    218
    219

AttributeError: 'Tensor' object has no attribute 'assign'
```

Figure 3.17: Error with constant

Now that the computational graph is ready let us execute these nodes in a session. Before we do that, we have to create one more node which is for initializing the variables:

```
[9]: #you need this when using Variables only
     #if you are using contants and placeholders - you do not need this line of code

     init_op=tf.global_variables_initializer()
```

Figure 3.18: Variable initialization

Anytime we use a variable in the code, we have to create this node/operation and execute it in the session before executing any other node. This is required only if we use variables. If we are using only constant or placeholder, then we need not perform this initialization.

Now, let us create the session:

```
[10]: sess=tf.Session()
```

Figure 3.19: Creating a session

As a first step, we run the initialization operation:

```
[13]: sess.run(init_op)

[14]: sess.run(const)
t[14]: 10

[15]: print(sess.run(var2))
      110

[16]: print(sess.run(sum))
      120
```

Figure 3.20: Initialization

And then run the other nodes:

```
[13]: sess.run(init_op)

[14]: sess.run(const)
t[14]: 10

[15]: print(sess.run(var2))
      110

[16]: print(sess.run(sum))
      120
```

Figure 3.21: To run the node const

Executing the node const in the session actually assigns the value 10 to **const** and then displays the value. We can also explicitly use the **print** function to print the values of **var1** and **sum**, as shown here:

```
[29]: print(sess.run(var1))
      100

[30]: print(sess.run(sum))
      110
```

Figure 3.22: The print function

This was a very good example of how to handle constant and variable. Next, let us see how placeholder works.

Let us create a placeholder **a**:

```
[31]: #not initialized to any value - unlike constants and variables
      a=tf.placeholder(tf.float32)

[32]: a
t[32]: <tf.Tensor 'Placeholder:0' shape=<unknown> dtype=float32>

[33]: b=a*2
```

Figure 3.23: Creating placeholder

Even though **a** has no value in it, you can treat it like a regular variable and perform computations on it. For example, you can create a node **b** which is **a*2**.

However, when you try to execute this node in the session, you will get an error:

```
[34]: sess.run(b)
```

```
InvalidArgumentError                     Traceback (most recent call last)
E:\Continuum\anaconda3\envs\tensorflow\lib\site-packages\tensorflow\python\client\session.py in
   _call(self, fn, *args)
   1277         try:
-> 1278           return fn(*args)
   1279         except errors.OpError as e:

E:\Continuum\anaconda3\envs\tensorflow\lib\site-packages\tensorflow\python\client\session.py in _ru
n fn(feed_dict, fetch_list, target_list, options, run_metadata)
   1262           return self._call_tf_sessionrun(
-> 1263               options, feed_dict, fetch_list, target_list, run_metadata)
   1264
```

Figure 3.24: Placeholder node

That is because you need to populate the placeholder at runtime while running it in the session. There is a certain way of executing the placeholder in a session. We have to "**feed**" the values into the placeholder at runtime using a parameter by the name **feed_dict** (short for feed dictionary). The syntax for executing a placeholder is like this:

```
[40]: print(sess.run(a,feed_dict={a:3.0}))
      3.0
```

```
[41]: sess.run(b,feed_dict={a:3.0})
t[41]: 6.0
```

Figure 3.25: Feeding values for placeholder

You feed the value of the placeholder in the form of a dictionary. In this case, we fed the placeholder a with 3.0. Note that when we want to execute **b,** which in turn contains **a**, we have to feed a once again.

So, every time you execute a node containing a placeholder, you have to feed the placeholder. And if there are multiple placeholders in a node, you have to feed all the placeholders at the time of execution.

Here is another example:

```
[43]: pl1=tf.placeholder(tf.float32)

[44]: pl2=tf.placeholder(tf.float32)

[45]: prod=pl1*pl2

[47]: sess.run(prod,feed_dict={pl1:2.0,pl2:3.0})
[47]: 6.0
```

Figure 3.26: Executing all placeholders

Note that the values are not stored. They are used for the computation and then discarded. So, if you try to print the value of **pl1** or **pl2** directly, it will give an error again:

```
[48]: sess.run(pl1)
```

```
InvalidArgumentError                    Traceback (most recent call last)
E:\Continuum\anaconda3\envs\tensorflow\lib\site-packages\tensorflow\python\cli
   call(self, fn, *args)
   1277        try:
-> 1278            return fn(*args)
   1279        except errors.OpError as e:

E:\Continuum\anaconda3\envs\tensorflow\lib\site-packages\tensorflow\python\cli
 n_fn(feed_dict, fetch_list, target_list, options, run_metadata)
   1262            return self._call_tf_sessionrun(
-> 1263                options, feed_dict, fetch_list, target_list, run_metadata)
```

```
[49]: sess.run(pl2)
```

```
InvalidArgumentError                    Traceback (most
E:\Continuum\anaconda3\envs\tensorflow\lib\site-packages\t
   call(self, fn, *args)
   1277        try:
-> 1278            return fn(*args)
   1279        except errors.OpError as e:

E:\Continuum\anaconda3\envs\tensorflow\lib\site-packages\t
```

Figure 3.27: error while executing placeholders

You have to feed the placeholder at runtime in the session and every time needs to run it. However, there are different ways of feeding the placeholders. Let us take a look at the variations. First of all, the values we pass need not be regular numbers (scalars); they can be arrays or multidimensional arrays. Here are some examples:

```
[50]: sess.run(b,feed_dict={a:[1,2,3,4]})
[50]: array([2., 4., 6., 8.], dtype=float32)
```

Figure 3.28: *feed dictionary*

And you can also prepare the dictionary in advance and use it in the session like in this example:

```
[51]: dictionary={a:[[[1,2,3],[4,5,6],[7,8,9],[10,11,12]],[[13,14,15],[16,17,18],
                     [19,20,21],[22,23,24]]]}
```

```
[52]: result=sess.run(b,feed_dict=dictionary)
      print(result)
      [[[ 2.  4.  6.]
        [ 8. 10. 12.]
        [14. 16. 18.]
        [20. 22. 24.]]

       [[26. 28. 30.]
        [32. 34. 36.]
        [38. 40. 42.]
        [44. 46. 48.]]]
```

Figure 3.29: *Dictionary preparation*

Let us take a couple of more variations of the placeholder examples:

```
[1]: import tensorflow as tf

[2]: a=tf.placeholder(tf.float32)

[3]: b=tf.placeholder(tf.float32)

[4]: c= a+b

[5]: sess=tf.Session()

[6]: result=sess.run(c,feed_dict={a:10,b:20})

[7]: print(result)
     30.0
```

Figure 3.30: *Addition of two placeholders*

In the preceding example, we are adding two placeholders. In the next example, we are adding two vectors (arrays) instead of scalars:

[12]: `avalues=[1,2,3]`
`bvalues=[4,5,6]`

[13]: `result=sess.run(c,feed_dict={a:avalues,b:bvalues})`

[14]: `#c=a+b`
`print(result)`

`[5. 7. 9.]`

[15]: `#d=a*c ....why are we feeding a and b instead of a and c ?!`
`result=sess.run(d,feed_dict={a:avalues,b:bvalues})`

[16]: `print(result)`

`[ 5. 14. 27.]`

Figure 3.31: Adding two vectors (arrays)

Hope these examples gave a good insight into how to use constant, variable, and placeholder.

In the next example, we will try to use them in a more meaningful way. Let us say we want to implement a mathematical expression:

Z=X**2*Y+Y+2

Using TensorFlow and solve it for

X=3

Y=4

There are multiple ways of doing it. Let us try a couple of variations. The first one is by creating **X** and **Y** as **Variables**:

```
Demo code to implement a simple function
x^2*Y+Y+2

X =3, y =4, C= 2
```

In [1]: `import tensorflow as tf`

In [2]: `X=tf.Variable(3)`

In [4]: `Y=tf.Variable(4)`

In [5]: `C=tf.constant(2)`

In [6]: `Z=X*X*Y+Y+C`

In [7]: `init_op=tf.global_variables_initializer()`

Figure 3.32: Implementing mathematical expression

In the preceding code, we have created the computational graph. **X** and **Y** are Variables initialized to 3 and 4, respectively, and **C** is the constant initialized to 2. **Z** is the required mathematical expression or formula.

Next, we have to execute this graph and node **Z** in a session to get the results:

[8]: `sess=tf.Session()`

[9]: `sess.run(init_op)`

[10]: `print(sess.run(Z))`
      42

[ ]: `#Z = 3*3*4+4+2 = 42`

Figure 3.33: Executing a session

Although there is nothing wrong with this implementation – this cannot be generic. If we have changed the values of **X** and **Y** – we have to reinitialize and run the entire code. So, an extension of this is to use placeholders. In this case, there is no re-initialization required, but at the runtime, you feed the required values, and the value of **Z** is computed.

The following is the code using placeholders:

Demo code to implement a simple function in tensorflow using placeholders

```
[1]: import tensorflow as tf

[2]: X=tf.placeholder(tf.float32)

[3]: Y=tf.placeholder(tf.float32)

[4]: C=tf.constant(2.0)

[5]: Z=X*X*Y+Y+C

[6]: init_op=tf.global_variables_initializer()

[7]: sess=tf.Session()

[8]: sess.run(init_op)

[9]: print(sess.run(Z,feed_dict={X:3,Y:4}))
     42.0
```

Figure 3.34: A demo code in TensorFlow using placeholders

As you can see, the results are the same.

Now, if you want to assign a different set of values to **X** and **Y**, you can do it in the feed dictionary shown as follows:

```
[10]: print(sess.run(Z,feed_dict={X:5,Y:10}))
      262.0
```

Figure 3.35: Feeding values in the dictionary

An even more sophisticated way is to accept the inputs from the user:

Demo code to implement a simple function in tensorflow using placeholders

```
[1]: import tensorflow as tf

[2]: X=tf.placeholder(tf.float32)

[3]: Y=tf.placeholder(tf.float32)

[4]: C=tf.constant(2.0)

[5]: Z=X*X*Y+Y+C

[6]: sess=tf.Session()

[7]: xinput=input("input x: ")
     input x: 3

[8]: yinput=input("input y: ")
     input y: 4
```

Figure 3.36: To accept input from a user

In this variation, we take inputs from the end-user using the standard Python **input** function. Then the feed dictionary is constructed and used in the session.

```
[9]: mydict={X:xinput,Y:yinput}

[10]: print(sess.run(Z,feed_dict=mydict))
      42.0
```

Figure 3.37: Feed dictionary in session

If a different set of inputs are required from the user, you once again get the inputs and feed them in the session:

```
[12]: xinput=input("input x: ")
      input x: 10

[13]: yinput=input("input y: ")
      input y: 20

[14]: mydict={X:xinput,Y:yinput}

[15]: print(sess.run(Z,feed_dict=mydict))
      2022.0
```

Figure 3.38: To feed different set of data

So far, we have been using a simplified version of the session creation where we create an object named **sess** and assign it to the session created by the method **tf.Session()**.

In this format, you have to make sure that the session is closed at the end using the method **sess.close()**:

```
[16]: sess.close()
```

Figure 3.39: Closing session

You must have seen this in the Jupyter notebook files. While you may not get an error if you do not close the session, it can cause problems if you run several Jupyter notebooks in parallel. Every time a session is created, certain resources are assigned to it. And when you close the session, these resources are released.

One way of avoiding this is to create and use the session in a **with** block. This is a more professional way of writing the code. Here is the **Hello World** code using a **with** block:

```
[1]:  #Hello world program for Tensorflow - using session in with block

[2]:  #import the tensorflow library
      import tensorflow as tf

[3]:  #define a string
      hello=tf.Variable("Hello World")

[4]:  init_op=tf.global_variables_initializer()

[5]:  with tf.Session() as sess:
          sess.run(init_op)
          result=sess.run(hello)
          print(result)

      b'Hello World'
```

Figure 3.40: Code to Print "Hello world" using "with"

The session is created in the with block and is valid within the with block. The moment we exit the with block, the session gets automatically closes. So, we do not have to perform an explicit session close.

Hopefully, by now, you get a good hang of how the TensorFlow program is written and executed. Before we move forward, let us take another real-world example. In this example, we will implement the equation of motion:

$s=u*t+(1/2)*a*t**2$

We will do this for $u=50$ m/s, $a=40$ m/s**2, and t needs to be requested from the end-user at runtime.

This is how we create the computational graph and prepare the data:

```
[1]: import tensorflow as tf

[2]: #using a with block

[3]: u=tf.constant(50.0)
     a=tf.constant(40.0)
     t=tf.placeholder(tf.float32)

[4]: distance=u*t+.5*a*t**2

[5]: time=input("input time: ")
     input time: 20

[6]: mydict={t:time}
```

Figure 3.41: Creating computational graph and preparing data

And then execute the graph in a session in the **"with"** block:

```
[9]: with tf.Session() as sess:
         #sess.run(init)
         result=sess.run(distance,feed_dict=mydict)
         print(result)
     9000.0
```

Figure 3.42: Executing the graph

Note that *u* and *a* are created as constants and not variables or placeholders as their values do not change in this case.

Let us now see how we use TensorFlow to perform some Linear Algebra in the next section.

Linear algebra with TensorFlow

The most important linear algebra function that will be used in Neural Networks is matrix multiplication. In this section, we will first explain how matrix multiplication works and then use TensorFlow's built-in functions to solve some matrix multiplication examples. This is essential in preparation for Neural Networks in the upcoming chapter.

How does matrix multiplication work? You might have studied this as a part of your high school but let us do a quick recap.

Let us take a simple example. If we have to perform a matrix multiplication between two matrices A and B where,

A =

$$\begin{vmatrix} 1 & 2 & 3 \\ 4 & 5 & 6 \end{vmatrix}$$

B =

$$\begin{vmatrix} 7 & 8 \\ 9 & 10 \\ 11 & 12 \end{vmatrix}$$

The first step is to check whether this is possible. There is a pre-requisite for matrix multiplication. Remember this as C=R; that is, the number of columns (C) in the first matrix should be equal to the number of rows (R) in the second matrix.

And remember, the sequence matters here. A×B is not equal to B×A.

In this particular example, C =3 and R=3. So, multiplication is possible.

The resultant matrix would have the number of rows equal to that in A and the number of columns equal to that in B.

So, in this case, the resultant matrix would be 2×2. You take the elements of the first row of A and the elements of the first column of B:

AR_1 =   [1 2 3]

BC_1 =

$$\begin{vmatrix} 7 \\ 9 \\ 11 \end{vmatrix}$$

Get the sum of the element-wise products, i.e., (1×7)+(2×9)+(3×11) = 58.

This will be the first element in the 2×2 resultant matrix:

$$\begin{vmatrix} 58 & \end{vmatrix}$$

Repeat this with the first row of A and second column of B:

$AR_1 = $ [1 2 3]

$BC_2 = $

$$\begin{vmatrix} 8 \\ 10 \\ 12 \end{vmatrix}$$

Get the sum of the products of the corresponding elements, that is, (1×8)+(2×10)+(3×12) = 64

This will be the second element in the resultant matrix:

$$\begin{vmatrix} 58 & 64 \end{vmatrix}$$

Repeat the same with the second row to get the final result:

$$\begin{vmatrix} 58 & 64 \\ 139 & 154 \end{vmatrix}$$

TensorFlow offers a method named **matmul** to perform matrix multiplication. Let us write the code to execute the preceding example in TensorFlow:

Demo code to perform matrix multiplication

```
In [1]: import tensorflow as tf

In [2]: A=tf.Variable([[1,2,3],[4,5,6]])

In [3]: B=tf.Variable([[7,8],[9,10],[11,12]])

In [4]: init_op=tf.global_variables_initializer()

In [5]: sess=tf.Session()

In [6]: sess.run(init_op)
```

Figure 3.43: Initializing matrices as values

Note how the matrices are created as variables. To make sure they are created correctly, we will execute each of the nodes **X** and **Y** in a session so that they can be printed and visualized:

```
[7]: print(sess.run(A))

     [[1 2 3]
      [4 5 6]]

[8]: print(sess.run(B))

     [[ 7  8]
      [ 9 10]
      [11 12]]
```

Figure 3.44: To print matrices

We see that the matrices are created correctly. We perform matrix multiplication by calling the method **matmul()** and passing **A** and **B** as parameters:

```
[9]:  c1=tf.matmul(A,B)

[10]: sess.run(c1)

[10]: array([[ 58,  64],
             [139, 154]])
```

Figure 3.45: A×B matrix using matmul ()

We can perform B×A and see that the results are different:

```
[12]: c2=tf.matmul(B,A)
      sess.run(c2)

[12]: array([[ 39,  54,  69],
             [ 49,  68,  87],
             [ 59,  82, 105]])
```

Figure 3.46: Matrix B×A using matmul ()

While we are at it, let us try out a few other tensor-related functionalities offered by TensorFlow, like shape and reshape. In order to find the shape of a tensor, we call the shape attribute of the tensor like this:

```
[13]: A.shape
t[13]: TensorShape([Dimension(2), Dimension(3)])

[14]: B.shape
t[14]: TensorShape([Dimension(3), Dimension(2)])
```

Figure 3.47: Shape of matrices

TensorFlow offers a way to change the shape of a tensor, which will rearrange the elements of a given tensor into a different configuration. This is known as **reshape**. And it is frequently used in Neural Networks, so it is a good idea to understand it right now. Let's take an example and create a few tensors and try to reshape them:

```
[1]: import tensorflow as tf

[2]: x=tf.Variable([2,50,3,10,4,5,6,7])

[3]: y=tf.Variable([[1,2],[3,4],[5,6]])

[4]: z=tf.Variable([[1,9],[8,2],[8,7]])

[5]: sess=tf.Session()

[6]: initop=tf.global_variables_initializer()

[7]: sess.run(initop)

[8]: sess.run(x)
t[8]: array([ 2, 50,  3, 10,  4,  5,  6,  7])

[9]: x.shape
[9]: TensorShape([Dimension(8)])

10]: sess.run(y)
10]: array([[1, 2],
            [3, 4],
            [5, 6]])

11]: y.shape
```

Figure 3.48: Creating tensors

Observer that **x** has a shape of **[8]** and is a one-dimensional array. Although *y* is a 2×3 matrix. We can reshape **x** to either a 2×4 matrix or a 4×2 matrix as follows:

```
[23]: sess.run(tf.reshape(x,[2,4]))
t[23]: array([[ 2, 50,  3, 10],
              [ 4,  5,  6,  7]])

[24]: sess.run(tf.reshape(x,[4,2]))
t[24]: array([[ 2, 50],
              [ 3, 10],
              [ 4,  5],
              [ 6,  7]])
```

Figure 3.49: Presenting matrix using reshape()

Note the following:

- The number of elements cannot be changed. So, the new configuration should be compatible. For example, we cannot reshape *x* to 3×4 or 3×5 since the total elements in these cases would be 12 and 15, respectively.
- The sequence of the elements remains unchanged.
- The elements are rearranged in the new configuration.

Let us reshape **y**:

```
[12]: sess.run(tf.reshape(y,[2,3]))
t[12]: array([[1, 2, 3],
              [4, 5, 6]])
```

Figure 3.50: To reshape y

The other two possibilities are 1×6 and 6×1:

```
[25]: sess.run(tf.reshape(y,[1,6]))
t[25]: array([[1, 2, 3, 4, 5, 6]])

[26]: sess.run(tf.reshape(y,[6,1]))
t[26]: array([[1],
              [2],
              [3],
              [4],
              [5],
              [6]])
```

Figure 3.51: reshape

These were matrices. You can also reshape it to a single dimension array like this:

```
[27]: sess.run(tf.reshape(y,[6]))
t[27]: array([1, 2, 3, 4, 5, 6])
```

Figure 3.52: Reshaping a single-dimension array

It should be noted that the original shape of *x* and *y* are not modified in these cases:

```
[28]: sess.run(x)
t[28]: array([ 2, 50,  3, 10,  4,  5,  6,  7])

[29]: sess.run(y)
t[29]: array([[1, 2],
              [3, 4],
              [5, 6]])
```

Figure 3.53: No change in the original shape of *x* and *y*

In case you want to save the new shape, you have to reassign the new values:

```
[31]: x=sess.run(tf.reshape(x,[2,4]))

[33]: x
[33]: array([[ 2, 50,  3, 10],
             [ 4,  5,  6,  7]])
```

Figure 3.54: Reassigning the values

Before we move on, one more important function that will be used in Neural Networks is the **argmax()**. This method gives the index value of the maximum value in a tensor. Let us see how this works with an example:

```
: sess.run(x)
: array([ 2, 50,  3, 10,  4,  5,  6,  7])

: sess.run(tf.argmax(x))
: 1
```

Figure 3.55: To get index value using argmax()

The **argmax** takes the tensor as the first parameter and the second parameter is the axis value which is defaulted to 0 if not provided.

And the index value that it returns starts from 0. So, in the preceding example, **argmax** of **x** resulted in a value of 1 since the second position has the highest value, which is 50.

It is re-emphasized that argmax returns the index/position of the maximum value and not the maximum value itself (which is 50 in this case), and the index starts from 0.

Let us take one more example:

```
[18]: sess.run(z)
t[18]: array([[1, 9],
              [8, 2],
              [8, 7]])

[19]: sess.run(tf.argmax(z,axis=0))
t[19]: array([1, 0], dtype=int64)
```

Figure 3.56: argmax

In this case, argmax returns two values, one for each column. And it must be noted that if there are multiple positions where the maximum value is present, it returns the position of the first occurrence.

If you need row-wise values, you need to pass **axis=1**:

```
: sess.run(tf.argmax(z,axis=1))
: array([1, 0, 0], dtype=int64)
```

Figure 3.57: To display row-wise values

In this case, it returns three values, one for each row. And this can be extended to multidimensional arrays.

In the next section, we will introduce the concept of an optimizer which is very important in implementing and training Neural Networks.

Optimizer

Now that you have a good idea of how TensorFlow programming works, in general, let us see how we apply this in machine learning and specifically for training a model. For this, we will take the very basic ML algorithm – simple linear regression, which is represented in the simplest form as an equation of a straight line as follows:

$Y = w^*X+b$

For a given data set, training of this model means – finding the right values of **w** and **b**.

One way of doing this is using brute force and try all possible values for **w** and **b**. These are also referred to as trainable parameters. Let us write the code for this:

```
[1]: import tensorflow as tf
```

```
[2]: #variables
     #first run
     W=tf.Variable([.2],tf.float32)
     b=tf.Variable([-.2],tf.float32)
     #second run
     #W=tf.Variable([-1.0],tf.float32)
     #b=tf.Variable([1.0],tf.float32)
```

```
[3]: #placeholders
     x=tf.placeholder(tf.float32)
     #label
     y=tf.placeholder(tf.float32)
```

```
[4]: #linear model
     linear_model=W*x+b
```

```
[5]: #loss
     squared=tf.square(linear_model-y)
     loss=tf.reduce_sum(squared)
```

Figure 3.58: Code for trainable parameters

We start by initializing variables for **w** and **b** to some random values (.2 and –.2):

```
[1]: import tensorflow as tf

[2]: #variables
     #first run
     W=tf.Variable([.2],tf.float32)
     b=tf.Variable([-.2],tf.float32)
     #second run
     #W=tf.Variable([-1.0],tf.float32)
     #b=tf.Variable([1.0],tf.float32)

[3]: #placeholders
     x=tf.placeholder(tf.float32)
     #label
     y=tf.placeholder(tf.float32)

[4]: #linear model
     linear_model=W*x+b

[5]: #loss
     squared=tf.square(linear_model-y)
     loss=tf.reduce_sum(squared)
```

Figure 3.59: *Placeholders for x and y*

We create placeholders **x** and **y** for training data. **X** is the feature, and **y** are the label/target:

```
[1]: import tensorflow as tf

[2]: #variables
     #first run
     W=tf.Variable([.2],tf.float32)
     b=tf.Variable([-.2],tf.float32)
     #second run
     #W=tf.Variable([-1.0],tf.float32)
     #b=tf.Variable([1.0],tf.float32)

[3]: #placeholders
     x=tf.placeholder(tf.float32)
     #label
     y=tf.placeholder(tf.float32)

[4]: #linear model
     linear_model=W*x+b

[5]: #loss
     squared=tf.square(linear_model-y)
     loss=tf.reduce_sum(squared)
```

Figure 3.60: *Defining the linear model*

Then we define our model. Keep in mind that we are first creating the computational graph, and then we will execute it in the session:

```
[1]: import tensorflow as tf
```

```
[2]: #variables
     #first run
     W=tf.Variable([.2],tf.float32)
     b=tf.Variable([-.2],tf.float32)
     #second run
     #W=tf.Variable([-1.0],tf.float32)
     #b=tf.Variable([1.0],tf.float32)
```

```
[3]: #placeholders
     x=tf.placeholder(tf.float32)
     #label
     y=tf.placeholder(tf.float32)
```

```
[4]: #linear model
     linear_model=W*x+b
```

```
[5]: #loss
     squared=tf.square(linear_model-y)
     loss=tf.reduce_sum(squared)
```

Figure 3.61: loss function

Next, we create the error or loss function. Cell 5 needs some additional explanation.

Linear_model is the predicted value. That is, during the training process, we pass the value of **x,** and the output is predicted by the model. Note that it is not *y* which is the label. This is the predicted value. Therefore, the difference between the predicted value (**linear_model**) and **y** (label) gives the error.

This error can be +ve or –ve based on whether the predicted value is larger than the label value or vice versa. **tf.square()** squares the error so that all the values are positive.

The next line is simply the sum of all these squares. Do not get confused by the name of the method **reduce_sum**. **tf.reduced_sum** (squared) provides the sum of squares of the errors of the data set:

```
6]:  init=tf.global_variables_initializer()

7]:  sess=tf.Session()
     sess.run(init)

8]:  print(sess.run(loss,feed_dict={x:[1,2,3,4],y:[0,-1,-2,-3]}))
     20.16
```

Figure 3.62: Session

After the creation of the graph, we create the session and initialize the variables before executing the graph in the session:

```
6]:  init=tf.global_variables_initializer()

7]:  sess=tf.Session()
     sess.run(init)

8]:  print(sess.run(loss,feed_dict={x:[1,2,3,4],y:[0,-1,-2,-3]}))
     20.16
```

Figure 3.63: Initializing variables

This line is the actual execution of the graph. Let us spend some time to understand this.

The node we are executing is loss which is a function of the node squared, which in turn is a function of **linear_model** and y. **linear_model** is in turn dependent on x. Therefore, the loss is dependent on x and y, which are placeholders. Therefore, we feed x and y using the **feed_dict**. And the values being fed are as follows:

X=[1,2,3,4]

And

Y=[0, –1, –2, –3]

This is the training data. And the loss calculated is 20.16. We have to minimize this value by changing the values of the trainable parameters W and b.

Now, let us try to manually change the values of **W** and **b** by reinitializing them to different values and running the session again.

```
[15]:  #variables
       #first run
       W=tf.Variable([.3],tf.float32)
       b=tf.Variable([-.3],tf.float32)
       #second run
       #W=tf.Variable([-1.0],tf.float32)
       #b=tf.Variable([1.0],tf.float32)
```

Figure 3.64: Re-run the session

W and b are reinitialized to .3 and −.3, respectively:

```
[24]:  print(sess.run(loss,feed_dict={x:[1,2,3,4],y:[0,-1,-2,-3]}))
       23.66
```

Figure 3.65: To print loss value

Now we get the loss value of 23.66 which is higher than the previous value. Let us try one more set of values for **W** and **b**:

```
[25]:  #variables
       #first run
       #W=tf.Variable([.3],tf.float32)
       #b=tf.Variable([-.3],tf.float32)
       #second run
       W=tf.Variable([-1.0],tf.float32)
       b=tf.Variable([1.0],tf.float32)
```

Figure 3.66: initializing

W and b are reinitialized to −1.0 and 1.0, respectively.

```
[31]:  print(sess.run(loss,feed_dict={x:[1,2,3,4],y:[0,-1,-2,-3]}))
       0.0
```

Figure 3.67: Loss value = 0

And the loss is finally reduced to 0.

This is what happens behind the scenes during the training process. The values of the parameters *W* and *b* are being updated continuously in order to reduce the loss. If we have to automate this process, we can use an optimizer provided by TensorFlow. In order to do that, we update the code as shown here:

```
#Loss
squared=tf.square(linear_model-y)
loss=tf.reduce_sum(squared)

#select an optimizer
optimizer=tf.train.GradientDescentOptimizer(0.01)

#minimize loss
train=optimizer.minimize(loss)
```

Figure 3.68: Applying Optimizer

An instance of the optimizer is created and named optimizer. It takes a parameter called learning rate—in this case, it is .01. We will discuss about learning rate later on.

Then we use the minimize method of the optimizer to minimize the loss. The node **train**, when executed in a recursive manner in a session, will automatically change the trainable parameters **W** and **b** in order to reduce the loss:

```
[35]: for i in range(1000):
          sess.run(train,{x:[1,2,3,4],y:[0,-1,-2,-3]})

[36]: print(sess.run([W,b]))
      [array([-1.], dtype=float32), array([1.], dtype=float32)]
```

Figure 3.69: To use train()

The node **train** is executed in a session in a loop for 1000 iterations. When we print W and b, we find that it found the correct values of **W (−1.0)** and **b(1.0)**, which we have seen earlier gave a loss value of 0.

This can be verified by executing the node **loss** in the session:

```
[38]: print(sess.run(loss,{x:[1,2,3,4],y:[0,-1,-2,-3]}))
      0.0
```

Figure 3.70: To calculate loss value

It returns 0. Although we have used the `GradientDescentOptimizer` in this case, TensorFlow offers a variety of optimizers. The functioning of `GradientDescentOptimizer` will be explained in the Neural Networks chapter. Here, the focus is on writing the code, and hence, the detailed explanation of the functioning of the `GradientDescentOptimizer` is deferred to the next chapter.

Applying optimizer to solve simple mathematical problems

In order to help us get a better understanding of the use of the optimizer, let us take a very simple mathematical example of solving a quadratic equation using the `GradientDescent` optimizer.

In this demo, we will solve the following quadratic equation:

(i.e., in code, x**2-10*x + 25)

And the code is here:

```
[1]: import tensorflow as tf

[2]: x=tf.Variable(0.0)
     #x=tf.Variable(10.0)

[3]: cost=x**2-10*x+25

[4]: #select an optimizer
     optimizer=tf.train.GradientDescentOptimizer(0.01)

[5]: #minimize loss
     train=optimizer.minimize(cost)

[6]: init=tf.global_variables_initializer()
     sess=tf.Session()
     sess.run(init)
```

Figure 3.71: Solving quadratic equation

We first start building the computational graph. Initialize **x** to 0 and any other random value. And create a node called **cost** that defines the left side of the quadratic equation, which needs to be minimized (to 0):

```
[1]: import tensorflow as tf

[2]: x=tf.Variable(0.0)
     #x=tf.Variable(10.0)

[3]: cost=x**2-10*x+25

[4]: #select an optimizer
     optimizer=tf.train.GradientDescentOptimizer(0.01)

[5]: #minimize loss
     train=optimizer.minimize(cost)

[6]: init=tf.global_variables_initializer()
     sess=tf.Session()
     sess.run(init)
```

Figure 3.72: instantiate optimizer

Next, we create an instance of the optimizer and the **train** node to minimize the cost function:

```
[42]: for i in range(500):
          sess.run(train)

[43]: print(sess.run(x))
      4.9999886
```

Figure 3.73: result after 500 iterations

If we execute this for 500 iterations in a session, it determines the value of x, which is 5 (4.9999886)—the solution to this quadratic equation.

You can try this out with another example:

Conclusion

This brings us to the end of this chapter. TensorFlow programming can be tricky even for experienced programmers, but once you get the hang of it, it is really very powerful for developing and training Neural Networks. In case you feel some parts are still fuzzy, it may be a good idea to read through this chapter once again and also run the demo code examples in your development environment. It is very important to get a good understanding of these concepts of TensorFlow before you move forward.

In the upcoming chapter, you will learn about Neural Networks. In *Chapter 5: TensorFlow 2*, we will introduce TensorFlow 2.

Questions

1. What is TensorFlow?
2. What is the difference between – constant, variable, and placeholder?
3. Can you initialize a placeholder to a value of 100.0?
4. Explain what is meant by Lazy execution?
5. Write a code snippet to perform the following:

    Create a variable named x and initialize it to 100. Create a placeholder named y. Add a node named z and perform $z = x*y$. Execute the node z in a session and find the result for $y = 48.197$.

CHAPTER 4
Neural Networks

Introduction

This is the beginning of the deep learning section. In this chapter, you will learn about Neural Networks, which is the core component of deep learning. Instead of only discussing theory, we will take a practical approach to help you understand the concepts quickly and apply them. And that is also the reason this book is structured in such a way that TensorFlow programming was dealt with prior to starting this chapter.

In this chapter, you will learn about the working of Neural Networks. We start with the smallest component of Neural Networks, which is an artificial neuron also referred to as a perceptron. Then, we move to a layer with multiple neurons, followed by multilayer Neural Networks.

This step-by-step approach with code examples will help in grasping this complex topic in an easy way.

Just a quick caution that Neural Networks is a complex topic, and do not get discouraged if you do not understand everything in one go. That is quite natural as in the case of TensorFlow, you may have to iterate this chapter maybe a couple of times.

And there is still a huge debate out there as to whether we fully understand the working of a Neural Network. Very often, they work and give the required results, but it is difficult to explain why those results are obtained. And we just consider the Neural Network as a black box. Therefore, approach it with an open mind, be inquisitive and keep asking "why?" and be prepared that there are no answers yet for all the questions.

With that, let us get started.

Structure

In this chapter, the following topics will be covered:

- What are neural networks?
- Structure of a perceptron
- Creating and training a perceptron with TensorFlow
- Step by step process of developing multilayer deep neural networks with TensorFlow
- Code demos and examples

Objective

After studying this chapter, you will be able to work on Neural Networks, learn about the most basic unit called **perceptron**, implement deep neural networks with multiple layers work, and build multilayer Neural Networks with TensorFlow and Keras.

About Neural Networks

The general meaning of a Neural Network is a network of interconnected neurons. Neurons can be biological (that exist in the human brain) or artificial. In the current context, we are referring to **Artificial Neural Networks** (**ANN**), which are modeled after the human brain, which is a Biological Neural Network. The term artificial intelligence is derived from the fact that natural intelligence exists in the human brain (or any brain for that matter!), and we humans are trying to simulate this natural intelligence artificially.

It may be noted that ANN was originally based on the human brain and the biological neurons, but today it has greatly evolved, and some of the forms of Neural Networks, such as CNN and RNN, cannot be directly mapped to the functioning of the human brain and biological neurons. Even the output of an artificial neuron can be programmed to different values, whereas a biological neuron has only two possible states—on and off.

However, for ease of understanding and as per tradition, we will begin by drawing an analogy between the biological neuron and an artificial neuron.

The human brain consists of billions of biological neurons interconnected with each other, and they are constantly communicating with each other by sending minute electrical binary signals by turning themselves on or off. It is believed that despite all the scientific advances, we still do not have a good understanding of the working of the human brain. According to some of the early research, a simplified version of the biological brain is represented as in *figure 4.1*:

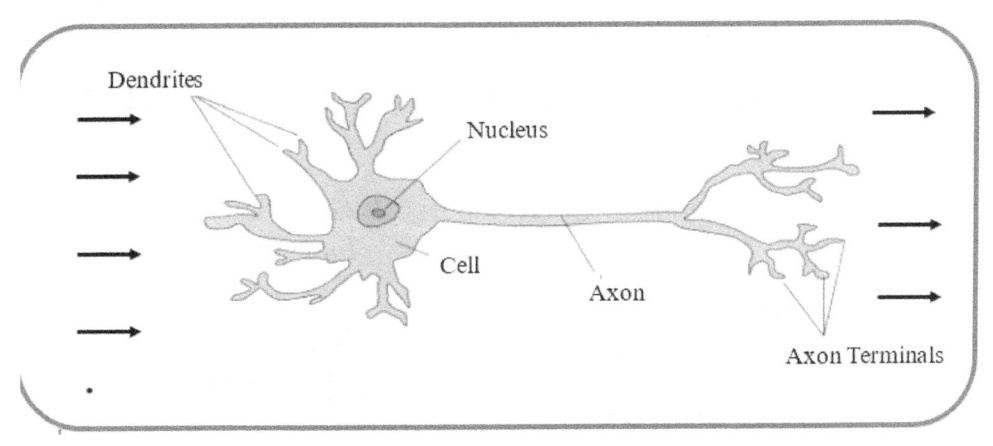

Figure 4.1: Biological neuron

This is a highly simplified representation. There are the following three main components:

- The dendrites that received the input signals
- The cell body where the signal is processed in some form
- The tail-like Axon through which it transfers the signal out to the next neuron.

An artificial neuron is also represented in a similar way, although it is not a physical entity but just a mathematical model. *Figure 4.2* is a high-level representation of an artificial neuron:

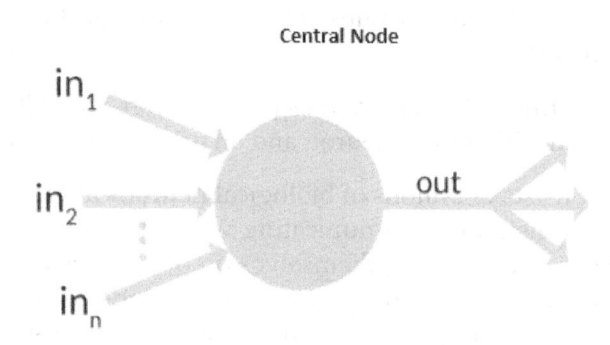

Figure 4.2: Representation of an artificial neuron

A more detailed representation of an artificial neuron or perceptron is shown in *figure 4.3*:

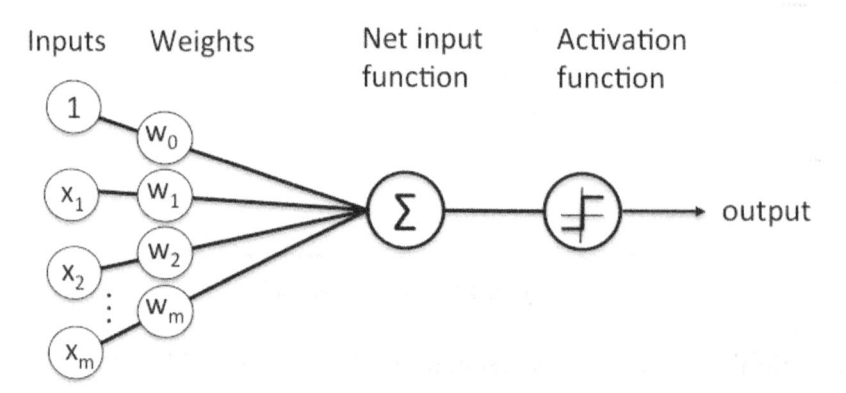

Figure 4.3: Representation of an Artificial Neuron or Perceptron

A perceptron has the following components:
1. Inputs ($x_1, x_2, ..., x_m$)
2. Weights ($w_1, w_2, ..., w_m$)
3. Bias (w_0)
4. Net Input Function
5. Activation function
6. Output

Inputs

Every neuron receives input data which is represented by $X_1, X_2,...,X_m$. The input data can be structured data (like a CSV file) or unstructured data like an image. These inputs are called **features**. In the beginning, this can be confusing. It should be understood that if it is structured data, then $X_1,...,X_m$ refers to the columns and not rows. Let us illustrate it with an example.

If the data is in the form of a table as follows:

x_1	x_2	x_3	x_4	x_5
0.02	0.0371	0.0428	0.0207	0.0954
0.0453	0.0523	0.0843	0.0689	0.1183
0.0262	0.0582	0.1099	0.1083	0.0974
0.01	0.0171	0.0623	0.0205	0.0205
0.0762	0.0666	0.0481	0.0394	0.059
0.0286	0.0453	0.0277	0.0174	0.0384
0.0317	0.0956	0.1321	0.1408	0.1674
0.0519	0.0548	0.0842	0.0319	0.1158
0.0223	0.0375	0.0484	0.0475	0.0647
0.0164	0.0173	0.0347	0.007	0.0187

Table 4.1: Sample data

Then the inputs to the neuron are the columns $x_1, x_2, x_3, x_4,$ and x_5, which correspond to one row. At this point, it may be difficult to comprehend, but for now, accept that the data is fed one row at a time in an iterative manner, which is a part of the overall perceptron training process.

Weights

Every neuron has weights. There are as many weights as the number of inputs. So in the above example, because there were 5 inputs $(x_1,...,x_5)$, there will be 5 weights. If you use another set of data where let us say there 20 inputs $(X_1,...,X_{20})$ then there will be 20 weights represented as $w_1, w_2,...,w_{20}$.

So, in general, if there are m inputs $(X_1, X_2,...,X_m)$, then there will be m weights $(W_1, W_2,...,W_m)$. Weight is nothing but a real number; it can be positive or negative. Here are some sample values:

$$w_1 = 0.712$$

$$w_2 = -0.3548$$

$$w_3 = 0.2681$$

$$w_4 = 0.112$$

$$w_5 = -0.8548$$

Table 4.2: Sample values of weights

These values are not predetermined, but they get assigned during the training process. We will see how perceptron training works in the next section, and this will become clear.

Note that w_0 is not a weight, though it is represented by a w.

Bias

Every neuron has one bias. In earlier representation, it was denoted by b, but in the newer representation, it is denoted by w_0. There is always only one bias per neuron, irrespective of the number of inputs. But like the weights, this is also a real number.

Net input function (F)

Net input function, also commonly referred to as input function, can be described as the sum of the products of the inputs and their corresponding weights and the bias. The mathematical expression is as follows:

As you can see, this is the reason why there are as many weights as there are inputs. And this is where matrix multiplication will be used. We will see this when we go into the code demo.

Since all of the variables are numbers, the result of the Net Input Function is just a number, a real number.

Activation function (G)

The output of the net input function is fed as input to the activation function. And the output of the activation function is the final output of the neuron. The activation function provides non-linearity. There are a variety of activation functions available, but we will start with the oldest one, known as *Sigmoid activation function*, which provides a binary output, thereby making the perceptron behave like a biological neuron that has binary status—on or off.

The mathematical equation of sigmoid function is :

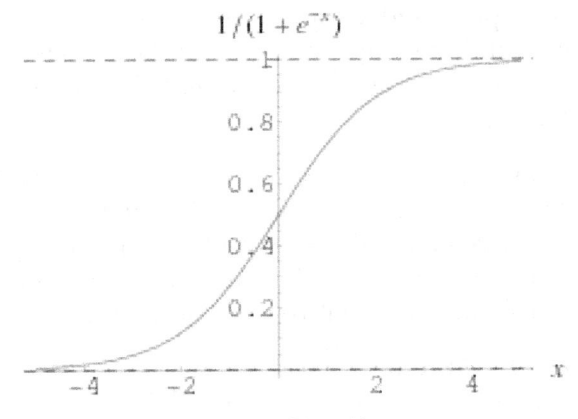

Figure 4.4: Sigmoid curve

As seen in *figure 4.4*, the output of a sigmoid function will always be between 0 and 1 no matter what the input is. And if we set a threshold (say, 0.5), we can convert this into a binary output. Any output greater than equal to 0.5 is considered 1, and any value less than 0.5 is considered 0.

Thus, the final output of the perceptron when using a sigmoid activation function is either 0 or 1, just like the biological neuron. This is just the structure of a perceptron. Let us implement this in our code before we move on to understand how perceptron training works.

Before writing the code, we need to freeze the design parameters. We will implement our first neural network in TensorFlow using the following design parameters:

Number of layers = 1

Number of neurons (units) = 1

Number of features (inputs) = 2 (X_1, X_2)

Activation function = sigmoid

Label = Y

Here goes the code:

```
[1]: import tensorflow as tf

[2]: # defining the perceptron
     #define place holder for features and labels
     x=tf.placeholder(tf.float32,[None,2])  #2 features

     y=tf.placeholder(tf.float32,[None,1])  #labels
```

Figure 4.5: Placeholder for features

We begin by creating a placeholder for features. The **tf.float32** function in the placeholder declaration indicates the data type of the placeholder is **float32**. Let us take a closer look at the parameter value [None,2] because we have so far never come across such a format.

Typically, while creating/declaring a placeholder, we can specify the shape of the placeholder along with the data type. And in this case, the parameter value [None,2] indicates the placeholder is a 2-dimensional array (or matrix) with two columns—but an unknown number of rows. None indicates that we do not know how many rows will be in the placeholder, which is decided at run time.

This is a very powerful feature of placeholder, and we will see how this is used in the perceptron training section. And we defined 2 columns because there are 2 features (X_1, X_2) as per our design. If the data has 10 features, then the placeholder needs to have 10 columns, and the shape would be given as [None,10], or if it has 100 features, then the shape needs to be [None,100].

It is to be noted that before we begin implementing any new neural network, we have to know our data, especially how many features we are dealing with. The number of rows is not as important at this point. We will see in *figure 4.6* that how the number of rows plays a role in the perceptron training section:

```
[1]: import tensorflow as tf

[2]: # defining the perceptron

     #define place holder for features and labels
     x=tf.placeholder(tf.float32,[None,2])  #2 features

     y=tf.placeholder(tf.float32,[None,1])  #labels
```

Figure 4.6: Placeholder for labels

Next, we define a placeholder for the label. This can sometimes be confusing because **y** is usually considered as the output. Recall that in the case of labeled data, the label is already available, and this needs to be fed along with the features (X_1 and X_2). This should not be confused with the output of the neuron, which is known as the predicted value.

Then, we initialize the weights and bias as follows:

```
[3]: # weights and bias

     weight=tf.Variable(tf.zeros([2,1]))

     bias=tf.Variable(tf.zeros([1]))
```

Figure 4.7: Initialization of weights and bias

Recall that since there are 2 inputs (X_1, X_2), we will need two weights as well. However, instead of creating them as separate variables, we just create a matrix of shape [2,1]. This makes the code scalable and re-usable. You will see very soon how this makes sense.

Number 2 in shape corresponds to the number of inputs-2 in this case, and Number 1 indicates the number of neurons-1 in this case. Since there is only one neuron, we need just one bias. Hence, the bias is initialized like a variable. However, once again, this is created as a matrix of one element—just to make the code re-usable later.

Defining the weights and bias as matrixes also helps in leveraging the matrix multiplication function that is offered by TensorFlow. Another important aspect is that while weights and bias are created as variables, inputs and labels are created as placeholders. The reason being inputs labels are fed at run time; that is why they are placeholders. Weights and bias are internally initialized, re-assigned, and updated during the training process, and hence, they cannot be constants or placeholders, and hence, they are variables.

The next step is to calculate the Net **input** function (refer to *figure 4.8*). Just to remind you that we are just creating the computational graph. Nothing is getting computed as of now:

```
# input function
#mult= tf.matmul(x,weight)
#I= tf.add(mult,bias)

I=tf.add(tf.matmul(x,weight),bias)

#activation function
output=tf.sigmoid(I)
```

Figure 4.8: Calculating Net input function

Net input function (**I**) has two parts: the matrix multiplication of **x** and weight, which will result in .

This is how it works. Assuming we pass one row of data, **NONE = 1**. The shape of **x** is **[1,2]**:

$$x = [X_1 \ X_2]$$

weight =

$$\begin{vmatrix} w_1 \\ w_2 \end{vmatrix}$$

Recall how matrix multiplication works: **x** weight

The result of the matrix multiplication would be as follows:

$$X_1 * w_1 + X_2 * w_2$$

$$bias = [b]$$

The function `tf.add` adds bias to the result of the matrix multiplication, so the final result **I** is as follows:

$$X_1 * w_1 + X_2 * w_2 + b$$

And if multiple rows of data are fed, the output is a columnar matrix with as many rows. Here is an example output if we feed 5 rows of data:

$$\begin{vmatrix} X_{11} * w_1 + X_{12} * w_2 + b \\ X_{21} * w_1 + X_{22} * w_2 + b \\ X_{31} * w_1 + X_{32} * w_2 + b \\ X_{41} * w_1 + X_{42} * w_2 + b \\ X_{51} * w_1 + X_{52} * w_2 + b \end{vmatrix}$$

And since all the X values, w values, and b are real numbers, the output might look like this:

$$\begin{vmatrix} 3.123 \\ -2.34 \\ 103.4533 \\ -302.345 \\ 566.333 \end{vmatrix}$$

Now, the activation function is as follows:

```
#activation function
output=tf.sigmoid(I)
```

Figure 4.9: Activation function

The final output of the perceptron is the output of the activation function (sigmoid in this case). The net input function, as calculated earlier, is fed as input (**I**) to the sigmoid function. Recall that the output of the sigmoid is always between 0 and 1 no matter what the input. In this example, let us consider the elements of the preceding columnar matrix:

3.123 > 0.5 -> output will be 1

−2.34 <0.5 -> output will be 0

103.4533 >0.5 -> output will be 1

−302.345 <0.5 -> output will be 0

566.333>0.5 -> output will be 1

So, the final output of this perceptron for these 5 rows would be as follows:

$$\begin{vmatrix} 1 \\ 0 \\ 1 \\ 0 \\ 1 \end{vmatrix}$$

Putting all of this together, this is the complete code for the implementation of a perceptron:

```python
import tensorflow as tf

# defining the perceptron

#define place holder for features and labels
x=tf.placeholder(tf.float32,[None,2])   #2 features

y=tf.placeholder(tf.float32,[None,1])   #labels

# weights and bias

weight=tf.Variable(tf.zeros([2,1]))

bias=tf.Variable(tf.zeros([1]))

# input function
#mult= tf.matmul(x,weight)
#I= tf.add(mult,bias)

I=tf.add(tf.matmul(x,weight),bias)

#activation function
output=tf.sigmoid(I)
```

Figure 4.10: Code for perceptron

And this is just the creation of the computational graph. This needs to be executed in a session. The purpose of a perceptron is to learn. Executing this graph as it is will not make any sense. We have to write additional code to train this perceptron by feeding some data. We will do this in two parts. First, we will look at the code for training the perceptron. Then, we will take some toy data to train this perceptron to classify the data:

```
# define the cost/ loss fns and the optimizer
individual_loss=tf.nn.sigmoid_cross_entropy_with_logits(labels=y,logits=output)
loss=tf.reduce_mean(individual_loss)

gdo=tf.train.GradientDescentOptimizer(learning_rate=0.01)
train=gdo.minimize(loss)
```

Figure 4.11: Defining Cost/Loss function

This cell contains the additional code required to train a perceptron. As we have seen earlier, to train a model, we have to define the loss function and then try to minimize this loss by changing the trainable parameters. In this case, the weights and bias are the trainable parameters. Recall the simple linear regression example we implemented in the previous chapter using the gradient descent optimizer since the code is very similar. Let us go line-by-line:

```
# define the cost/ loss fns and the optimizer
individual_loss=tf.nn.sigmoid_cross_entropy_with_logits(labels=y,logits=output)
loss=tf.reduce_mean(individual_loss)
```

Figure 4.12: Loss function

This line of code calculates the error. TensorFlow offers a readily available method **tf.nn.sigmoid_cross_entropy_with_logits** to calculate this error.

Do not get intimidated by these weird-sounding function names. What it is doing is simple. It takes two parameters: labels and logits. Recall we declared **y** as a placeholder to capture the labels. It may be noted that **y** has not been used so far in our code. It is only used for comparing the error here. The other parameter logits take the output of the perceptron. And it calculates the error

Y—output

For each of the observations,

```
loss=tf.reduce_mean(individual_loss)
```

Figure 4.13: Calculation of average loss for the batch

This line calculates the mean. Once again, the term **reduce_mean** may be confusing, but it is just the mean error value. And it takes the output of the previous line (**individual_loss**) as the parameter:

```
gdo=tf.train.GradientDescentOptimizer(learning_rate=0.01)
train=gdo.minimize(loss)
```

Figure 4.14: Optimizer with learning rate

In these two lines, we instantiate a gradient descent optimizer and create a node to minimize the loss calculated in the previous line. Now the entire computational graph is ready to be executed in a session. However, we cannot execute it without data. We need some data to train this perceptron.

A single perceptron may not be of much practical value, but we will use it with some dummy data just to understand how the perceptron training process works. There is a CSV file named **data.csv** which has 3 columns (label, x_1, x_2) and 21 rows; x_1 and x_2 are the features, and label is the target. And the data belong to two classes. The labels for these classes are 0 and 1, which are stored in the column label. We will train our perceptron to classify this data.

Let us read and prepare the data first. For this, we will make use of some of the libraries like scikit learn, NumPy, and pandas. Let us import these libraries:

```
import tensorflow as tf
import pandas as pd
import numpy as np
import matplotlib.pyplot as plt
%matplotlib inline

from sklearn.metrics import confusion_matrix
from sklearn.metrics import accuracy_score
```

Figure 4.15: Importing libraries

Then read the CSV file:

```
data=pd.read_csv('data.csv')
data.head()
```

Figure 4.16: To read data

The **data.head()** function displays the data. This is to check whether the CSV file can read properly. It will display the top 5 rows like:

	label	x1	x2
0	1	2.6487	4.5192
1	1	1.5438	2.4443
2	1	1.8990	4.2409
3	1	2.4711	5.8097
4	1	3.3590	6.4423

Figure 4.17: Output using data.head()

Next, separate the features and the labels:

```
X_input=data[['x1','x2']]
Y_label=data[['label']]
```

Figure 4.18: Code to display features and labels

This is how the features would look:

X_input

	x1	x2
0	2.6487	4.5192
1	1.5438	2.4443
2	1.8990	4.2409
3	2.4711	5.8097
4	3.3590	6.4423
5	3.2406	5.8097

Figure 4.19: List of features

And this how the labels are:

```
Y_label
```

	label
0	1
1	1
2	1
3	1
4	1
5	1

Figure 4.20: To display labels

A scatter plot of the data looks as shown in *figure 4.21*, and it can be seen that the data can be easily separated into two distinct classes:

```
plt.scatter(data.x1,data.x2,c=data.label)
```
```
<matplotlib.collections.PathCollection at 0x267bd6116d8>
```

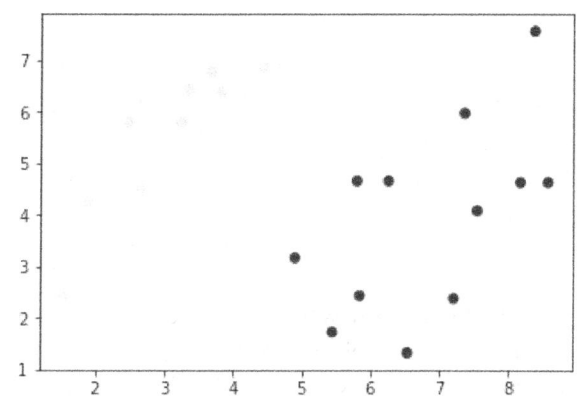

Figure 4.21: Scatter plot of the data

Now that we have data in the required format and the entire computations graph is ready, we will create the session and execute the computational graph for training the perceptron. Let us create a session and initialize the variables:

```
#initialize the variables
init=tf.global_variables_initializer()

sess=tf.Session()
sess.run(init)
```

Figure 4.22: Session

As mentioned earlier, training a perceptron is nothing but finding the right values of the weights and bias.

Before we train the perceptron, let us check what are the values of the weights and bias:

```
sess.run(weight)
array([[0.],
       [0.]], dtype=float32)
```

```
sess.run(bias)
array([0.], dtype=float32)
```

Figure 4.23: Weights and bias

Weights are initialized to 0, and bias is initialized to 0 as they should be. Now we train the perceptron for 100 iterations to start with:

```
for i in range(100):
    final_train=sess.run(train,feed_dict={x:X_input,y:Y_label})
```

Figure 4.24: Training perceptron for 100 iterations

By now, you should be able to figure out what is happening. We are executing the node train, which in turn takes the placeholders **x** and **y** as parameters. And since these are placeholders, we use the **feed_dict** and feed the data through **X_input** and **Y_label,** which are the features and labels, respectively.

If there was any learning by our perceptron, its weights and bias would have changed their values. Let us check it out:

```
sess.run(weight)
array([[-0.2642073 ],
       [-0.00197102]], dtype=float32)
```

```
sess.run(bias)
array([-0.01742139], dtype=float32)
```

Figure 4.25: Updated weights and bias

As we can see here, weights and bias have new values now.

This means our perceptron got trained, and it learned. But we do not know if it is trained enough to classify the data. To check that, we have to test our trained perceptron and measure the accuracy.

One simple way of doing it is to feed the features and see if it predicts the output correctly:

```
result=sess.run(output,feed_dict={x:X_input})
```

```
result
```

```
array([[0.32604352],
       [0.39409712],
       [0.37109783],
       [0.33586967],
       [0.28544888],
       [0.29212976],
       [0.26165408],
       [0.23056372],
       [0.26860726],
       [0.11732043],
       [0.12718327],
       [0.14845484],
       [0.18833707],
       [0.1727153 ],
       [0.21119347],
       [0.17357723],
       [0.12186671],
       [0.15704852],
       [0.09588055],
       [0.0919378 ],
       [0.10114945]], dtype=float32)
```

Figure 4.26: Predicted values

This is done by executing the preceding piece of code. We first execute the node output but feed the features **X_input,** and this is saved to results. The result has the exact value calculated by the sigmoid function. In order to get the corresponding binary values, we use the **round()** function to round off the values to 0 or 1.

```
ypred=result.round()
ypred
array([[0.],
       [0.],
       [0.],
       [0.],
       [0.],
       [0.],
       [0.],
       [0.],
       [0.],
       [0.],
       [0.],
       [0.],
       [0.],
       [0.],
       [0.],
       [0.],
       [0.],
       [0.],
       [0.]], dtype=float32)
```

Figure 4.27: Rounded off predicted values

This shows that our perceptron has predicted all of them as 0's, which is incorrect. It means that our perceptron needs further training. We ran the training for only 100 iterations. Let us re-run the training for 500 iterations:

```
for i in range(500):
    final_train=sess.run(train,feed_dict={x:X_input,y:Y_label})
```

Figure 4.28: Training perceptron for 500 iterations

Now, if the run the test once again, we notice that some of the predictions and 0 and some are 1. It looks like our perceptron has learned to classify the data. We would like to now measure the accuracy. Scikit-learn library offers a function **accuracy_score** to calculate the accuracy but passing the labels and the predicted values as parameters:

```
accuracy_score(Y_label, ypred)
```
1.0

Figure 4.29: Accuracy

Wow! It shows that our perceptron got perfectly trained. It predicted all the data correctly, which is 100% accuracy. We can also use the confusion matrix. Once again, there is a readily available function from scikit-learn, which we can call and pass the same two parameters:

```
confusion_matrix(Y_label, ypred)

array([[12,  0],
       [ 0,  9]], dtype=int64)
```

Figure 4.30: confusion matrix

Once again, this shows that the predictions are 100% correct. This is how you train a basic perceptron.

How do we extend this to perform multiclass classification? This is where we introduce a new kind of activation function called the Softmax activation function.

The Softmax activation function is a special type of activation function which is used in combination with 3 or more neurons. Keep in mind that this is not used with individual neurons. It is used for multiclass classification. If we want to build a multiclass classifier with 3 classes, we will need 3 neurons connected to a Softmax activation function:

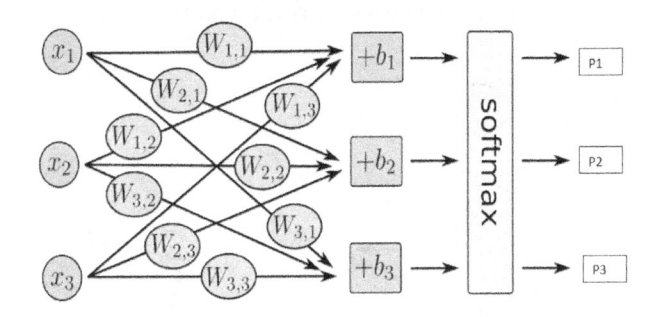

Figure 4.31: Softmax activation function

As seen in *figure 4.31*, the net input function of each of the 3 neurons is fed to the common Softmax activation function instead of individual sigmoid functions.

The Softmax activation functions give 3 outputs *P1*, *P2*, and *P3*, which are the probabilities of the 3 classes.

Hence,

- P1, P2, P3 are each less than 1.
- P1 + P2 + P3 = 1

This network is trained in such a way that P1 has a maximum value when an object of class 1 is fed, and P2 has the maximum value when an object of class 2 is fed, and similarly, P3 will have the maximum value when an object of class 3 is fed.

Here is an example. After the model is trained, if the features of an object of Class 2 are fed to this model, the output would be something like this:

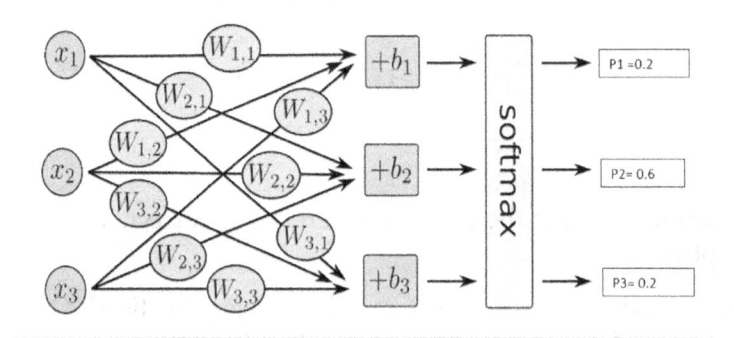

Figure 4.32: Sample output

P2 has the highest value, which means the prediction is correct. An associated concept is one hot encoding. To make the results quick and easy to interpret, the output is further processed to a one-hot encoded format. In this case, the output which has the maximum value is set to 1, and all others are set to 0. The one-hot encoded output of the previous example would be as follows:

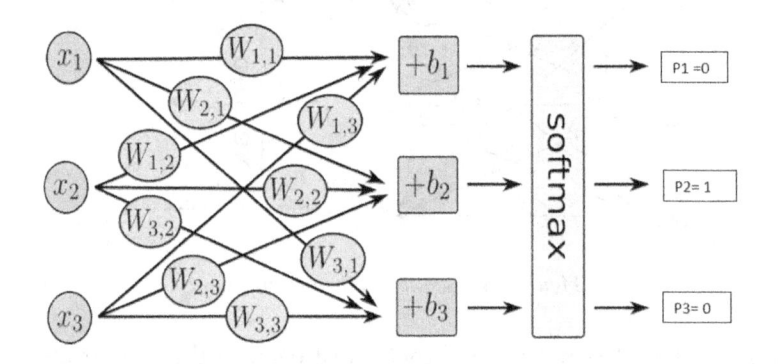

Figure 4.33: One hot encoded output

The labels of the training data also need to be one-hot encoded. And if they have a different format, it needs to convert to one-hot encoded before training the model, like in the following code example.

Let us see a code demo of this model. We will take the iris data set, which has 3 classes for this demo:

```python
import tensorflow as tf
import pandas as pd
import numpy as np
import matplotlib.pyplot as plt
%matplotlib inline

from sklearn.metrics import confusion_matrix
from sklearn.metrics import accuracy_score
from pandas import get_dummies
```

Figure 4.34: Import libraries and packages

We import the required libraries and then load the data:

```python
data=pd.read_csv('iris.csv')
data.head()
```

	petallength	petalwidth	sepallength	sepalwidth	species
0	5.1	3.5	1.4	0.2	0
1	4.9	3.0	1.4	0.2	0
2	4.7	3.2	1.3	0.2	0
3	4.6	3.1	1.5	0.2	0
4	5.0	3.6	1.4	0.2	0

Figure 4.35: To load data

A quick display of the top 5 rows shows the data is properly loaded. As always, we separate the features and the target:

```python
X_input=data.drop(labels='species', axis=1)
Y_label=data['species']
```

Figure 4.36: To separate features and target

Let us display the labels:

```
     Y_label
0       0
1       0
2       0

27      0
28      0
29      0
       ..
120     2
121     2
122     2
123     2
```

Figure 4.37: Displaying labels

The labels have values 0, 1, and 2, respectively, for Classes 1, 2, and 3. As mentioned earlier, this needs to be converted to a one-hot encoded format. There is a readily available function called **get_dummies** to do this conversion:

```
y_hot = get_dummies(Y_label)

y_hot
```

	0	1	2
0	1	0	0
1	1	0	0
2	1	0	0
3	1	0	0

Figure 4.38: One hot encoding of labels

Now the data is ready. We create the model with three neurons:

```
# defining the neural network / perceptron

#define place holder for input and label
x=tf.placeholder(tf.float32,[None,4])
#labels
y=tf.placeholder(tf.float32,[None,3])  #labels
```

Figure 4.39: Placeholders

We start by defining the placeholders **x** and **y** for the features and labels. There are features, and hence, the shape of **x** is [None,4]. The one-hot encoded format of the labels has 3 columns, and hence, the share of **y** is [None,3].

```
# weights and bias

weight=tf.Variable(tf.truncated_normal([4,3],stddev=0.1))
bias=tf.Variable(tf.truncated_normal([3],stddev=0.1))
#tf.truncated_normal
# input function

netinput=tf.add(tf.matmul(x,weight),bias)
#activation function
output=tf.nn.softmax(netinput)
```

Figure 4.40: Weights and bias

Next, we define the weights and bias. Since there are 4 features and 3 neurons, the shape of the weight variable is [4,3]. And there are 3 bias values since there are three neurons. If you have noticed, this time, weight and bias are not initialized to zeros like before, but random values.

The function **tf.truncated_normal** will generate a set of random numbers with a normal distribution and truncated at a standard deviation of 0.1, which is indicated by the parameter **stddev=0.1**.

```
# input function
netinput=tf.add(tf.matmul(x,weight),bias)
#activation function
output=tf.nn.softmax(netinput)
```

Figure 4.41: Input function and activation function

Then we create the net input function, which is fed to the Softmax activation function using **tf.nn.softmax** function. This is an example of a single-layer multi-neuron neural network. Now that the network is configured, lets us add the code loss function and training:

```
# define the cost/ loss fns and the optimizer
loss=tf.reduce_mean(tf.nn.softmax_cross_entropy_with_logits_v2(labels=y,logits=output))

#optimizer
gdo=tf.train.GradientDescentOptimizer(learning_rate=0.01)
train=gdo.minimize(loss)
```

Figure 4.42: Loss function and optimizer

The loss function is different from what we used earlier. Instead of **tf.nn.sigmoid_cross_entropy_with_logits**, we use **tf.nn.softmax_cross_entropy_with_logits_v2** which is used along with the Softmax activation function. The next step is to train this model:

```
for i in range(100):
    sess.run(train,feed_dict={x:X_input,y:y_hot})
```

Figure 4.43: Training for 100 iterations

We do not know how many iterations will be required to properly train the model, so we randomly start with 100 iterations:

```
predict=sess.run(output,feed_dict={x:X_input})
```

```
predict
        [0.4286547 , 0.3079394 , 0.26340592],
        [0.48475736, 0.2826661 , 0.23257647],
        [0.4707907 , 0.28943017, 0.23977917],
        [0.47036526, 0.28662512, 0.2430096 ],
        [0.44348344, 0.29113457, 0.26538202],
        [0.44173566, 0.28241193, 0.2758523 ],
        [0.43997645, 0.29778394, 0.26223958],
        [0.4227679 , 0.28532517, 0.29190692],
```

Figure 4.44: Predicted values

When we run the test, we get an output like shown above. However, in order to use the **accuracy** function, we need to convert it into a one-dimension array. We can do this using the **argmax** functionality, remember we learned in the previous chapter:

```
result=sess.run(tf.argmax(predict,1))
```

```
result
array([0, 0, 0, 0, 0, 0, 0, 0, 0, 0, 0, 0, 0, 0, 0, 0, 0, 0, 0, 0, 0,
       0, 0, 0, 0, 0, 0, 0, 0, 0, 0, 0, 0, 0, 0, 0, 0, 0, 0, 0, 0, 0,
       0, 0, 0, 0, 0, 0, 2, 2, 2, 2, 2, 2, 2, 2, 2, 2, 2, 2, 2, 2, 2,
       2, 2, 2, 2, 2, 2, 2, 2, 2, 2, 2, 2, 2, 2, 2, 2, 2, 2, 2, 2, 2,
       2, 2, 2, 2, 2, 2, 2, 2, 2, 2, 2, 2, 2, 2, 2, 2, 2, 2, 2, 2, 2,
       2, 2, 2, 2, 2, 2, 2, 2, 2, 2, 2, 2, 2, 2, 2, 2, 2, 2, 2, 2, 2,
       2, 2, 2, 2, 2, 2, 2, 2, 2, 2, 2, 2, 2, 2, 2, 2, 2], dtype=int64)
```

Figure 4.45: Class label

After running argmax on predict, the output is a one-dimensional array similar to the labels in **Y_label**. Now, these two values can be passed as parameter values to the accuracy function to calculate the accuracy:

```
accuracy_score(result,Y_label)
```

0.6666666666666666

Figure 4.46: Calculating accuracy

We observe that our model has achieved 66.66% accuracy. In order to improve the accuracy let us train the model for 10,000 iterations and then check the results:

```
for i in range(10000):
    sess.run(train,feed_dict={x:X_input,y:y_hot})
```

Figure 4.47: Retrain for 10000 iterations

Now, we get 98% accuracy which is pretty good. We can also check the confusion matrix by calling the function **confusion_matrix** and passing the same parameter values:

```
confusion_matrix(result,Y_label)

array([[50,  0,  0],
       [ 0, 47,  0],
       [ 0,  3, 50]], dtype=int64)
```

Figure 4.48: To run confusion_matrix()

We observe that 3 of the items are getting miss-classified. If this model needs to be extended for multiclass classification problems with more classes, all that is needed to be done is add as many neurons as there are classes, and the rest of the code remains the same. For example, if the problem has 10 classes, then we will need 10 neurons. Therefore, the code needs to be modified to change the shape of the weight and bias to correspond to 10 neurons:

```
# weights and bias
weight=tf.Variable(tf.truncated_normal([4,10],stddev=0.1))
bias=tf.Variable(tf.truncated_normal([10],stddev=0.1))
#tf.truncated_normal
# input function
netinput=tf.add(tf.matmul(x,weight),bias)
#activation function
output=tf.nn.softmax(netinput)
```

Figure 4.49: Classifier for 10 classes

The rest of the code remains the same. A good example of such a problem is the MNIST problem.

MNIST

MNIST is one of the most popular neural networks case studies. Before we work on it, let us get a little bit of background about this project. MNIST stands for Modified

120 ■ *Beginning with Deep Learning Using TensorFlow*

National Institute of Standards and Technology. Modified stands for the modified data set that the team led by *Yann LeCun* worked with at NIST. This project was aimed at handwritten digit recognition using neural networks.

We need to understand the data set before we get into writing the code. MNIST data set is integrated into the TensorFlow library. It consists of 70,000 handwritten images of digits 0 to 9:

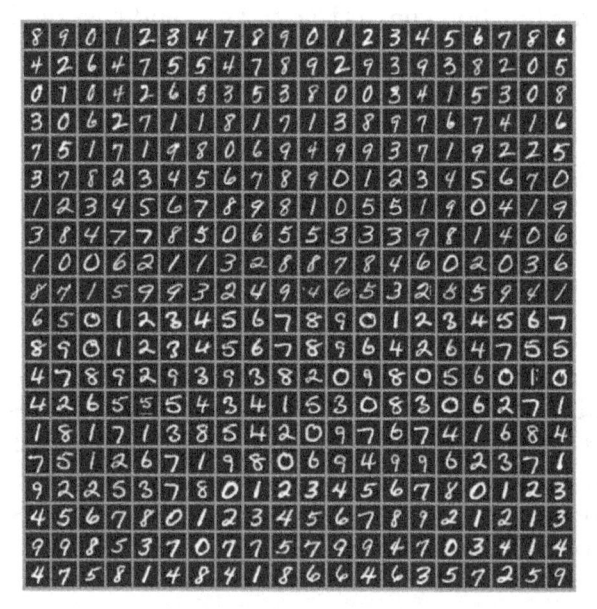

Figure 4.50: MNIST data

When we say images, you might think these are jpeg files, but they are not. They are actually stored in the form of pixel values. As far as the computer is concerned, an image is a bunch of numbers. These numbers are pixel values ranging from 0 to 255.

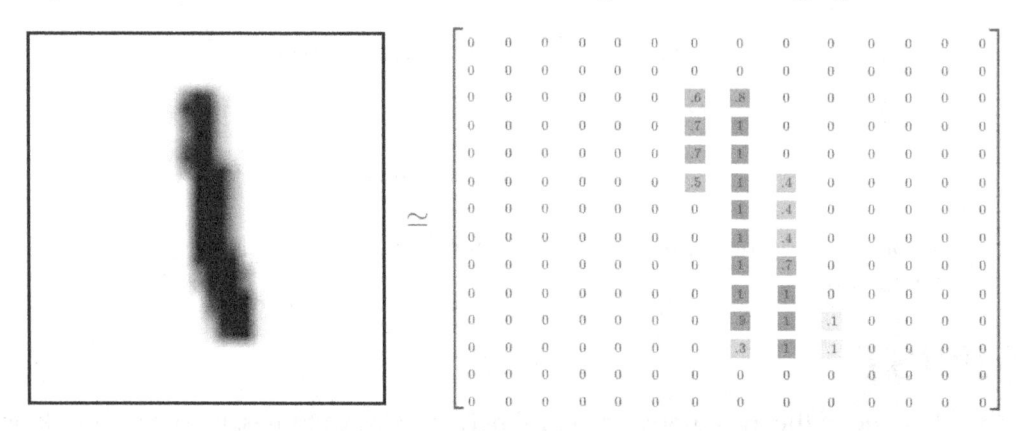

Figure 4.51: Matrix representation of number 1

Each of these images was of 28×28 dimension. The image is stored in the form of a 28×28 matrix, each cell containing a normalized pixel value ranging from 0 to 1. Real values range from 0 to 255, but these are normalized to 0 to 1. These are greyscale images (commonly known as black and white), 0 indicates white, and 1 indicates completely black, and a value in between indicates a certain shade of Gray. For example, in *figure 4.51*, the number 1 is represented in the form of a matrix.

The MNIST data set is split into 55,000 training images 10,000 test and 5000 validation images. And each image has a one-hot encoded label:

mnist.train.ys

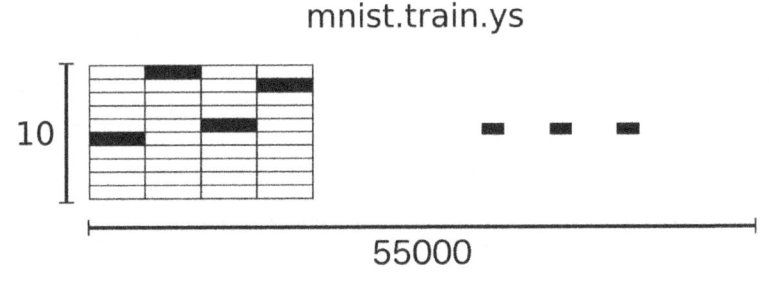

Figure 4.52: *Label information*

Each label has an array of 10 elements (shown along the vertical axis in *figure 4.52*), with exactly one of them set to 1 and the rest set to 0. The index value of the element set to 1 specifies the digit.

For example, in *figure 4.52*, the first image has the bit 4 set to 1, which means the label is 4. The second image has 9 sets to 1, which means the label is 9, and so on. Let us work on a demo to understand this data better before we start building the model for classifying this data:

```
import tensorflow as tf

from tensorflow.examples.tutorials.mnist import input_data

mnist = input_data.read_data_sets("MNIST_data/",one_hot=True)
```

Figure 4.53: *Load MNIST data*

This piece of code will download the MNIST data set to your local system. The parameter **one_hot=True** will make sure the labels are one-hot encoded. It takes a little while the first time you run this code. Subsequently, if the data is already available in your local system, it will not download again.

Let us explore the data to obtain the following output:

```
#28X28 images are flattened and stored as an array of 784 pixel values
mnist.train.images.shape
```

(55000, 784)

```
mnist.test.images.shape
```

(10000, 784)

```
mnist.validation.images.shape
```

(5000, 784)

Figure 4.54: The number of images in training, test, and validation.

When the MNIST team started this project, there were no sophisticated neural networks like CNN, which could accept the 2-dimensional images. So, the 28×28 matrix of pixel values was "*flattened*" to a one-dimensional array of 784 (28*28=784) pixel values:

```
: mnist.train.images[1].min()
: 0.0
```

```
: mnist.train.images[1].max()
: 1.0
```

Figure 4.55: Normalized pixel values range from 0 to 1

The pixel values are normalized, and hence, they go from a maximum of 1 to a minimum of 0. Using matplotlib, we can view the images:

```
import matplotlib.pyplot as plt
%matplotlib inline

plt.imshow(mnist.train.images[1000].reshape(28,28))

<matplotlib.image.AxesImage at 0x210ca861860>
```

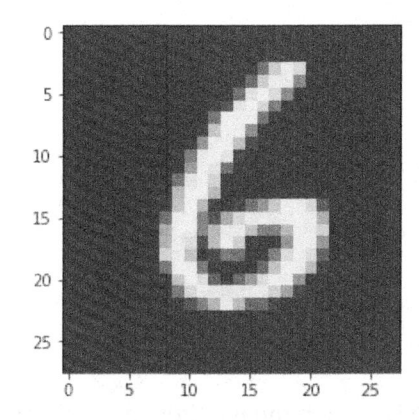

Figure 4.56: To display training data=6

The image in index location 1000 in the training data set is 6. Note that before displaying, we reshape the array to 28×28; therefore, we can view it like a regular image. We can try it with a different location by changing the index:

```
plt.imshow(mnist.train.images[2000].reshape(28,28))

<matplotlib.image.AxesImage at 0x1dd80729240>
```

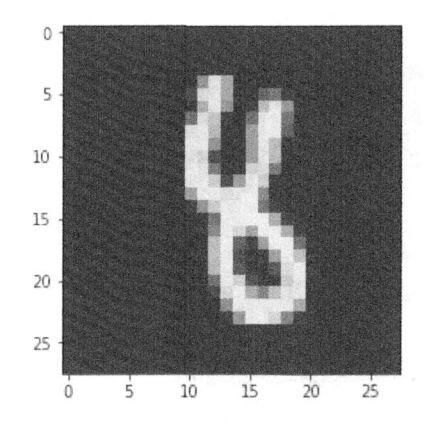

Figure 4.57: To display training data=8

Location 2000 has Number 8. In addition to data, MNIST also provides some easy-to-use functions. For example, **next_batch** takes a number as a parameter and fetches that many images.

This piece of code will fetch randomly selected 100 images from the training data set. It returns the pixel values in **batch_x** and the labels in **batch_y**:

```
batch_x , batch_y = mnist.train.next_batch(100)
```

```
batch_x.shape
```
(100, 784)

```
batch_y.shape
```
(100, 10)

Figure 4.59:

Figure 4.58: In built function — next_batch()

The shape of **batch_x** is [100, 784], which means there are 100 images in the flattened format of one-dimensional arrays of size 784. The shape of **batch_y** is [100,10], which means there are 100 one-hot encoded labels in the form of one-dimensional arrays of size 10 with exactly one cell set to 1 and others set to 0.

Let us examine some of the 10 images that are fetched:

```
plt.imshow(batch_x[50].reshape(28,28))
```
<matplotlib.image.AxesImage at 0x210cade6160>

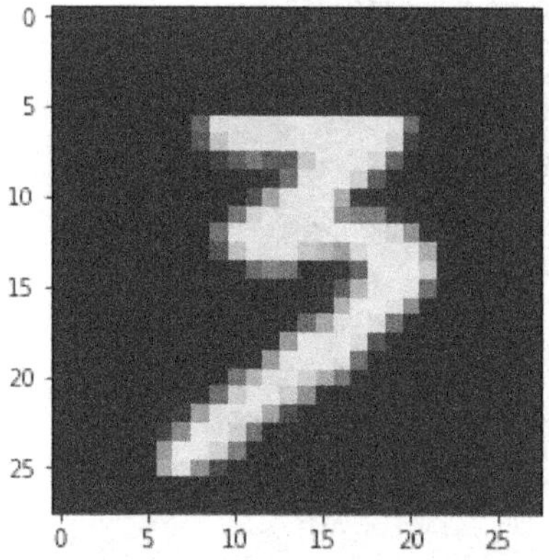

Figure 4.59: Image in 50th location

The image in the 50th location in this **batch_x** contains 3. Let us examine if the label corresponds to this.

```
batch_y[50]
```

```
array([0., 0., 0., 1., 0., 0., 0., 0., 0., 0.])
```

Figure 4.60: One hot encoded label

This is the corresponding one-hot encoded label. And as you can see, the location with Index 3 is set to 1, and all others are 0:

```
print(batch_y[50].argmax())
```

```
3
```

Figure 4.61: Digit in the image

We can use argmax to get the index location that also corresponds to the label value. Let us take one more example to illustrate this:

```
plt.imshow(batch_x[80].reshape(28,28))
```

```
<matplotlib.image.AxesImage at 0x1dd81788f28>
```

```
batch_y[80]
```

```
array([0., 0., 0., 0., 0., 0., 0., 0., 0., 1.])
```

```
print(batch_y[80].argmax())
```

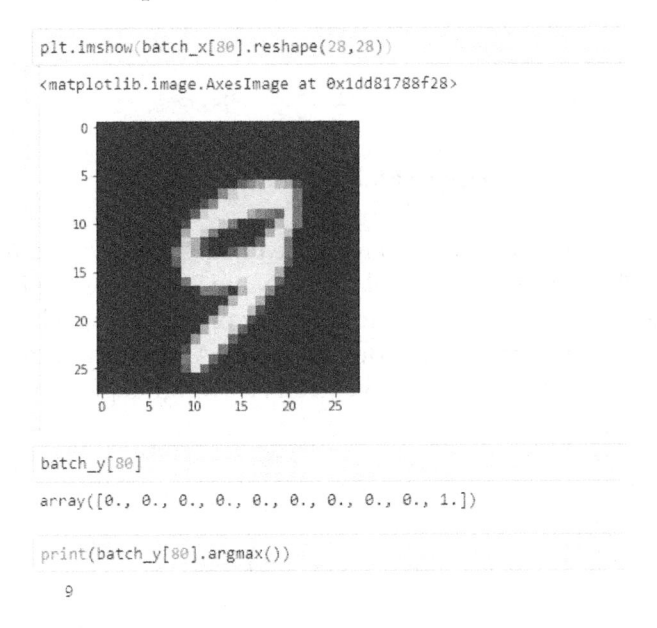

```
9
```

Figure 4.62: One more example

When we try this with the image in location 80, it is observed that the image is 9 and the label also is 9. Play around with this piece of code available in the notebook **MNIST-data.ipynb** on GitHub link provided to get a good understanding of the data. This is essential to understand the subsequent code where a single-layer Neural Network model is created and trained.

MNIST—single layer multi-neuron model

Now that you understand the MNIST data set and also understand how to create a single layer multiclass Neural Network, we will create and train a multiclass neural network and train it to classify the MNIST data set:

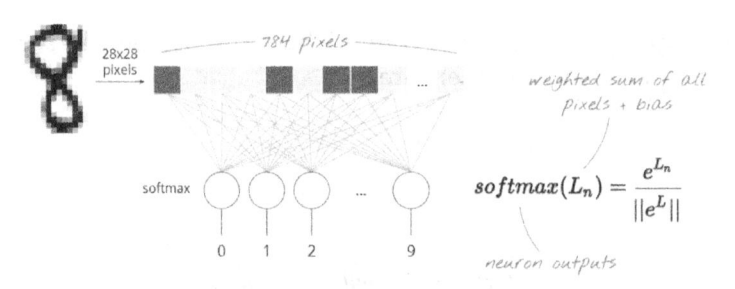

Figure 4.63: *A 10-Neuron Handwritten digit classifier*

$$softmax(L_n) = \frac{e^{L_n}}{||e^L||}$$

Figure 4.64 is the pictorial representation of this neural network. Let us start with the code:

```
x = tf.placeholder(tf.float32,shape=[None,784])
```

Figure 4.64: *To create a placeholder*

As a first step, create a placeholder to read the images and feed them to the network at runtime. The shape of this placeholder is [None,784] since the images are stored in the form of a flattened one-dimensional array of size 784. Each of these 784-pixel values is in the features/inputs for our neurons. And every input is fed to every neuron, as seen in *figure 4.63*. Hence, we need 784 weights per neuron:

```
# 10 sets of 784 weights
W = tf.Variable(tf.zeros([784,10]))
```

Figure 4.65: *weights*

The weight variable shape is [784,10] since there are 10 neurons, and each neuron needs 784 weights corresponding to the 784 inputs:

```
#10 biases - one for each neuron
b = tf.Variable(tf.zeros([10]))
```

Figure 4.66: *Bias*

Bias variable has just 10 elements, one for each neuron:

```
# Net input value
I = tf.matmul(x,W) + b
```

Figure 4.67: Net Input function

This is our net input function—nothing special:

```
#labels
y_true = tf.placeholder(tf.float32,[None,10])
```

Figure 4.68: Placeholder for labels

We create the placeholder to read in the labels and feed at runtime during the training process. The construction of the neural network is done. Then we add the code for loss function and optimizer:

```
individual_loss=tf.nn.softmax_cross_entropy_with_logits_v2(labels=y_true, logits=I)
loss_function = tf.reduce_mean(individual_loss)

#optimize the loss using gradient descent optimizer

optimizer = tf.train.GradientDescentOptimizer(learning_rate=0.5)

train = optimizer.minimize(loss_function)
```

Figure 4.69: Code for loss function and optimizer

With this, the graph is ready. We have to execute this in a session to train the model:

```
init = tf.global_variables_initializer()

sess=tf.Session()
sess.run(init)

#training
for step in range(1000):
    
    features , labels = mnist.train.next_batch(100)
    
    sess.run(train,feed_dict={x:features,y:labels})
```

Figure 4.70: To train model with 1000 iterations

We run the training for 1000 iterations, and in each iteration, we fetch 100 images using the **next_batch** function. Now that training is done, we have to check the accuracy of the model using the test data:

```
#pass the test data through the model
#NOTE: There will be no iteration for test
predict=sess.run(Output,feed_dict={x:mnist.test.images})
```

```
#output of 10,000 images
predict.shape
```

(10000, 10)

Figure 4.71: Predicted output

For testing, we use the entire test data **mnist.test.images** (10,000 images) and run the node **Output** to get the predictions from the model. The output **predict** will be 1000 rows of one hot encoded array of size 10.

In order to calculate the accuracy, it would be easier to convert this into a simpler format. We once again make use of the **argmax** functionality:

```
#argmax will give the predicted value in terms of a number
result=sess.run(tf.argmax(predict,1))
```

```
#predicted values
result
```

array([7, 2, 1, ..., 4, 8, 6], dtype=int64)

Figure 4.72: Output in regular digit format

Now **result** has all the predictions in the form of single-digit numbers:

```
#same way get the label value using argmax
label_number=tf.argmax(mnist.test.labels,1)
labels=sess.run(label_number)
```

```
labels
```

array([7, 2, 1, ..., 4, 5, 6], dtype=int64)

Figure 4.73: Labels in digit format

We convert the labels also into this format using argmax. Now, these two arrays can be used for calculating the accuracy:

```
accuracy_score(result,labels)
0.9067
```

Figure 4.74: To calculate accuracy

We observe that the model has achieved 90.67% accuracy. Let us train it for a few more iterations to see if the accuracy improves:

```
#training
for step in range(10000):
    features , labels = mnist.train.next_batch(200)
    sess.run(train,feed_dict={x:features,y:labels})
```

Figure 4.75: Retrain with 10000 iterations

Training the model for 10,000 iterations results in about 92.74% accuracy, as shown here:

```
accuracy_score(result,labels)
0.9274
```

Figure 4.76: New accuracy

This is pretty good, considering it is a very simple single-layer neural network with just 10 neurons. This entire code is available on GitHub link provided. Run this code and play around by changing the number of iterations and the batch size to see how the accuracy gets affected.

Multilayer Neural Network

In the previous example, we developed a single-layer Neural Network, often referred to as a shallow neural network. A pictorial representation is shown below:

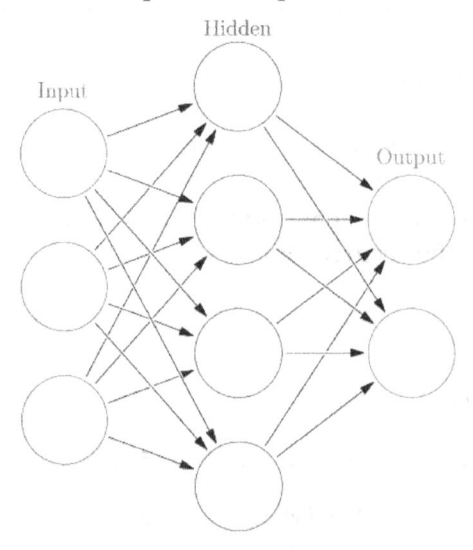

Figure 4.77: Shallow Neural Network

One layer of neurons is not sufficient to solve most of the deep learning problems. You need to stack up multiple layers. This is often referred to as **Deep Neural Network**. A pictorial representation is shown as follows:

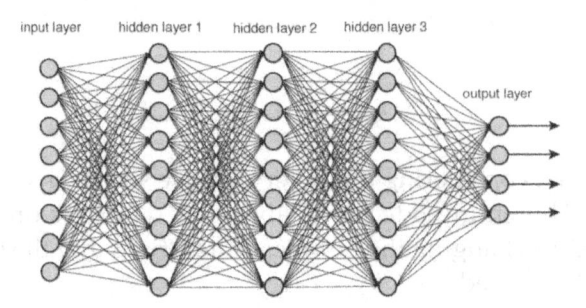

Figure 4.78: Deep Neural Network

Before we jump into the code, let us try to understand how this works. The hidden layers are where the neurons are there. The input layer is the input data and does not contain any neurons, even though it is common to represent this layer also with nodes. Similarly, the output does not actually have any neurons.

Input data is fed to the neurons in the first layer. It must be noted that every input is fed to every neuron in the first layer. And every neuron has one output. The output from each neuron in the first layer is fed to every neuron in the second layer. And the output of each neuron in the second layer is fed to every neuron in the third layer, and so on.

That is why this kind of network is also referred to as a Dense Neural Network or fully connected Neural Network. There are other types of neural networks like Convolutional Neural Network, where this is not true, but that will be discussed later.

There is no hard and fast rule about the number of neurons in each of the layers. This is usually determined by trial and error as a part of a process known as Hyper-Parameter tuning. However, there are some restrictions on the number of neurons in the last layer. The configuration of the last layer is determined as follows:

Binary classification	Multiclass classification
No. of Neurons = 1	No. of Neurons = number of classes
Activation function—Sigmoid	Activation function—Softmax

Table 4.3: Last layer configuration

Now let us get into the code. First, we will build a binary classifier with the same data we used to build our single perceptron. Then we will use the MNIST data set to extend the single layer 10 neuron network to a multilayer network.

Multilayer binary classifier

We will build a Binary classifier with a deep neural network of the following configuration:

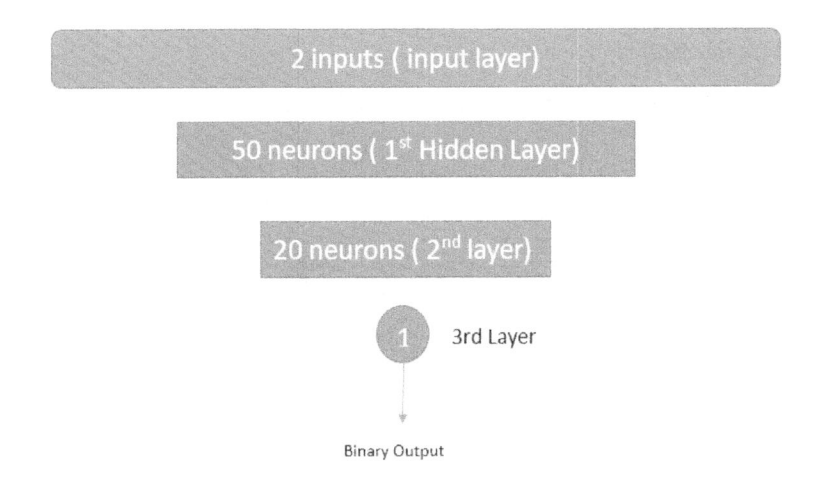

Figure 4.79: Multilayer neural network

The code is as follows:

```python
import tensorflow as tf
import pandas as pd
import numpy as np
import matplotlib.pyplot as plt
%matplotlib inline

from sklearn.metrics import confusion_matrix
from sklearn.metrics import accuracy_score
```

```python
data=pd.read_csv('data.csv')
data.head()
```

	label	x1	x2
0	1	2.6487	4.5192
1	1	1.5438	2.4443
2	1	1.8990	4.2409
3	1	2.4711	5.8097
4	1	3.3590	6.4423

```python
X_input=data[['x1','x2']]
Y_label=data[['label']]
```

Figure 4.80: Load data

This part of the code for loading and preparing the data remains the same:

```python
# defining the neural network / perceptron


#define place holder for input and label
x=tf.placeholder(tf.float32,[None,2])   #inputs/features - x1, x2
#labels
y=tf.placeholder(tf.float32,[None,1])   #labels

# weights and bias - layer1

weight=tf.Variable(tf.truncated_normal([2,100],stddev=0.1))
#tf.truncated_normal([784,200],stddev=0.1)
bias=tf.Variable(tf.truncated_normal([100],stddev=0.1))

# input function

netinput=tf.add(tf.matmul(x,weight),bias)
#activation function
output1=tf.nn.relu(netinput)
```

Figure 4.81: Placeholders

The creation of placeholders also remains the same:

```
# weights and bias - layer1
weight=tf.Variable(tf.truncated_normal([2,50],stddev=0.1))
bias=tf.Variable(tf.truncated_normal([50],stddev=0.1))
# input function
netinput=tf.add(tf.matmul(x,weight),bias)
#activation function
output1=tf.nn.relu(netinput)
```

Figure 4.82: First layer of neurons

We start by creating the first hidden layer. The weight variable has the shape [2,50] since there are 2 inputs and 50 neurons. And the bias variable has shape [50] since this layer has 50 neurons. The output of this layer is the output of the activation function. Observe that the activation function used here is **relu** and not sigmoid. We will discuss about this new kind of activation function a little later:

```
# weights and bias - layer2
weight2=tf.Variable(tf.truncated_normal([50,20],stddev=0.1))
bias2=tf.Variable(tf.truncated_normal([20],stddev=0.1))
# input function
netinput2=tf.add(tf.matmul(output1,weight2),bias2)
#activation function
output2=tf.nn.relu(netinput2)
```

Figure 4.83: Second layer

Then we add the second layer. We define a new set of variables for weights and bias. The shape of the weight variable (weight1) is [50,20] since this layer receives 50 inputs from each of the 50 neurons in the previous layer, and this layer has 20 neurons. The bias variable has shape [20] since there are 20 neurons. Let us take a closer look at the net-input function for this layer.

`netinput2=tf.add(tf.matmul(output1,weight2),bias2)`

The input here is the output from the previous layer (**output1**) and not **x**.

You will see this pattern in the next layer as well. The input for the next layer will be **output2**:

```
# weights and bias - Layer3
weight3=tf.Variable(tf.truncated_normal([20,1],stddev=0.1))

bias3=tf.Variable(tf.truncated_normal([1],stddev=0.1))

# input function
netinput3=tf.add(tf.matmul(output2,weight3),bias3)
output3=tf.sigmoid(netinput3)
```

Figure 4.84: *The third layer*

The third layer is the last layer. Since it is a binary classifier, it has only one neuron. It receives 20 inputs coming from each of the 20 neurons in the previous layer. The net-input function takes the output of layer 2 (**output2**) as its input.

Here we use the sigmoid activation function since we are expecting a binary output. Refer to *table 5.13*. The construction of the network is done. We just need to add the rest of the code for loss function and session:

```
# define the cost/ loss fns and the optimizer
loss=tf.reduce_mean(tf.nn.sigmoid_cross_entropy_with_logits(labels=y,logits=output3))

#optimizer
gdo=tf.train.GradientDescentOptimizer(learning_rate=0.01)
train=gdo.minimize(loss)

#initialize the variables
init=tf.global_variables_initializer()

sess=tf.Session()
sess.run(init)

for i in range(100):
        final_train=sess.run(train,feed_dict={x:X_input,y:Y_label})
```

Figure 4.85: *Code for loss function and session*

We run the training for 100 iterations:

```
accuracy_score(Y_label, ypred)
1.0
```

Figure 4.86: Training model for 100 iterations

Our model achieves 100% accuracy. The complete code is available on the GitHub link. You can play around by adding more layers and more neurons in each layer and see how the accuracy changes.

ReLu activation function

Before we go to the next demo with MNIST, let us see what this activation function ReLu is all about. ReLu is shortened form for rectified linear unit. The output of the ReLu function is always a non-negative value, that is, greater than or equal to 0:

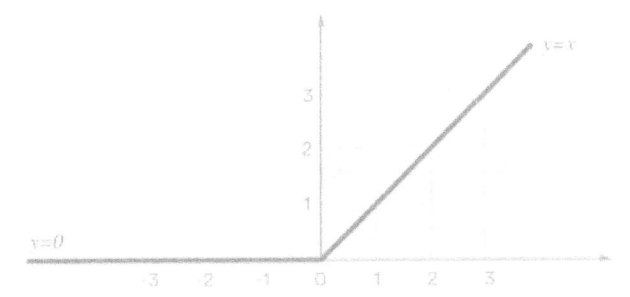

Figure 4.87: ReLu activation function

Mathematical expression for ReLu is:

This converges much faster than the sigmoid activation function, and therefore, it is by far the most widely used activation function. ReLu is used in almost every deep neural network. It is used in all the layers except only in the last layer, where either a Sigmoid or Softmax is used.

Multilayer multiclass neural network

Let us now build a multilayer neural network to solve the MNIST problem, which is a multiclass classification problem with 10 classes. We can re-use and mix and match the code from the previous example and the first MNIST example. This is the structure of the network that we will build:

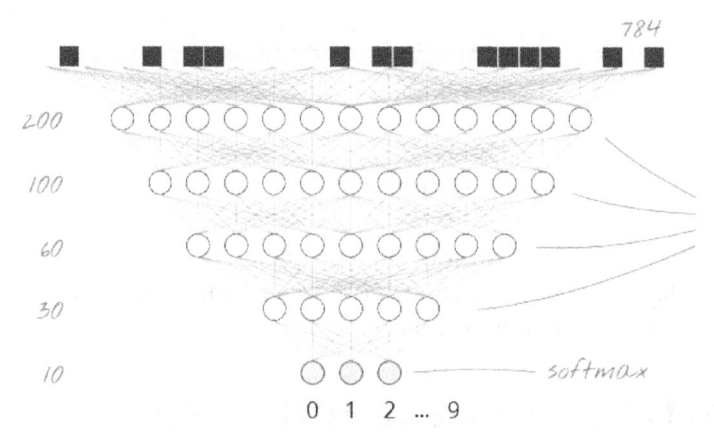

Figure 4.88: Multilayer multiclass

Hence, the code is given as follows:

```python
import tensorflow as tf

from tensorflow.examples.tutorials.mnist import input_data

mnist = input_data.read_data_sets("MNIST_data/",one_hot=True)

#input layer
x = tf.placeholder(tf.float32,shape=[None,784])

# first hidden layer
W1 = tf.Variable(tf.truncated_normal([784,200],stddev=0.1))
b1 = tf.Variable(tf.zeros([200]))

#output of first hidden layer
y1 = tf.nn.relu(tf.matmul(x,W1) + b1)

# second hidden layer
W2 = tf.Variable(tf.truncated_normal([200,100],stddev=0.1))
b2 = tf.Variable(tf.zeros([100]))

#output of second hidden layer
y2 = tf.nn.relu(tf.matmul(y1,W2) + b2)

# third hidden layer
W3 = tf.Variable(tf.truncated_normal([100,60],stddev=0.1))
b3 = tf.Variable(tf.zeros([60]))

#output of third hidden layer
y3 = tf.nn.relu(tf.matmul(y2,W3) + b3)

# fourth hidden layer
W4 = tf.Variable(tf.truncated_normal([60,30],stddev=0.1))
b4 = tf.Variable(tf.zeros([30]))

#output of fourth hidden layer
y4 = tf.nn.relu(tf.matmul(y3,W4) + b4)

#softmax layer

# 10 because 0-9 possible numbers
W5 = tf.Variable(tf.truncated_normal([30,10],stddev=0.1))

b5 = tf.Variable(tf.zeros([10]))

#Net input function of last layer
y = tf.matmul(y4,W5) + b5

#activation function
output=tf.nn.softmax(y)
```

Figure 4.89: Code for multilayer multiclass

All the five layers are created like before. The last layer has a Softmax activation function. The main structure is ready. Now we add the loss function and the session to run the training.

```python
y_true = tf.placeholder(tf.float32,[None,10])

# Cross Entropy

cross_entropy = tf.reduce_mean(tf.nn.softmax_cross_entropy_with_logits(labels=y_true, logits=output))

optimizer = tf.train.GradientDescentOptimizer(learning_rate=0.5)

train = optimizer.minimize(cross_entropy)
```

Create Session

```python
init = tf.global_variables_initializer()

sess=tf.Session()
sess.run(init)

# Train the model for 1000 steps on the training set
# Using built in batch feeder from mnist for convenience

for step in range(10000):
    batch_x , batch_y = mnist.train.next_batch(100)
    sess.run(train,feed_dict={x:batch_x,y_true:batch_y})

#pass the test data through the model
#NOTE: There will be no iteration for test
predict=sess.run(output,feed_dict={x:mnist.test.images})

#argmax will give the predicted value in terms of a number
result=sess.run(tf.argmax(predict,1))

#same way get the label value using argmax
label_number=tf.argmax(mnist.test.labels,1)
labels=sess.run(label_number)

from sklearn.metrics import accuracy_score

accuracy_score(result,labels)

0.9699
```

Figure 4.90: Adding loss function and session to run the training

As you can see, this model offers an accuracy of almost 97%:

This code is available on the GitHub link. Play around by increasing the number of layers and the number of neurons in each layer. It will be interesting for you to check what happens if you use the Sigmoid instead of ReLu activation function.

Conclusion

In this chapter, you learned how neural networks work, starting from the basic element, which is a perceptron, to multilayer deep neural networks. You have learned how to design and train neural networks using TensorFlow and Keras.

In the upcoming chapter, you will learn about TensorFlow 2, followed by an advanced type of neural network called **Convolutional Neural Network (CNN)** and how it is used for image recognition in the chapter.

Questions

1. How is an artificial neural network similar to the human brain?
2. What are the components of an artificial neuron?
3. What is the difference between a shallow neural network and deep neural network?
4. Name three activation functions.
5. Which activation function is used in the last layer of a binary classifier?

CHAPTER 5
TensorFlow 2

Introduction

Google announced the major new release of TensorFlow 2 in early 2019 and made the final release in October 2019. Although TensorFlow 1.x was very powerful and became very popular, it had a very steep learning curve. Even experienced Python programmers were finding it hard to learn and understand the programming construct. The two-step process of creating the graph and then executing it in a session was a bit confusing and difficult to understand. With TensorFlow 2, the whole programming construct has been simplified, making it very easy to learn.

However, there is still a lot of code out there already written in TF1.x, and hence, there is a demand for TF1.X developers. Therefore, in this book, we started with TF1.x. In this chapter, we will introduce TF2.0. Since by now you have a good understanding of how TF1.x works, learning TF2.0 will be much easier.

Structure

In this chapter, the following topics will be covered:

- How to install TensorFlow 2?
- What is new in TensorFlow 2?

- Eager execution
- @tf.function—decorator
- Keras API

Objective

After reading this chapter, you will be able to install TensorFlow 2 and will understand the new features of the newer version. This is important because the code in the subsequent chapters is based on TensorFlow 2.

Installing TensorFlow 2

There are two ways you can locally install TensorFlow 2:

- Using the Anaconda Navigator
- The Anaconda command prompt

Using Anaconda Navigator

We can install TensorFlow2 using the following steps:

1. Open Anaconda Navigator:

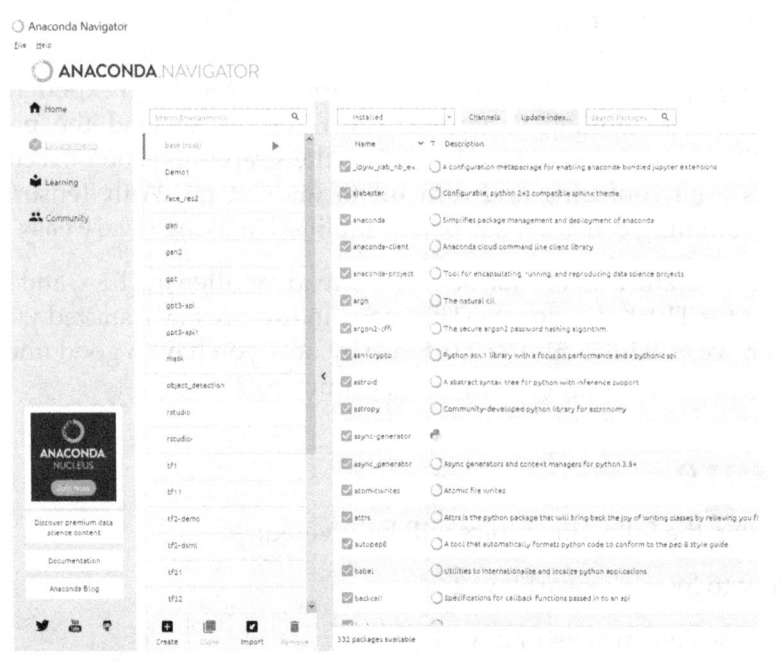

Figure 5.1: Environment's page

2. Click on **Create** as shown in *figure 5.2*:

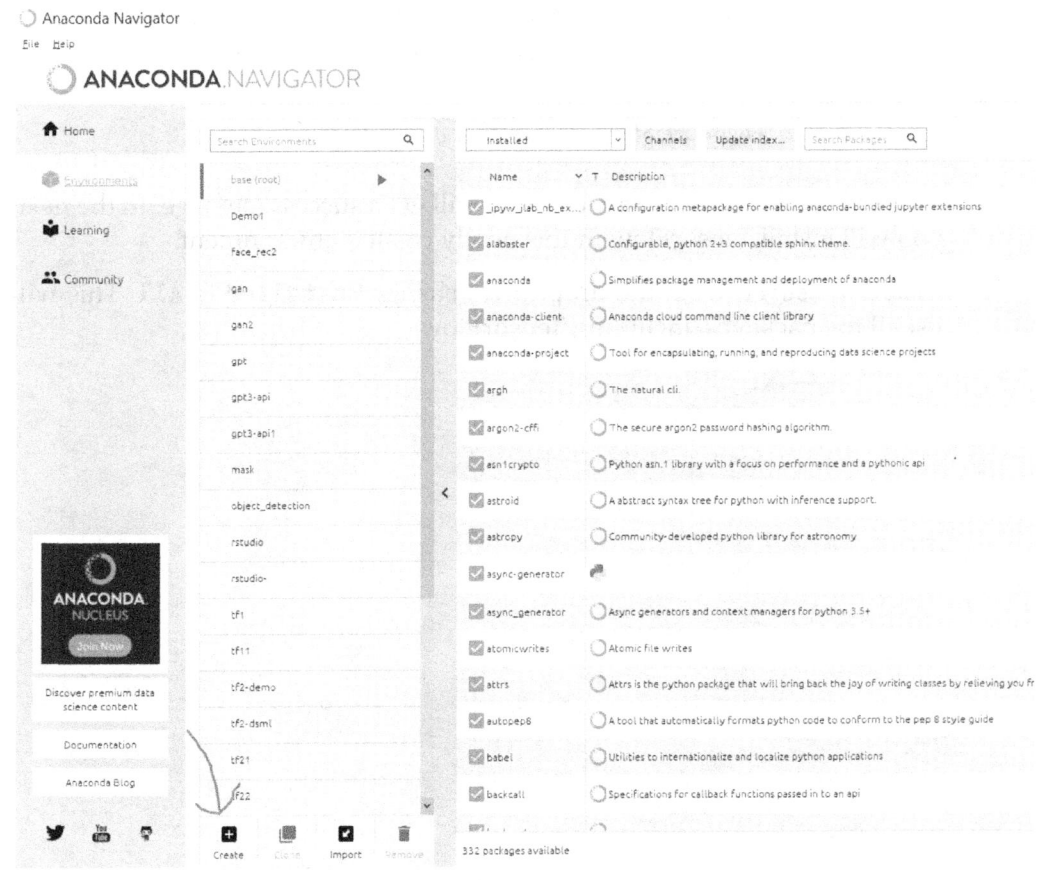

Figure 5.2: Step to click on "Create"

3. Create a new environment with a name like **BPBDemo** as follows. Leave the default python version; in this case, it is 3.6, but you may get a newer version like 3.8:

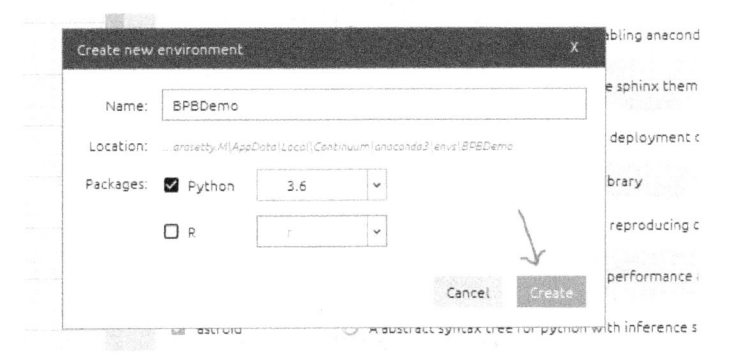

Figure 5.3: Environment name is given as BPBDemo

4. After clicking on **Create**, the status is shown as follows:

Figure 5.4: Status while creating new environment

Once the environment is created, you will get a success message. In the next, you will install TensorFlow in this newly created environment.

5. **Install TensorFlow**: In the dropdown, change **Installed** to **All**. This will list all the packages, including TensorFlow:

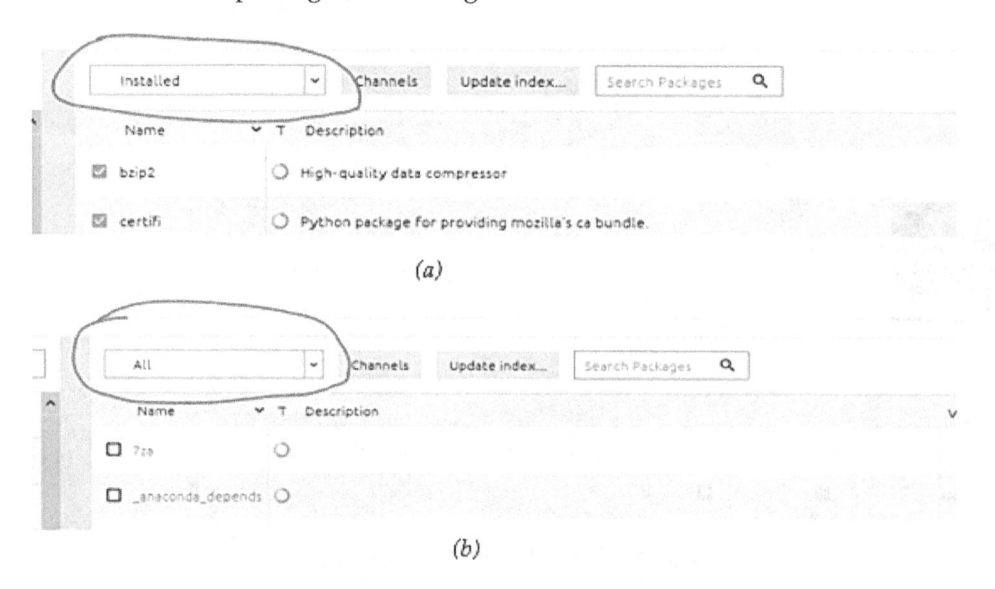

Figure 5.5: (a) "Installed" changed to (b) "All"

6. Now select **tensorflow**:

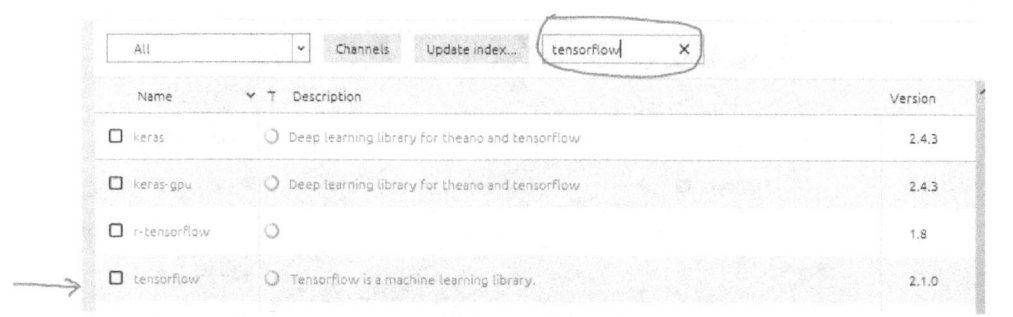

Figure 5.6: Select TensorFlow

7. Click on **Apply**.

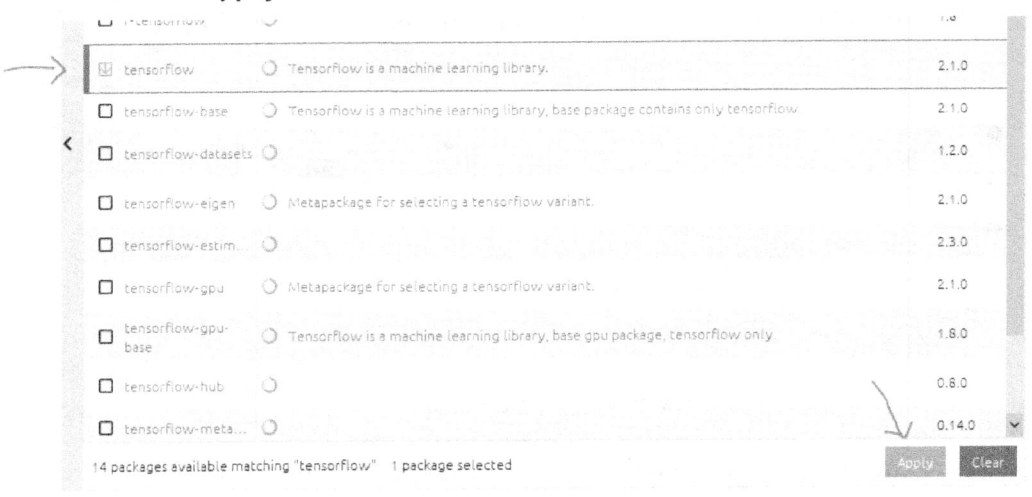

Figure 5.7: Clicking "Apply"

8. **Install Packages** window will be opened; it displays the packages that will be installed:

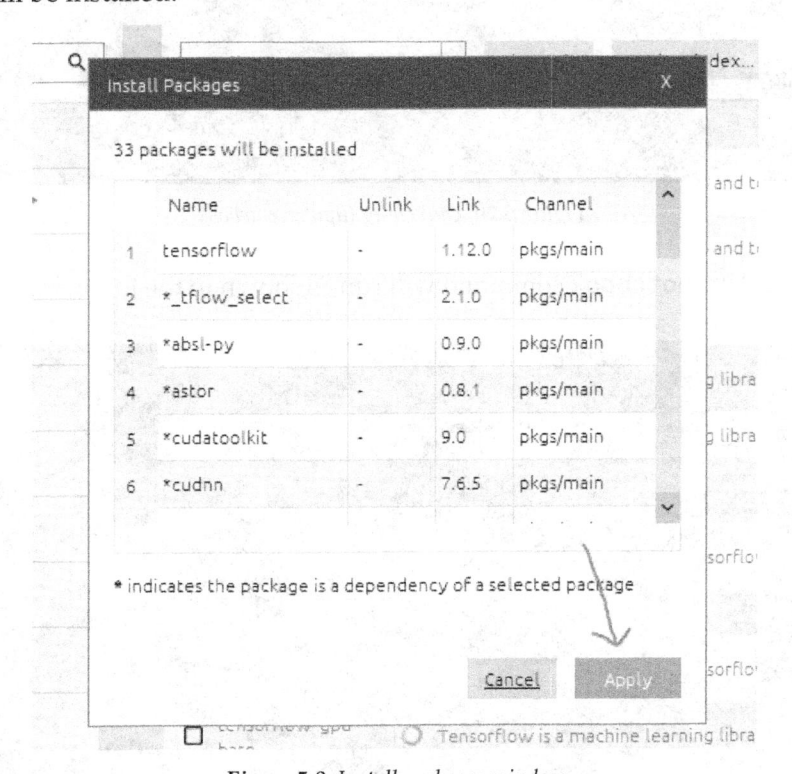

Figure 5.8: Install packages window

144 ■ *Beginning with Deep Learning Using TensorFlow*

9. **The n**ext step is to install Jupyter notebook. Click on **Home** on the left navigation bar. It will show Jupyter Notebook. Click on **Install**:

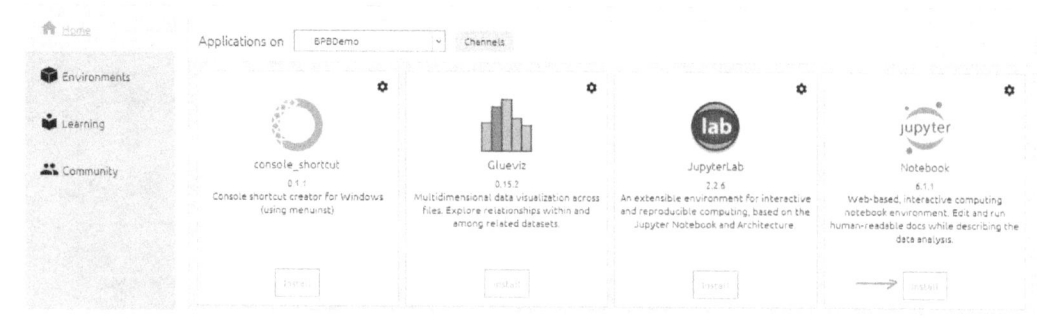

Figure 5.9: *Selecting Jupyter notebook*

10. Launch Jupyter notebook from anaconda prompt as follows:

Figure 5.10: *Launching Jupyter notebook*

11. **Jupyter notebook** command will run as shown in the following screenshot:

Figure 5.11: *Jupyter notebook command is working*

12. Check for the successful installation of TensorFlow 2:

```
In [1]: import tensorflow as tf

In [2]: tf.__version__
Out[2]: '2.0.1'

In [ ]:
```

Figure 5.12: Test for successful installation of TensorFlow 2

Congratulations! TensorFlow 2 is installed.

Please note if you have installed TensorFlow successfully by the above method, then there is no need to install again using the steps given below. You can skip to the next section *What is new is TensorFlow 2*.

From Anaconda command prompt

For installing TensorFlow 2 from the Anaconda command prompt, perform the following steps:

1. Open Anaconda command prompt:

```
Anaconda Prompt (anaconda3)
(base) C:\Users\Silaparasetty.M>
```

Figure 5.13: Anaconda command prompt

2. Create a new environment named **BPBDemo2** using the command:
   ```
   Conda create –name BPBDemo2 python=3.6
   ```

146 ■ *Beginning with Deep Learning Using TensorFlow*

You can use a newer version of Python, for example, 3.8:

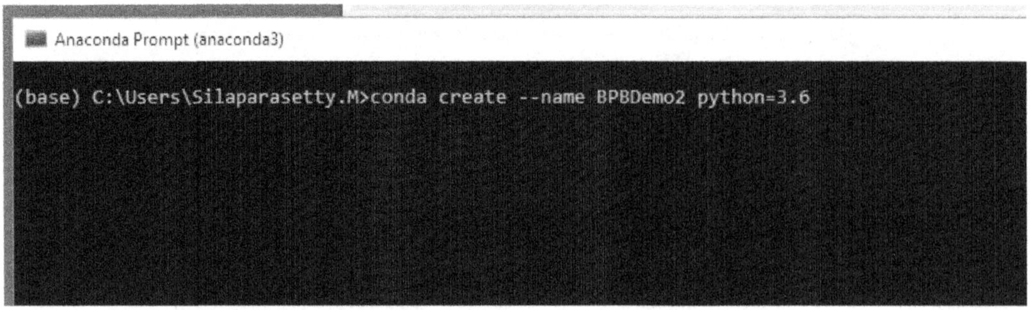

Figure 5.14: Creating an environment named BPBDemo2

3. Now, the following result will be displayed:

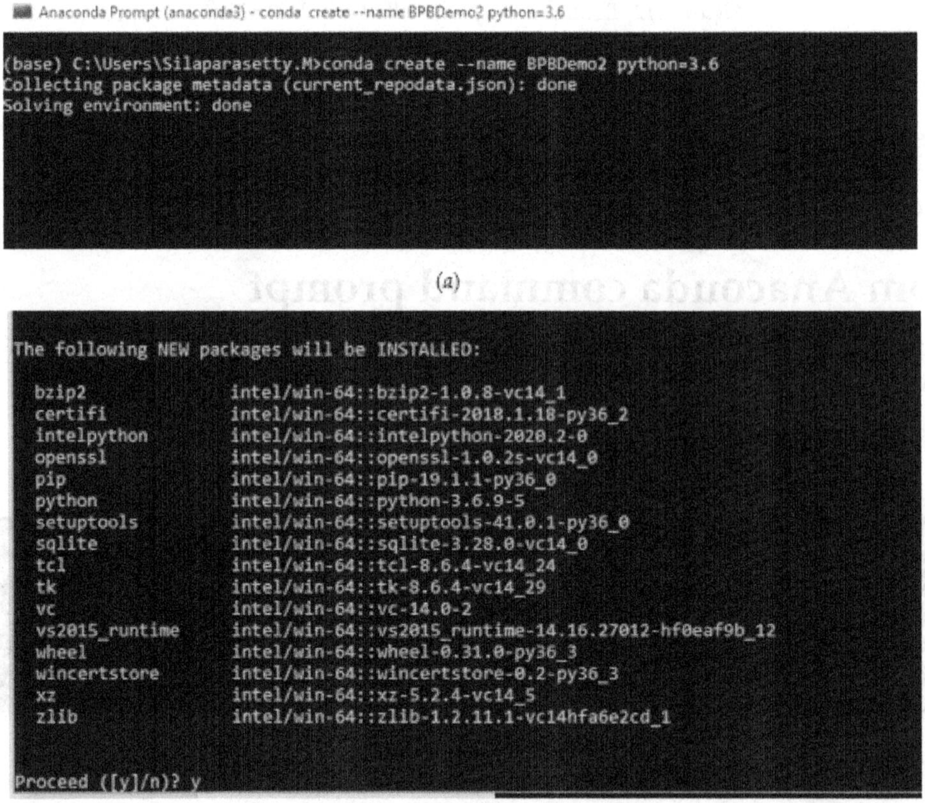

Figure 5.15: Steps to show (a) Conda create (b) Installed packages

4. **y** should be entered to proceed. To activate/deactivate the environment, steps are shown in the following figure:

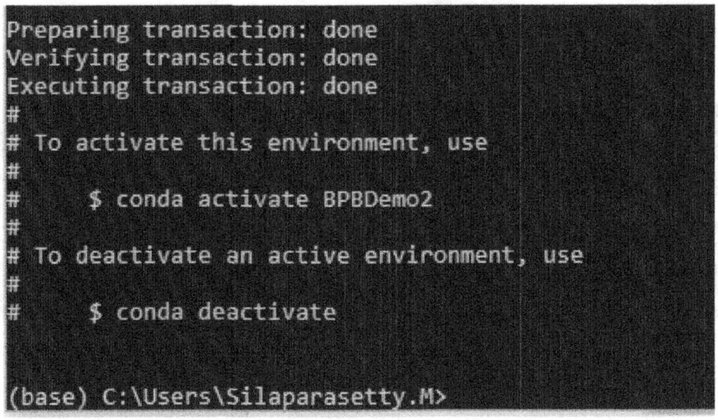

```
Preparing transaction: done
Verifying transaction: done
Executing transaction: done
#
# To activate this environment, use
#
#     $ conda activate BPBDemo2
#
# To deactivate an active environment, use
#
#     $ conda deactivate

(base) C:\Users\Silaparasetty.M>
```

Figure 5.16: Activating/deactivating the new environment

5. To install TensorFlow, use the command **pip install tensorFlow**:

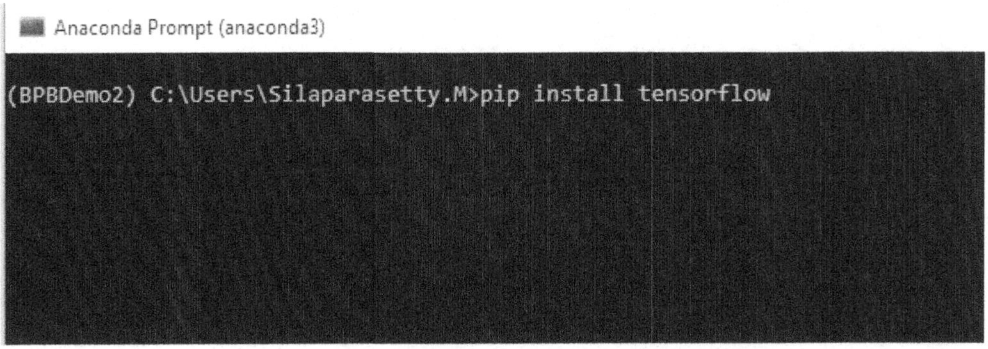

```
(BPBDemo2) C:\Users\Silaparasetty.M>pip install tensorflow
```

(a)

```
(BPBDemo2) C:\Users\Silaparasetty.M>pip install tensorflow
Collecting tensorflow
  Downloading https://files.pythonhosted.org/packages/8b/5d/b6ecf195081353e5dfbe71c6289
/tensorflow-2.3.0-cp36-cp36m-win_amd64.whl (342.5MB)
                                   | 17.6MB 2.2MB/s eta 0:02:30
```

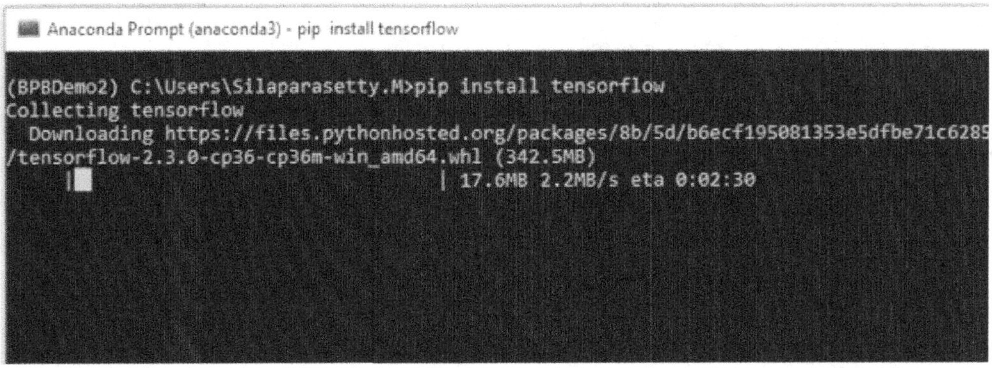

(b)

Figure 5.17: Installing TensorFlow: (a) pip install TensorFlow and (b) downloading TensorFlow

6. Install Jupyter notebook using the command:
   `pip install notebook`

Figure 5.18: Installing Jupyter notebook

7. Launch Notebook and check for successful installation:

Figure 5.19: Successful installation of TensorFlow

Google Colab

In case you have trouble installing TensorFlow 2 locally, you can always use the Google Colab as shown here:

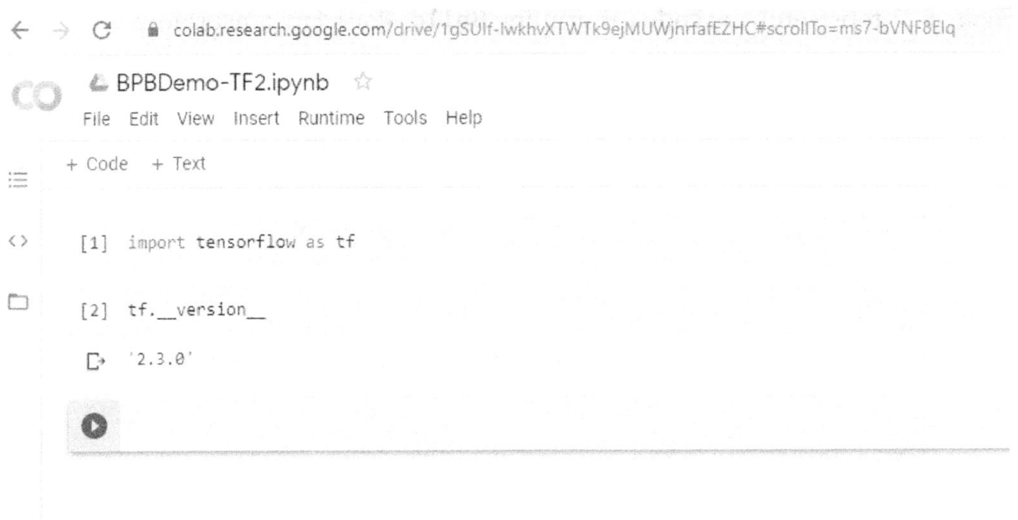

Figure 5.20: Google Colab

By default, TensorFlow 2.x is imported.

What is new in TensorFlow 2?

Google made major changes in the new release; a lot of it is behind the scenes, like improving the performance and cleaning up the API's. In addition, there are a few changes that impact the way we write code, and these are listed below and will be demonstrated with code examples.

Eager execution: TensorFlow 1.x worked in lazy execution mode by default. In the later versions, it was possible to explicitly turn the eager execution on, but in earlier versions, even that was not possible. This made learning TensorFlow not very intuitive. It was a two-step process; you create the computation graph and executed the graph in a session. The code does not look like a regular Python code.

TensorFlow 2 works in Eager execution mode. This makes learning TensorFlow much easier. The code looks like a regular Python code. Let us check how to write the `Hello World` program.

Figure 5.21 represents the code for printing **Hello World** in TensorFlow 2:

```
#import the tensorflow library
import tensorflow as tf
```

```
#define a string
hello=tf.constant("Hello World")
```

```
#it shows the value of hello unlike in TF1.0
hello
```

```
<tf.Tensor: id=2, shape=(), dtype=string, numpy=b'Hello World'>
```

```
#prints more elegantly
tf.print(hello)
```

```
Hello World
```

```
#Congratulations!!! - this is your first tensorflow program
```

Figure 5.21: Code to print "Hello World" in TensorFlow 2

Recall the Hello World program that we wrote in TensorFlow 1.x. It was much more complicated due to the creation of the session and execution of the graph in the session:

`@tf.function decorator`

There was a reason why computational graphs were introduced in the first place in TensorFlow1. It was to improve distributed computing, and thereby performance.

So now, with eager execution, does it mean we can make use of the graph technique? No, we can still make use of the graph technique when there is computationally intensive code like training a multilayer neural network. However, there are no more sessions. In TensorFlow 2, we use Functions instead of sessions.

Here is a comparison:

```
# TensorFlow 1.X
outputs = session.run(f(placeholder), feed_dict={placeholder: input})
# TensorFlow 2
outputs = f(input)
```

There are two by-products as a result of this:

1. There are no placeholders anymore
2. You do not have to initialize the variables

The second point is a big relief to many of us because while learning TensorFlow1, this was a very common mistake we used to make—not initializing the variables and then get errors while executing the graph in the session.

The good news is, we can still get the performance of graph execution by using the `tf.function()` decorator.

Here is a code example for the usage of this decorator:

```
Demo code to implement a simple function x^2*Y+Y+C

x =3, y =4, c= 2

import tensorflow as tf

X=3

Y=4

C=2

@tf.function
def myfunc(x,y,c):
    z=x*x*y+y+c
    return z

Z=myfunc(10,15,2)

tf.print(Z)
1517
```

Figure 5.22: Using the tf.function() decorator

In general, however, we will not be using a lot of this syntax because for all the multilayer Neural Network training, it is advisable to use Keras, which is even more tightly integrated with TensorFlow 2, and Keras takes care of this behind the scenes.

Kera API

Keras is a higher-level API that helps in developing neural network models much faster and thereby reducing the development time in projects. Keras is available with TensorFlow1 as well, but it has been much more tightly integrated and built into TensorFlow 2.

One of the most common and popular functions of Keras is the sequential model. Using sequential model, it is very easy to create complicated multilayer neural networks, including some advanced types like **Convolutional Neural Networks (CNN)**, which we will see in the upcoming chapter.

Let us start with the very simple MNIST example and create a classifier with a single hidden layer as we did in the previous chapter, but this time using Keras. As always, the first step is to import the TensorFlow library. MNIST is available as a part of Keras package; we load the MNIST data set:

```
import tensorflow as tf
mnist = tf.keras.datasets.mnist


(x_train, y_train),(x_test, y_test) = mnist.load_data()


#Normalize the data
x_train, x_test = x_train / 255.0, x_test / 255.0
```

Figure 5.23: Loading MNIST data set

Next, we separate the training and test data sets using the inbuild function **load_data()**. This function returns two tuples, one each for training and test data:

```
import tensorflow as tf
mnist = tf.keras.datasets.mnist


(x_train, y_train),(x_test, y_test) = mnist.load_data()


#Normalize the data
x_train, x_test = x_train / 255.0, x_test / 255.0
```

Figure 5.24: Use of load_data()

The **x_train** contains the training images, and **y_train** contains the training labels. Similarly, **x_test** contains the test images, and **y_test** contains the test labels.

It may be noted that the way the labels are not in one hot encoded format like we saw in the previous chapter where we used the MNIST data set from TensorFlow.

Let us take a look at the labels:

```
y_train
array([5, 0, 4, ..., 5, 6, 8], dtype=uint8)
```

Figure 5.25: Labels

As you can see, the labels are integers between 0 and 9. We then normalize the data and keep it ready to be fed into the model:

```
#Normalize the data
x_train, x_test = x_train / 255.0, x_test / 255.0
```

Figure 5.26: Normalizing the data

Building the model with Keras is very easy. We us the sequential model, which is extremely easy to understand and use. We start by creating an instance of the model and adding layers one-by-one using the **add** method:

```
mymodel = tf.keras.models.Sequential()

mymodel.add(tf.keras.layers.Flatten(input_shape=(28, 28)))
```

Figure 5.27: Creating model using add()

The second line of the previous code is not really a layer of neurons. The **Flatten** function reshapes the input into a one-dimensional tensor. This is needed because the hidden layer which will be added next can take only one-dimensional input. The out is an array of 784 elements (28*28=784). This will go as input to the single hidden layer of 10 neurons:

```
mymodel.add(tf.keras.layers.Dense(10, activation=tf.nn.softmax))
```

Figure 5.28: Input to a hidden layer of 10 neurons

In the preceding syntax, a layer of fully connected or dense neurons is added. The number of neurons in the layer is 10, and the activation function is Softmax.

Next, we have to provide the details for training the network. For this Keras, provides a function call compile, where inputs like the type of optimizer, the loss function, and so on. are provided:

```
mymodel.compile(optimizer='adam',
            loss='sparse_categorical_crossentropy',
            metrics=['accuracy'])
```

Figure 5.29: Use of compile function

We selected the type of optimizer as **adam**, which is the most used optimizer in Keras. The loss function used here is **sparse_categorical_crossentropy**. The other loss function that can be used is **categorical_crossentropy**.

It is important to note the difference between these two variants. Which one to use depends on the label information. If the labels are in a one-hot encoded format, then we use **categorical_crossentropy**. But if the labels are in regular numbers like in this case, we have to use **sparse_categorical_crossentropy**.

The last parameter metrics are almost always set to the value **['accuracy']**. This tells how the results of the training should be displayed.

There is very detailed documentation for each and every parameter available on the keras website keras.io – you can go through it if you are interested. Now that the model is ready before we start training, we can check the configuration of the model using the summary function:

```
mymodel.summary()
Model: "sequential"
_____
Layer (type)                 Output Shape              Param #
=================================================================
flatten (Flatten)            (None, 784)               0
_____
dense (Dense)                (None, 10)                7850
=================================================================
Total params: 7,850
Trainable params: 7,850
Non-trainable params: 0
_____
```

Figure 5.30: Use of summary()

As seen in *figure 5.30*, the summary displays the configuration of the model and provides details of each layer, especially about what type of layer and how neurons in the layer and the number of trainable parameters—which is the sum of weights and biases. Since this is a very simple configuration, you can cross-check the number of parameters. There are 784 inputs for each neuron—which means there are 784 weights per neuron. Since there are 10 neurons, the total number of weights is 784*10 = 7840.

And each neuron has a single bias—so there are total 10 biases. That makes the total number of parameters = 7840+10= 7850. In more complex networks like CNN, which we will say later, there will be some parameters that are not trainable, and that is what is referred to as non-trainable parameters.

Now, it is time to train our model. Unlike in the regular TensorFlow program, training a model in Keras is just a function call. The fit method trains the model with the training data. We need to provide some parameters like a number of epochs, and so on:

```
#training
mymodel.fit(x_train, y_train, epochs=5)

Train on 60000 samples
Epoch 1/5
60000/60000 [==============================] - 5s 91us/sample - loss: 0.4661 - accuracy: 0.8778
Epoch 2/5
60000/60000 [==============================] - 3s 53us/sample - loss: 0.3036 - accuracy: 0.9152
Epoch 3/5
60000/60000 [==============================] - 3s 50us/sample - loss: 0.2831 - accuracy: 0.9207
Epoch 4/5
60000/60000 [==============================] - 3s 52us/sample - loss: 0.2732 - accuracy: 0.9234
Epoch 5/5
60000/60000 [==============================] - 3s 51us/sample - loss: 0.2663 - accuracy: 0.9256
```

Figure 5.31: Use of fit()

The **fit** function takes three parameters—training images, training labels, and the number of epochs. In this case, **x_train** has the training images, and **y_train** has the training labels. We set the number of epochs to 5. Results of each epoch are displayed in the output. Loss and accuracy are the important parameters here. As can be seen from the previous image, loss keeps decreasing with each epoch, and accuracy keep increasing. At the end of the fifth epoch, the training accuracy is 0.9256% or 92.56%.

Let us now test the model with the test data. For this, Keras offers the function **evaluate**. This works very similarly to **fit,** but there are no epochs. Why?—I am sure you know the answer by now:

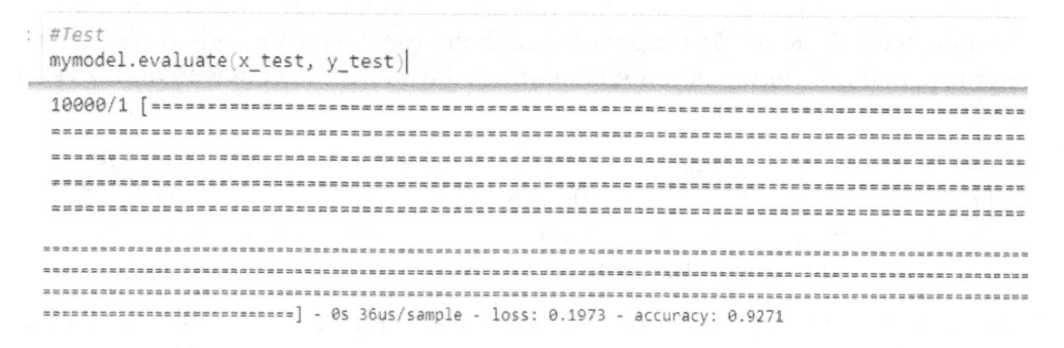

```
#Test
mymodel.evaluate(x_test, y_test)
10000/1 [==============================] - 0s 36us/sample - loss: 0.1973 - accuracy: 0.9271
```

Figure 5.32: Use of evaluate()

The "**evaluate**" takes two parameters—the test images and the corresponding labels. The test loss and accuracy are 0.1973% and 92.71%, respectively. As you can see, with just about 10 lines of code, we were able to build, train and test a model using Keras.

Let us take a couple of more examples. What if we want to increase the accuracy further and hence want a multilayer neural network? With Keras, it is very easy to do this. Remember this configuration from the previous chapter.

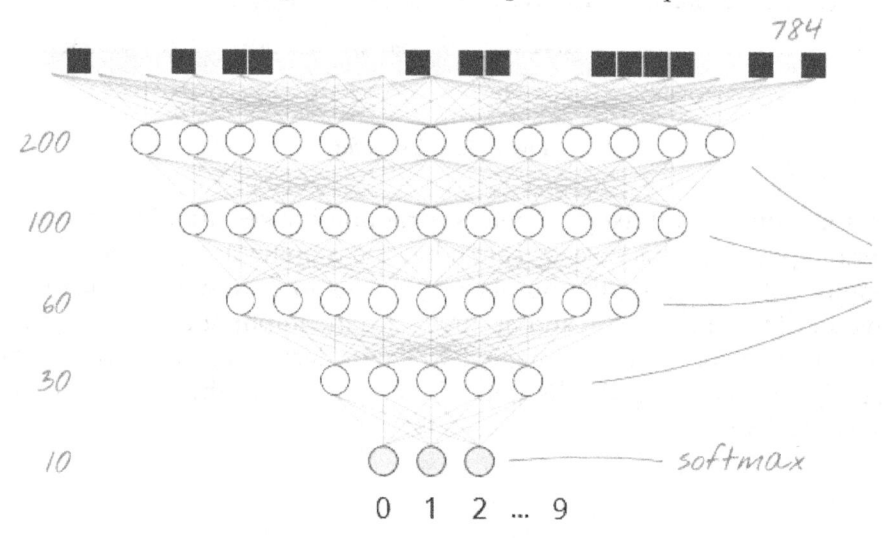

Figure 5.33: Multilayer neural network

Let us build this model and train and test it with Keras:

```python
import tensorflow as tf
mnist = tf.keras.datasets.mnist

#load and prepare the data

(x_train, y_train),(x_test, y_test) = mnist.load_data()
x_train, x_test = x_train / 255.0, x_test / 255.0

#build the model

mymodel = tf.keras.models.Sequential()
mymodel.add(tf.keras.layers.Flatten(input_shape=(28, 28)))
mymodel.add(tf.keras.layers.Dense(200, activation='relu'))
mymodel.add(tf.keras.layers.Dense(100, activation='relu'))
mymodel.add(tf.keras.layers.Dense(60, activation='relu'))
mymodel.add(tf.keras.layers.Dense(30, activation='relu'))
mymodel.add(tf.keras.layers.Dense(10, activation= 'softmax'))

mymodel.compile(optimizer='adam',
            loss='sparse_categorical_crossentropy',
            metrics=['accuracy'])
```

Figure 5.34: The first part of the code to build the model

This is how the first part of the code looks. As you can see, just one line of code is required for adding each layer. We can check the summary of the model:

```
mymodel.summary()

Model: "sequential_2"
_____
Layer (type)                 Output Shape              Param #
=================================================================
flatten_2 (Flatten)          (None, 784)               0
_____
dense_10 (Dense)             (None, 200)               157000
_____
dense_11 (Dense)             (None, 100)               20100
_____
dense_12 (Dense)             (None, 60)                6060
_____
dense_13 (Dense)             (None, 30)                1830
_____
dense_14 (Dense)             (None, 10)                310
=================================================================
Total params: 185,300
Trainable params: 185,300
Non-trainable params: 0
_____
```

Figure 5.35: Summary of the model

There are many more parameters in this model, and it may be an interesting exercise for you to calculate the number of parameters in each layer and compare them with the above. Now let us train and test this model:

```
mymodel.fit(x_train, y_train, epochs=3)

Train on 60000 samples
Epoch 1/3
60000/60000 [==============================] - 6s 104us/sample - loss: 0.2437 - accuracy: 0.9262
Epoch 2/3
60000/60000 [==============================] - 6s 94us/sample - loss: 0.0997 - accuracy: 0.9706
Epoch 3/3
60000/60000 [==============================] - 6s 102us/sample - loss: 0.0724 - accuracy: 0.9770
```

Figure 5.36: Testing the model

With three epochs, we get a training accuracy of 97.7% which is higher than the 92.56% we got with the single layer.

Time to test the model with the test data:

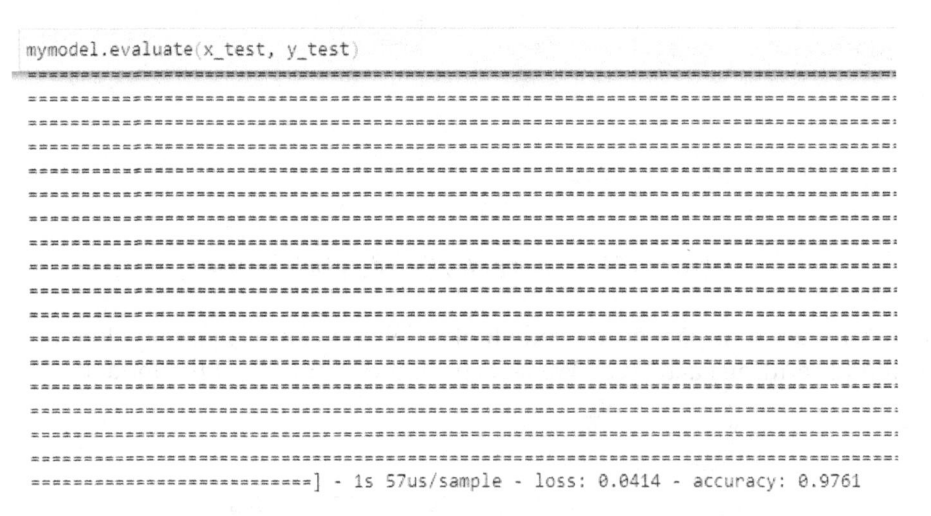

```
mymodel.evaluate(x_test, y_test)
=================================================================================
=================================================================================
=================================================================================
=================================================================================
=================================================================================
=================================================================================
=================================================================================
=================================================================================
=================================================================================
=================================================================================
=================================================================================
=================================================================================
=================================================================================
=================================================================================
=================================================================================
=================================================================================
==========================] - 1s 57us/sample - loss: 0.0414 - accuracy: 0.9761
```

Figure 5.37: Testing the model with the test data

Here again, the test accuracy is 97.61%, which is higher than the test accuracy of 92.71% we got with the single layer.

Classification with Iris data set

In this last example, we will see how to import external data and train a model with Keras. The data set we are going to take is the famous iris data set, which consists of three classes. And here, we use a slight variation in the code to make it easier to understand and look elegant. Before we start with the code, let us take a quick look at the data which is available in CSV format.

petallength	petalwidth	sepallength	sepalwidth	species
5.1	3.5	1.4	0.2	0
4.9	3	1.4	0.2	0
4.7	3.2	1.3	0.2	0
4.6	3.1	1.5	0.2	0
5	3.6	1.4	0.2	0
5.4	3.9	1.7	0.4	1
4.6	3.4	1.4	0.3	2
5	3.4	1.5	0.2	0
4.4	2.9	1.4	0.2	1
4.9	3.1	1.5	0.1	0
5.4	3.7	1.5	0.2	1
4.8	3.4	1.6	0.2	0
4.8	3	1.4	0.1	0
4.3	3	1.1	0.1	2
5.8	4	1.2	0.2	1
5.7	4.4	1.5	0.4	2
5.4	3.9	1.3	0.4	0
5.1	3.5	1.4	0.3	2
5.7	3.8	1.7	0.3	0
5.1	3.8	1.5	0.3	2
5.4	3.4	1.7	0.2	0

Figure 5.38: Data in CSV format

The last column species contains the label. And the values are not one-hot encoded, very similar to the MNIST example we saw earlier. It is important to make a note of it since that will determine the loss function we are going to use while training the model.

Now let us get started with the code. As always, begin with importing the required libraries. In this case, apart from TensorFlow, we also import Pandas and Matplotlib, which are used to load data and visualize it:

```python
import tensorflow as tf
import pandas as pd

import matplotlib.pyplot as plt
%matplotlib inline
```

Figure 5.39: Importing Pandas and Matplotlib

In addition, we will import a couple of additional packages, which will make our coding easy and look elegant. These are sequential and dense. Later in, you will see how this makes it easy to code:

```python
##Import Keras libraries
from tensorflow.keras.models import Sequential
from tensorflow.keras.layers import Dense
```

Figure 5.40: Importing Keras

Next, we load and visualize the data:

```
dataframe = pd.read_csv('iris.csv')
dataframe.head()
```

	petallength	petalwidth	sepallength	sepalwidth	species
0	5.1	3.5	1.4	0.2	0
1	4.9	3.0	1.4	0.2	0
2	4.7	3.2	1.3	0.2	0
3	4.6	3.1	1.5	0.2	0
4	5.0	3.6	1.4	0.2	0

```
plt.scatter(dataframe.sepallength,dataframe.sepalwidth,c=dataframe.species)
<matplotlib.collections.PathCollection at 0x1d8c36b6438>
```

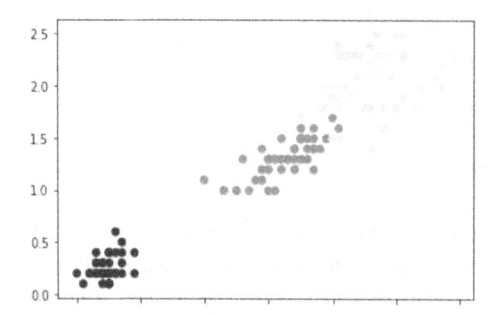

Figure 5.41: Visualizing the data

As seen in the preceding figure, the data has three features and one target or label. And the scatter plot helps in visualizing the three classes.

We have to prepare the data before it is fed to the model. To keep this exercise simple, and since the data is not large, we will not split this into training and test data sets. We will use all the 150 observations for training. However, we need to split the features and the labels:

```
x_input=dataframe.drop('species',axis='columns').values
y_label=dataframe[['species']].values
```

Figure 5.42: Splitting features and labels

Now, **x_input** has the features, and **y_label** has the labels. If the data is ready, we will build the model:

```
mymodel = Sequential()
mymodel.add(Dense(units = 50,input_dim=4, activation = 'relu'))
mymodel.add(Dense(units = 20 , activation = 'relu'))
mymodel.add(Dense(units = 3, activation = 'softmax'))
```

Figure 5.43: Building model

As mentioned earlier, this is a slight variation from the earlier code, and we are making use of the imported packages to simplify the code. This is a model with three hidden layers, including the Softmax layer. The first hidden layer consists of 50 neurons. We specify the number of inputs or features using the parameter **input_dim**. The next layer has 20 neurons, and we do not have to provide the number of inputs because it automatically fetches this information from the previous layer. And the Softmax layer has three neurons since there are three classes.

Next, we provide the training parameters using the compile function:

```
## Compiling
mymodel.compile(optimizer = 'adam', loss = 'sparse_categorical_crossentropy', metrics = ['accuracy'])
```

Figure 5.44: Training parameters

There is nothing new here. Observer that we use the loss function **sparse_categorical_crossentropy** since the labels are regular numbers and not one-hot encoded. We can check the configuration of the model by calling the **summary** function:

```
mymodel.summary()
Model: "sequential_1"
_____
Layer (type)                 Output Shape              Param #
=================================================================
dense_3 (Dense)              (None, 50)                250
_____
dense_4 (Dense)              (None, 20)                1020
_____
dense_5 (Dense)              (None, 3)                 63
=================================================================
Total params: 1,333
Trainable params: 1,333
Non-trainable params: 0
```

Figure 5.45: Configuration of the model

Now, we run training by calling the **fit** method with 100 epochs:

```
mymodel.fit(x_input, y_label, epochs=15)
```

```
Epoch 1/15
150/150 [==============================] - 1s 5ms/sample - loss: 1.1743 - accuracy: 0.3333
Epoch 2/15
150/150 [==============================] - 0s 107us/sample - loss: 0.9351 - accuracy: 0.3533
Epoch 3/15
150/150 [==============================] - 0s 107us/sample - loss: 0.8332 - accuracy: 0.6667
Epoch 4/15
150/150 [==============================] - 0s 147us/sample - loss: 0.7895 - accuracy: 0.7067
Epoch 5/15
150/150 [==============================] - 0s 73us/sample - loss: 0.7539 - accuracy: 0.6867
Epoch 6/15
150/150 [==============================] - 0s 107us/sample - loss: 0.7095 - accuracy: 0.7333
Epoch 7/15
150/150 [==============================] - 0s 53us/sample - loss: 0.6725 - accuracy: 0.7267
Epoch 8/15
150/150 [==============================] - 0s 107us/sample - loss: 0.6382 - accuracy: 0.6733
Epoch 9/15
150/150 [==============================] - 0s 107us/sample - loss: 0.6070 - accuracy: 0.6800
Epoch 10/15
150/150 [==============================] - 0s 134us/sample - loss: 0.5781 - accuracy: 0.7400
Epoch 11/15
150/150 [==============================] - 0s 107us/sample - loss: 0.5564 - accuracy: 0.7600
Epoch 12/15
150/150 [==============================] - 0s 107us/sample - loss: 0.5381 - accuracy: 0.8333
Epoch 13/15
150/150 [==============================] - 0s 160us/sample - loss: 0.5194 - accuracy: 0.8400
Epoch 14/15
150/150 [==============================] - 0s 107us/sample - loss: 0.5025 - accuracy: 0.8667
Epoch 15/15
150/150 [==============================] - 0s 164us/sample - loss: 0.4875 - accuracy: 0.8867
```

Figure 5.46: Running training using the fit method

We see that the training accuracy is close to 89%. This brings us to the end of this chapter. The code is available on the GitHub link.

Conclusion

In this chapter, you learned how to install and set up TensorFlow 2 environment and build deep neural networks using Keras. In the upcoming chapter, we will discuss computer vision and image classification, which is an important subdomain of artificial intelligence. A special type of Neural Networks called CNN will be introduced.

Points to remember

1. TensorFlow 2 is the newer release of TensorFlow.

2. There are two ways of installing TensorFlow on your local system—Anaconda Navigator and Anaconda command prompt.

3. Keras code written with TensorFlow1.x works with TensorFlow 2 without any major changes.

CHAPTER 6
Image Recognition

Introduction

Image recognition and speech recognition are the two main sub-domains within artificial intelligence and deep learning today. In this chapter, we will see how image recognition works and what are some of its applications. Image recognition is also considered as a part of the broader domain of computer vision which is the technique used by my machines to simulate human vision. For example, robots use computer vision with the help of cameras to detect obstacles in their path or identify objects. Similarly, self-driving cars use computer vision and image recognition to detect obstacles in their path, identify lane markings and check for traffic lights. Computer vision has existed for a very long time. What is new is the application of neural networks. In this chapter, we will explore how a particular type of neural network called **Convolutional Neural Networks (CNN)** is used for image recognition.

Structure

In this chapter, the following topics will be covered:

- Introduction to CNN
- CNN architecture
- Pre-trained CNN models

- Building CNN models with Keras and TensorFlow
- Image classification with CNN
- Code demos and examples

Objective

After reading this chapter, you will be able to understand what Convolutional Neural Networks (CNN) is and how they work. You will be able to use CNN's for image classification. In addition, you will learn about the concept of transfer learning and object detection.

Introducing Convolutional Neural Networks (CNN)

We have already seen how neural networks are modeled around the human brain. Dense Neural Networks, which are the most common form of neural networks, consist of an input layer, one or more hidden layers, and an output layer:

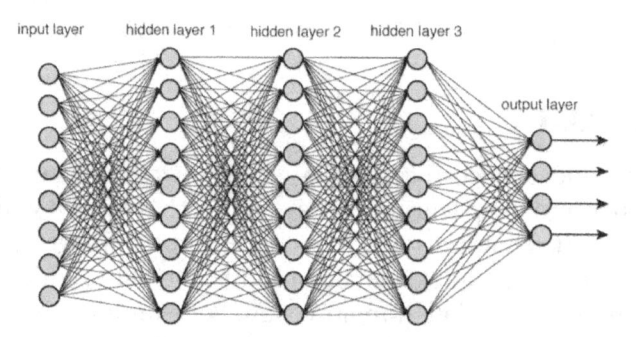

Figure 6.1: Dense Neural Network

Although dense Neural Networks are extremely useful, they are still not the most preferred method for solving problems related to image recognition. This is where the concept of Convolutional Neural Networks comes in. In Convolutional Neural Networks, all the outputs of all the nodes are not interconnected. Only a portion of the outputs is connected to some of the inputs of the succeeding layer. This is how Convolutional Neural Networks differ from a normal fully connected or dense Neural Network.

Convolutional Neural Networks are predominantly used for image recognition. The common architecture of these neural networks consists of a few convolutional layers and a few pooling layers. Typically, a pooling layer follows a convolutional layer, and there are multiple such pairs, and toward the end, there is one or more than one dense layer, followed by what is known as a classification layer.

There are quite a few pre-trained CNN models that are readily available for us to use in developing applications. These models include:

- LeNet
- AlexNet
- ZFNet
- GoogleNet
- VGGNet
- ResNet

All of these models are open-sourced, which means that anybody can use them to develop various applications. Training a Convolutional Neural Network requires a lot of computational power, and thus, if we want to develop an image recognition application, we will need to use some of these pre-trained networks and develop our applications. However, if we have to train our models for something very specific, then we would need to create our own Convolutional Neural Network and train it. We will see how to do this with the help of some examples.

First, we need to know how a CNN works. As mentioned earlier, a CNN has multiple layers. So, when it takes an image, each layer of the network identifies some features in that image. It starts with very low-level features such as edges, curves, vertical lines, horizontal lines, slanting lines, and so on. After this, the subsequent layers start identifying higher-level features.

Let us consider a simple example. Suppose we are working with the image of a dog; the convolutional neural network will first identify higher-level features like the eyes, ears, mouth, paws, and so on, along with the relative positions of these features. After this, the last few layers will identify the complete object. In this way, the Convolutional Neural Network recognizes the image of the dog.

There are multiple variations of the CNN architecture, but by and large, they all follow a certain pattern. There are two sections; there is a convolution block followed by the fully connected block:

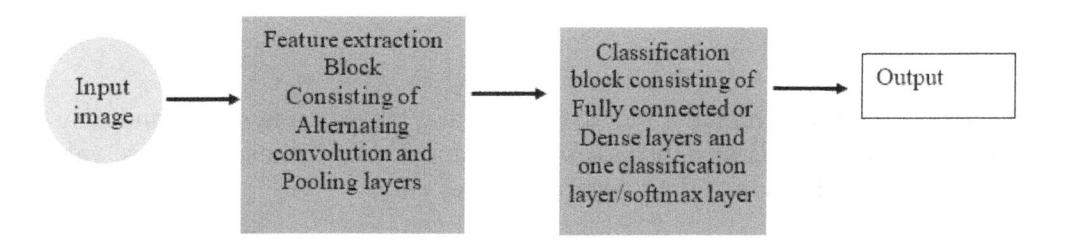

Figure 6.2: CNN structure

Let us have a look at the structure of the LeNet model, which was used for the MNIST data set. This Convolutional Neural Network consists of two convolutional layers, followed by two pooling layers, which together form the feature extraction section. Toward the end, it consists of one fully connected layer, followed by a classification layer (or Softmax layer), which together form the classification section. The Softmax layer has 10 neurons as this is a 10-class classification problem:

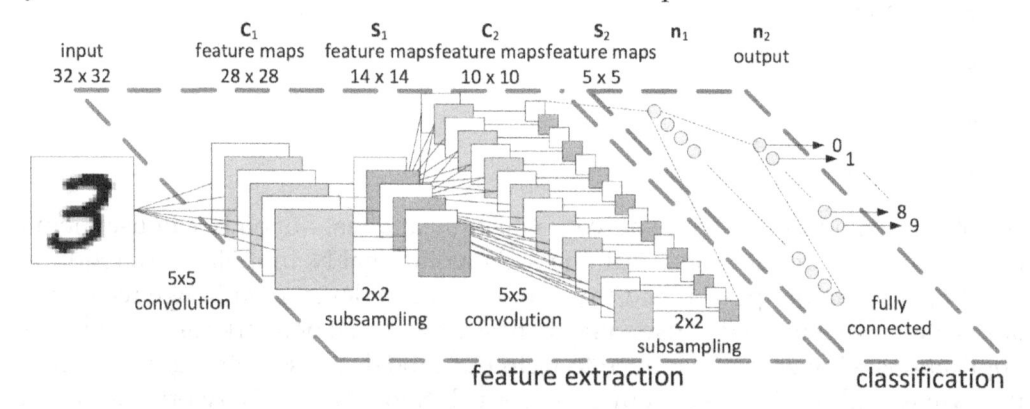

Figure 6.3: LeNet architecture

Let us understand in detail the convolution and pooling layers with a small specific example.

Convolution layer

Before we begin, you need to first understand some of the terms used. The first one is filter or kernel —this is nothing but a square matrix. Each cell in the matrix has some number which is known as the **weight**. That is also the reason sometimes it is referred to as the weighted matrix:

Here is an example.

0	1	1
1	0	0
1	0	1

This is a 3×3 filter or kernel. For the sake of keeping the example simple and easy to understand, the weights have been kept as 0's and 1's, but otherwise, these values are some real numbers, including negative values.

And each convolution layer can have many filters, and the combination of these weights in each filter is unique. This means not two filters in a given convolution layer will have exactly the same weights. For the sake of illustration, let us assume there is an image of 6×6. Machines see images as a bunch of pixel values. So, this image is a 6×6 matrix with some pixel values as shown here:

81	2	209	44	71	58
24	56	108	98	12	112
91	0	189	65	79	232
12	200	100	5	1	78
2	32	23	58	8	209
49	98	81	120	5	90

Figure 6.4: Sample image pixel values

The process of convolution is like a scan. The filter scans the image from left to right and top to bottom and produces an output known as **feature map**. The feature map is, in turn, another matrix of numbers. The numbers in the new matrix are the outcome of certain calculations, as shown in the following example. Note that this is not matrix multiplication:

81	2	209	44	71	58
24	56	108	98	12	112
91	0	189	65	79	232
12	200	100	5	1	78
2	32	23	58	8	209
49	98	81	120	5	90

0	1	1
1	0	0
1	0	1

Figure 6.5: First step of convolution

The first number is calculated as follows:

(81×0 + 2×1 + 209×1) + (24×1 + 56×0 + 108×0) + (91×1 + 0×0+189×1) = 515

The filter moves by one pixel to the right and performs the same calculations once again, which gives the value of the second cell in the feature map:

81	2	209	44	71	58
24	56	108	98	12	112
91	0	189	65	79	232
12	200	100	5	1	78
2	32	23	58	8	209
49	98	81	120	5	90

0	1	1
1	0	0
1	0	1

Figure 6.6: Next step

The second number is derived as follows:

$(2 \times 0 + 209 \times 1 + 44 \times 1) + (56 \times 1 + 108 \times 0 + 98 \times 0) + (0 \times 1 + 189 \times 0 + 65 \times 1) = 374$

The feature map is created as follows:

515	374				

Figure 6.7: Feature map

This way, a complete feature map is created. And then, the next filter with another set of weights is used, the process is repeated, and a new feature map is created. Therefore, in a particular convolution layer, if there are five filters, the output of this convolution layer will have five feature maps.

The size of the feature map is either same as the size of the image or smaller than the image, depending on the stride. Stride is the number of pixels by which the pixel moves. By default, it is 1. And in this case, the size of the feature map is equal to the size of the image. But the stride can be increased to 2 or 3, in which case the size of the feature maps is smaller than the size of the image.

So, if in the preceding example if the stride is set to 2, then the second position of the filter will be as shown in the following figure:

81	2	209	44	71	58
24	56	108	98	12	112
91	0	189	65	79	232
12	200	100	5	1	78
2	32	23	58	8	209
49	98	81	120	5	90

0	1	1
1	0	0
1	0	1

Figure 6.8: Convolution with stride = 2

Now there is another problem. In this case, we observe that the last column has been left out. And the last row will also be left out because there are not enough pixels for the filter to move:

81	2	209	44	71	58
24	56	108	98	12	112
91	0	189	65	79	232
12	200	100	5	1	78
2	32	23	58	8	209
49	98	81	120	5	90

0	1	1
1	0	0
1	0	1

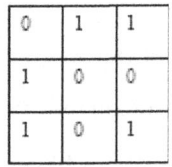

Figure 6.9: Problem with stride =2

This is where the concept of padding is used. When padding is used, a layer of dummy pixels is added to the image so that the filter can scan all the pixels of the image. This is how the image would look with padding. And the filter will work with stride 2 as well, and none of the information from the image is lost:

	81	2	209	44	71	58
	24	56	108	98	12	112
	91	0	189	65	79	232
	12	200	100	5	1	78
	2	32	23	58	8	209
	49	98	81	120	5	90

0	1	1
1	0	0
1	0	1

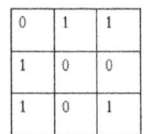

Figure 6.10: Image with padding

It is observed from above that for the convolution layer, there are some configurable parameters that are summarized as follows, and this will be handy and make it easy to understand when we are writing the code to build the model in Keras.

Summary of parameters:

- Kernel size—3×3 (min) and usually an odd number square matrix
- Number of kernels/filters = number of output feature maps
- Stride—1 by default can be increased.
- Padding—can be used optionally

The next layer is the pooling layer. This is relatively easy to understand. The output of the convolution layer, which is a bunch of feature maps, is fed as input to the pooling layer. The pooling layer is also known as the down sampling layer as that is what is exactly done here.

There different types of pooling, but *Maxpooling* is the most common type. We will use that for our example. There is an only filter like matrix used here, which does not have any weights. Only the size needs to be defined. Usually, it is one size smaller than the convolution filters. For example, if the filter size in convolution is 3, the size in pooling is 2, and if the filter size in convolution is 5, the pooling filter size is 4, and so on. Let us take the filter size of 2 and see how it works.

515	374	450	440	710	508
204	156	190	124	120	222
346	333	444	474	647	294
120	260	190	576	234	384
346	320	230	580	180	290
409	908	783	134	555	444

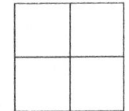

Figure 6.11: 2×2 max pooling

The filter scans the feature just like in the convolution layer, but there are no weights and no calculations. It picks the maximum value out of the four cells: in this case, the first number is 515. The output is once again a matrix-like in the case of the convolution layer, and in this case, the size of the output is always smaller than this feature map:

515	374	450	440	710	508
204	156	190	124	120	222
346	333	444	474	647	294
120	260	190	576	234	384
346	320	230	580	180	290
409	908	783	134	555	444

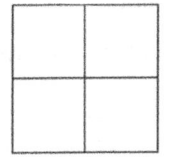

Figure 6.12: Step 2—max pooling

The next number is 450, and the third number is again 450, and so on. The final output would like this:

515	450	450	710	710
346	444	474	647	647
346	444	576	647	647
346	320	580	580	384
908	908	783	580	555

Figure 6.13: Maxpooling output

And there will be as many such outputs as the number of filters in the convolution layer. And you notice that the size of this output is 5×5 than the feature size 6×6. In addition to Maxpooling, there are other types of pooling, like Minpooling and Averagepooling, and as their number suggests, in these cases, the minimum number and the average of the number are taken, respectively, whereas scanning the feature map.

Let us now relate this to the LeNet architecture:

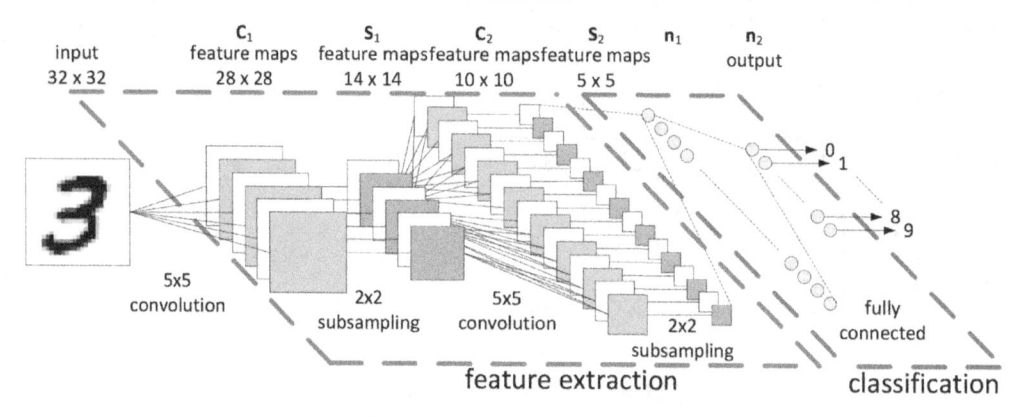

Figure 6.14: LeNet architecture

Going from the left, the input is an image of size 32×32. The image is fed to the first convolution layer, C1, which has six filters each of size 5×5. With stride=1, this will result in a feature map size of 28×28. Try this out manually if you are not convinced with the numbers!

The six feature maps are represented by the six squares. This is fed to the Maxpooling or subsampling layer with filter size 2. The output is 14×14, which is half the size of the feature maps (28×28).

This output is then fed to the next convolution layer, C2, which has 16 filters resulting in 16 feature maps of size 10×10 represented by the 16 boxes. This, in turn, is fed to subsampling layer S2, resulting in an output of size 5×5.

That is the end of the feature extraction section. This output is fed to the fully connected layer n1 followed by the classification layer n2 consisting of a Softmax layer of 10 neurons.

> **A couple of additional resources to understand convnets:**
> http://setosa.io/ev/image-kernels/
>
> https://ujjwalkarn.me/2016/08/11/intuitive-explanation-convnets/

Now that we got an understanding of how the convolution and pooling layers work let us look at how this is implemented in the code. We will start with some basic examples like MNIST and slowly move to more advanced examples.

MNIST with CNN

In this section, we will learn how to develop and train a CNN model for handwriting recognition. We will take the MNIST example, which we have already seen before. The advantage of using the MNIST data set is that it is tightly integrated into TensorFlow and Keras. Thus, we can easily use the Keras API with TensorFlow 2 to implement a basic multi-layer Convolutional Neural Network for handwriting recognition. Let us get started!

We will start with importing TensorFlow and the other necessary libraries and packages. You must be already familiar with some of these, which we used in the previous chapters. Some of the packages are new, like Conv2D and Maxpooling2D, which are used for creating the convolution and Maxpooling layers:

```
In [1]: import tensorflow as tf

        from tensorflow.keras.models import Sequential
        from tensorflow.keras.layers import Conv2D, MaxPooling2D
        from tensorflow.keras.layers import Activation, Dropout, Flatten, Dense

        import numpy as np
        from tensorflow.keras.preprocessing import image
        import matplotlib.pyplot as plt
        %matplotlib inline
```

Figure 6.15: *Import the required libraries*

After this, we import and prepare our data. There is nothing new here as we have done this in the previous chapter:

```
mnist = tf.keras.datasets.mnist

(train_images, train_labels),(test_images, test_labels) = mnist.load_data()


train_images, test_images = train_images / 255.0, test_images / 255.0
```

Figure 6.16: *Load MNIST data*

Model creation with Keras. The next step is to create our Convolutional Neural Network. This has two parts. One is the convolutional base, which consists of a sequence of convolutional layers and pooling layers. This is followed by a few dense layers. Finally, we end with a Softmax layer:

```
#conv layers
model = Sequential()
model.add(Conv2D(32, (3, 3), input_shape=(28,28,1),activation='relu'))
model.add(MaxPooling2D(pool_size=(2, 2)))

model.add(Conv2D(32, (3, 3), activation='relu'))
model.add(MaxPooling2D(pool_size=(2, 2)))

model.add(Conv2D(64, (3, 3), activation='relu'))
model.add(MaxPooling2D(pool_size=(2, 2)))
```

Figure 6.17: *Model creation*

Keras offers an easy and convenient way to create CNN models using **Sequential** class and other associate classes like **Conv2D** and **MaxPooling2D**. Let us go over these lines of code one-by-one:

```
model = Sequential()
```

Figure 6.18: Create an instance of sequential

An instance of the class **Sequential** is created and named as "**model**". As the name of the class, **Sequential** suggests, we can add the layers to the model in a sequential manner by calling the add method (**model.add**). The first layer is a convolution layer:

```
model.add(MaxPooling2D(pool_size=(2, 2)))
```

Figure 6.19: Add a convolution layer

Let us try to understand the various parameters of the Conv2D class. Number 32 indicates the number of filters or kernels—recall the convolution layer described previously. Although it is found that for the MNIST dataset 32 filters work very well, you can play around with this number and see how the accuracy changes.

The next parameter (3,3) is the size of the filter. The next parameter **input_shape** needs to be provided only for the first hidden layer. The value of this parameter is the shape of the images. For the MNIST data set, which consists of images of size 28 × 28 pixels, we take only grayscale, and thus, we require only one channel. This results in an input shape of (28, 28, 1).

This information needs to be provided to the Neural Network as a parameter for the first layer only. Each subsequent layer will take the output of the previous layer, and therefore, we need not provide any input shape.

The last parameter is the activation function which invariably is ReLU:

```
model.add(MaxPooling2D(pool_size=(2, 2)))
```

figure 6.20: Add a Maxpooling layer

Moving on to the next line of code, here we add the next layer, which will be a pooling layer. In this case, we use **MaxPooling**, and the size of the filter is 2 × 2, which is provided as a parameter. Two more such pairs of convolutions and Maxpooling layers are added.

Next, we add the dense layer and the Softmax layers:

```
#fully connected layers
model.add(Flatten())
model.add(Dense(64,activation='relu'))

model.add(Dense(10,activation='softmax'))
```

Figure 6.21: Add dense layers

Please note that convolution layers can accept multi-dimensional inputs, but dense layer requires a single dimensional input. However, the output from the convolution layer and Maxpooling layers are in the form of matrices (two dimensions). The **Flatten()** function reshapes the output of the previous Maxpooling layer into a one-dimensional array:

```
model.add(Flatten())
```

Figure 6.22: Add flatten

This line of code may appear like a new layer of neurons is added, but in fact, this is just reshaping the tensor. This is the power and convenience of Keras. There will be a few more such examples we will see as we move forward. The next line of code is adding a Dense layer or a fully connected layer of 64 neurons, each with ReLU **activation** function:

```
model.add(Dense(64,activation='relu'))
```

Figure 6.23: First dense layer

Finally, we add the classification layer or the Softmax layer. Since the MNIST data has 10 classes, we need 10 neurons and all of them linked to a single Softmax activate function:

```
model.add(Dense(10,activation='softmax'))
```

Figure 6.24: Softmax layer

That completes the creation of the multi-layer CNN model. Before we train the model, we have to compile it:

```
model.compile(optimizer='adam',
              loss='sparse_categorical_crossentropy',
              metrics=['accuracy'])
```

Figure 6.25: Compile

We use **adam** optimizer and the loss function `sparse_categorical_crossentropy`. The metrics parameter, as always, is set to **accuracy**. It may be noted that when we created the model directly in TensorFlow without Keras, the loss function used was `categorical_crossentropy`. This is because of the difference in the way the labels for the MNIST data are stored in TensorFlow and Keras.

In Keras, the MNIST labels are stored in one hot encoded format as shown below:

```
train_labels
array([5, 0, 4, ..., 5, 6, 8], dtype=uint8)
```

Figure 6.26: Labels

Now that our model is ready, we can have a look at its various parameters with the help of the **summary** function. This function displays a summary of the model, which shows the number of trainable and non-trainable parameters in each layer:

```
model.summary()

Model: "sequential"
_____
Layer (type)                 Output Shape              Param #
=================================================================
conv2d (Conv2D)              (None, 26, 26, 32)        320
_____
max_pooling2d (MaxPooling2D) (None, 13, 13, 32)        0
_____
conv2d_1 (Conv2D)            (None, 11, 11, 32)        9248
_____
max_pooling2d_1 (MaxPooling2 (None, 5, 5, 32)          0
_____
conv2d_2 (Conv2D)            (None, 3, 3, 64)          18496
_____
max_pooling2d_2 (MaxPooling2 (None, 1, 1, 64)          0
_____
flatten (Flatten)            (None, 64)                0
_____
dense (Dense)                (None, 64)                4160
_____
dense_1 (Dense)              (None, 10)                650
=================================================================
Total params: 32,874
Trainable params: 32,874
Non-trainable params: 0
```

Figure 6.27: Summary of the Neural Network

This relatively small Convolutional Neural Network that we have just built contains almost 33,000 parameters, and all of them are trainable. Typically, there are trainable parameters only in the convolution layer. The Maxpooling layer does not have any trainable parameters because it is just filtering out some of the values.

Before we feed the images to the model, we have to reshape it. The shape of the images is as follows:

```
X_test.shape
```

(10000, 28, 28)

Figure 6.28: Shape of the data

But convolution layer expects one more dimension— recall the input shape provided as **(28,28,1)**. Hence, we need to reshape before feeding the data to the model for training:

```
# Reshaping to format which CNN expects (batch, height, width, channels)
X_train = X_train.reshape(60000,28,28,1).astype('float32')
X_test = X_test.reshape(10000,28,28, 1).astype('float32')
```

Figure 6.29: Reshape

Next, we train our model by calling the fit method with three epochs:

```
#model.fit(x_train, y_train, epochs=1)
model.fit(X_train, Y_train, epochs=3)

Epoch 1/3
60000/60000 [==============================] - 38s 628us/sample - loss: 0.2333 - acc: 0.9282 3s - lo
Epoch 2/3
60000/60000 [==============================] - 41s 678us/sample - loss: 0.0830 - acc: 0.9744
Epoch 3/3
60000/60000 [==============================] - 42s 694us/sample - loss: 0.0620 - acc: 0.9812
```

Figure 6.30: Model training

The training accuracy is 98.12%. Then, we test the model to check the test accuracy:

```
model.evaluate(X_test, Y_test)
```

```
============================] - 2s 203us/sample - loss: 0.0504 - accuracy: 0.9707
```

Figure 6.31: Model test

The test accuracy is 97%. Let us run some inferences with this model using some test images. We can pick any image at random. In this case, if we take the image in index location 200:

```
test_image=X_test[200]
```

```
plt.imshow(test_image.reshape(28,28))
```

```
<matplotlib.image.AxesImage at 0x15484626160>
```

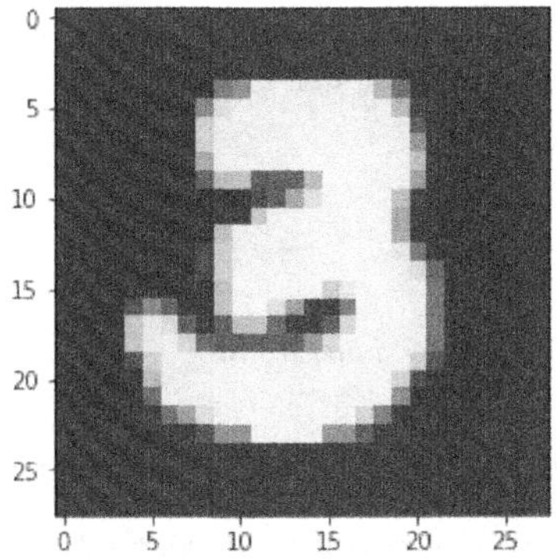

Figure 6.32: Display the image

We see that Number 3 is stored here. Let us check if the model predicts correctly.

Before feeding the image to the model for prediction, it needs some pre-processing. First, the image needs to be converted to an array using **img_to_array** and then add one extra dimension using reshape since the model expects 4-dimensional input:

```
test_image = image.img_to_array(test_image)

#predict expect a batch of images...we add a dummy dimension
test_image = test_image.reshape(1,28,28,1)
```

Figure 6.33: Prepare test image

We use this pre-processed image to run the **predict**:

```
result = model.predict(test_image)
```

```
result
```

```
array([[6.2312671e-07, 2.2274236e-05, 1.0856497e-03, 9.9804413e-01,
        1.2555657e-07, 1.1360716e-05, 2.2730499e-07, 3.2846776e-05,
        8.0189237e-04, 1.0082497e-06]], dtype=float32)
```

Figure 6.34: Inference result

The result of the prediction is Softmax output of 10 numbers. The numbers are between 0 and 1. If we round off, we will get the one-hot encoded value and running argmax in that gives the predicted number:

```
onehot= np.around(result)
onehot
```

```
array([[0., 0., 0., 1., 0., 0., 0., 0., 0., 0.]], dtype=float32)
```

```
onehot.argmax()
```

```
3
```

Figure 6.35: Final result

The model predicted it correctly. Let us try one more image in location 700.

Number 1 is stored here. Can our model predict correctly?

```
test_image = image.img_to_array(test_image)

#predict expect a batch of images...we add a dummy dimension
test_image = test_image.reshape(1,28,28,1)

result = model.predict(test_image)

result

array([[1.1352413e-04, 9.9889529e-01, 2.3837619e-04, 2.0383621e-04,
        1.2692001e-04, 2.4222916e-04, 1.3192258e-06, 9.2479837e-05,
        7.4455274e-05, 1.1606270e-05]], dtype=float32)

onehot= np.around(result)
onehot

array([[0., 1., 0., 0., 0., 0., 0., 0., 0., 0.]], dtype=float32)

onehot.argmax()

1
```

Figure 6.36: One more inference

Yes!

Binary image classification with Keras

So far, we have performed image classification with MNIST, which is an internal data set. This is a great way to start to understand how CNN works without worrying much about loading and preparing external data. In this section, we are going to import external data. Keras provides very powerful functionality to easily perform image classification. We start with binary classification using the legendary cat/dog data. This is like the "`Hello world`" of image classification. The data is in the form of JPEG files. They are split into training and test data sets. And each data set has several images of cats and dogs. Labeling of this data is very simple. All the images of dogs are stored in a folder named **dogs,** and all the images of cats are stored in a folder named **cats**. Keep in mind that there are several ways in which data can be labeled. This is one of the ways.

This is the folder structure of the data:

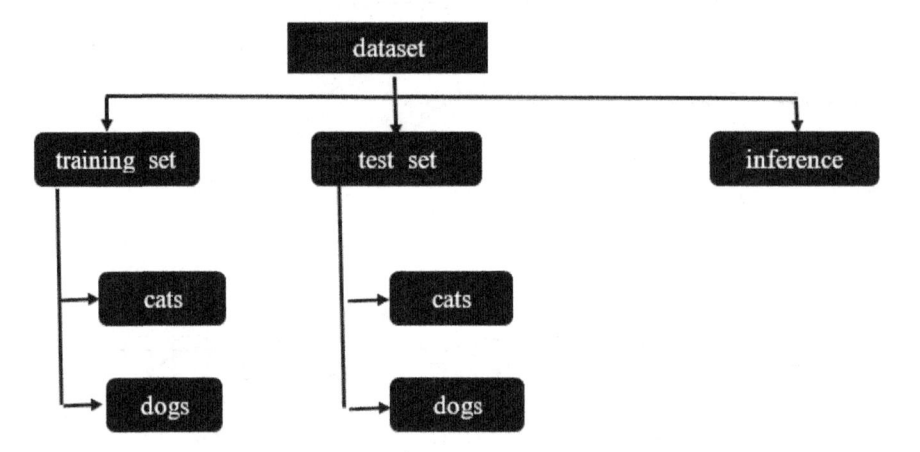

Figure 6.37: Folder structure of data

Now that we got an understanding of the data set let us jump into the code. The main difference between this example and the previous example is in the way the data is loaded and prepared. The CNN model building process remains the same.

So, as always, we import all the required libraries, and we can see that we are on TensorFlow 2:

```
import tensorflow as tf
tf.__version__
```

`'2.0.1'`

```
##Import libraries
from tensorflow.keras.models import Sequential
from tensorflow.keras.layers import Conv2D
from tensorflow.keras.layers import MaxPooling2D
from tensorflow.keras.layers import Flatten
from tensorflow.keras.layers import Dense
```

Figure 6.38: Load the libraries

Note that if we try **from tf.keras.models import Sequential** it will give an error—we have to use **tensoflow.keras.models**. Also, important to note that this is the only difference between TF1.x code and TF2.x code.

In TF1.x, the import looked like this:

```
##Import libraries
from keras.models import Sequential
from keras.layers import Conv2D
from keras.layers import MaxPooling2D
from keras.layers import Flatten
from keras.layers import Dense
```

Figure 6.39: TF1.x code

Rest of the code remains the same. Next, we build the CNN model, like in the case of MNIST. The code is pretty much the same except in two places:

- `input_shape`: In this case, the size of the input images is 64×64 color images; hence, the input shape is 64×64×3.
- The last layer has Sigmoid instead of Softmax. This was explained in the previous chapter. Since this is a binary classifier, we need one neuron with Sigmoid activation function. In the case of MNIST, it was a 10-class classifier, and hence, Softmax with 10 neurons was used.

```
## Initialising the CNN
classifier = Sequential()

## Convolution(64 filters of dimension 3 by 3), input shape 64x64x3 layer for color image)
classifier.add(Conv2D(64,(3,3),input_shape = (64,64,3), activation = 'relu'))
## MaxPooling
classifier.add(MaxPooling2D(pool_size = (2,2)))

## Add another layer
classifier.add(Conv2D(64,(3,3), activation = 'relu'))
classifier.add(MaxPooling2D(pool_size = (2,2)))

## Add another layer
classifier.add(Conv2D(64,(3,3), activation = 'relu'))
classifier.add(MaxPooling2D(pool_size = (2,2)))

## Flattening
classifier.add(Flatten())

## Fully connected ANN, Hidden ANN and output layer
classifier.add(Dense(units = 128, activation = 'relu'))

#output layer
classifier.add(Dense(units = 1, activation = 'sigmoid'))
```

Figure 6.40: Create the model

In compile, we add **adam** optimizer and use the loss function **binary_crossentropy**:

```
## Compiling
classifier.compile(optimizer = 'adam', loss = 'binary_crossentropy', metrics = ['accuracy'])
```

Figure 6.41: Compile

This is the configuration of the CNN model.

```
classifier.summary()
```

Model: "sequential"

Layer (type)	Output Shape	Param #
conv2d (Conv2D)	(None, 62, 62, 64)	1792
max_pooling2d (MaxPooling2D)	(None, 31, 31, 64)	0
conv2d_1 (Conv2D)	(None, 29, 29, 64)	36928
max_pooling2d_1 (MaxPooling2	(None, 14, 14, 64)	0
conv2d_2 (Conv2D)	(None, 12, 12, 64)	36928
max_pooling2d_2 (MaxPooling2	(None, 6, 6, 64)	0
flatten (Flatten)	(None, 2304)	0
dense (Dense)	(None, 128)	295040
dense_1 (Dense)	(None, 1)	129

Total params: 370,817
Trainable params: 370,817
Non-trainable params: 0

Figure 6.42: Model summary

This has 370,817 trainable parameters. Now that the model is ready let us import the data and prepare it to feed to the model for training.

Keras makes it really easy to do this. We import and create two instances of **ImageDataGenerator**, one each of training data and test data:

```
## data importing and transforming and scaling
from tensorflow.keras.preprocessing.image import ImageDataGenerator
train_datagen = ImageDataGenerator(rescale=1./255)
```

Figure 6.43: DataGenerator instances

Although creating these instances, we provide a normalization value to the parameter **rescale**. The function **flow_from_directory** is used to specify the path where the data is stored:

```
## Importing training data
train_set = train_datagen.flow_from_directory('dataset\\training_set',target_size=(64, 64),class_mode='binary')
```

Figure 6.44: Training data path

Recall the directory structure of the dataset mentioned above. The first parameter is the directory path. This can be either a relative path or an absolute path. The exact syntax can vary depending on whether you are running Windows or Mac/Linux. The above syntax is for Windows. In addition, we have to specify the **target_size**. This should be the same as the **input_size** specified for the model. Note that this need not be equal to the actual size of the images. Although you get the best performance when the actual size is equal to the **input_size** and **target_size**, this will work with images of any size. However, while loading the images, they are resized to **target_size**. If the **target_size** is different from the **input_size**, you will get an error while training the model.

The next parameter **class_mode** specifies what type of classification it is. In this case, since we are building a binary classifier, the value is set to **binary**.

When this cell is executed, it checks for the validity of the directory path and checks the number of images and the number of classes:

```
## Importing training data
train_set = train_datagen.flow_from_directory('dataset\\training_set',target_size=(64, 64),class_mode='binary')
Found 98 images belonging to 2 classes.
```

Figure 6.45: Training data

In this case, there are 98 images combined in two classes. It is interesting to note that the number of classes is determined by the number of sub-folders in the specified directory. In our case, there are only two subfolders, **cats** and **dogs**, and hence, it knows there are two classes. However, if you add additional subfolders, it will calculate the number of classes equal to the number of subfolders:

```
train_set.class_indices

{'cats': 0, 'dogs': 1}
```

Figure 6.46: Class indices

The class labels and the corresponding numeric values are stored in the attribute **class_indices**. As shown in the preceding class label is the name of the folder, and the numeric value is assigned in alphabetical order starting from 0. A similar process is followed for the test data set using the **test_datagen**, and the path for the test

```
## Importing test data
test_set = test_datagen.flow_from_directory('dataset\\test_set',target_size=(64, 64),class_mode='binary')

Found 38 images belonging to 2 classes.
```

Figure 6.47: Test data

The test data set has 38 images. Now that the data is prepared, the next step is to train the model:

```
## training the model
classifier.fit(
    train_set,
    epochs=50,
    validation_data=test_set
)
Epoch 1/50
4/4 [==============================] - 1s 150ms/step - loss: 0.7065 - accuracy: 0.4490 - val_loss: 0.6953 - val_accuracy: 0.5000
Epoch 2/50
4/4 [==============================] - 0s 105ms/step - loss: 0.7044 - accuracy: 0.5000 - val_loss: 0.7053 - val_accuracy: 0.5000
Epoch 3/50
4/4 [==============================] - 0s 95ms/step - loss: 0.6985 - accuracy: 0.5000 - val_loss: 0.6939 - val_accuracy: 0.5000
......
Epoch 49/50
4/4 [==============================] - 1s 176ms/step - loss: 4.8440e-04 - accuracy: 1.0000 - val_loss: 2.7154 - val_accuracy: 0.6316
Epoch 50/50
4/4 [==============================] - 1s 133ms/step - loss: 4.6983e-04 - accuracy: 1.0000 - val_loss: 2.7214 - val_accuracy: 0.6316
```

Figure 6.48: Model training

On executing this cell, the training process gets triggered. In this case we train the model for five epochs. At the end of the training process, it is seen that the model offers an accuracy of 63%.

Now that the model is trained let us run the inference with a test image of a dog. We start by loading the image from the path **\data\inference**:

```
#Load the image
test_image= image.load_img('dataset\\inference\\dog1.jpg',target_size =(64,64))
```

Figure 6.49: Load test image

By using the parameter target size, the image is resized to 64×64 to match with the input size provided while creating the model. Recall the parameter **input_shape** in the first layer of our CNN model. It was set to 64×64.

This will ensure we do not get an error in case the actual size of the image is different. Note that ideally, **input_shape** value should be equal to the actual size of the images of the train and test data set. However, in real life, it is not always possible to ensure this. Hence, this is a good way of overcoming the error.

Next, we check whether the image is loaded properly or not by displaying the image:

```
test_image
```

Figure 6.50: Display test image

We observe that the image of the dog is loaded properly. It is then converted to a NumPy array before feeding to the model:

```
## Convert image to array
test_image = image.img_to_array(test_image)
```

Figure 6.51: Data preparation

The model expects an array of images since that is how it has been trained. Since we have only one image, it needs to be converted into an array of one image. This is done by simply reshaping the image as follows:

```
## For single prediction change the dimension .
test_image=test_image.reshape(1,64,64,3)
```

Figure 6.52: Reshape

This completes the data preparation process. Now the image is ready to be fed to the model for inference. We run inference by calling the method **predict**:

```
result = classifier.predict(test_image)
```

Figure 6.53: Inference

This returns a Number 0 or 1 since this is a binary classifier. Where 0 indicates cat and 1 indicates dog. To make it easy for the user to understand, we write a small function to convert these numbers to the corresponding text as follows:

```
## covert result to the corresponding text label
if result == 1:
    prediction = 'dog'
else:
    prediction = 'cat'
```

```
prediction
```

```
'dog'
```

Figure 6.54: Result

The label is then printed. And in this case, it is seen that the model predicted the image correctly as a dog. Now, we can try with a different image of a cat to see if it is predicted correctly:

```
#Load the image
test_image= image.load_img('dataset\\inference\\cat.jpg',target_size =(64,64))

test_image

## Convert image to array
test_image = image.img_to_array(test_image)

## For single prediction change the dimension .
test_image=test_image.reshape(1,64,64,3)

result = classifier.predict(test_image)

## covert result to the corresponding text label
if result == 1:
    prediction = 'dog'
else:
    prediction = 'cat'

prediction

'cat'
```

Figure 6.55: Second inference

The same steps are followed once again, and it is seen the model predicts this image of a cat correctly.

Multiclass image classification

In this section, we will see how to build a multiclass classifier. Unlike the previous example where the images belonged only to two classes—**cats** and **dogs**. In this multiclass scenario, we will start with building a three-class classifier which can then be extended to any number of classes. Since we are using Keras, most of the process remains the same as the preceding. For example, the data is stored in the same folder like the preceding structure where we have the main subfolder, and under that, we have training data set and then the test data set, and within training, we have one folder for each class so in this case, we will take three classes one of the classes is images of um measures of four-wheelers then we have bikes and airplanes so these are the three classes the images are available for and accordingly the images are saved in the same folder structure. The primary difference between this example and the previous one is in the neural network model. We will see when we are building the neural network model that the difference is in the earlier example the last layer consists of the Softmax layer, which has three neurons since we are having three classes, whereas, in the previous example, it was a binary classifier therefore in the last layer there was just one neuron.

Before we start going into the code, let us take a look at how the folders are structured:

　　data
　　keras-multiclass-demo-TF20.ipynb

Figure 6.56: Root-level

The subfolders under data are as follows:

　　test
　　train
　　validation

Figure 6.57: Subfolders

And under the **train** folder,

] airplane
   car
   motorbike

Figure 6.58: "train" folder expanded

The image files are stored in the corresponding folders. For example, this is a sample of the images in the subfolder **airplane**:

Figure 6.59: Images in "airplane" folder

A similar structure exists for test data as well. Now let us get into the code. As always, we start by loading all the required libraries:

```
import tensorflow as tf
from tensorflow.keras.preprocessing.image import ImageDataGenerator
from tensorflow.keras.models import Sequential
from tensorflow.keras.layers import Conv2D, MaxPooling2D
from tensorflow.keras.layers import Activation, Dropout, Flatten, Dense


import numpy as np
from tensorflow.keras.preprocessing import image
```

Figure 6.60: Import libraries and packages

Next, we will build the neural network model. The first section has the convolution layers:

```
#conv layers
model = Sequential()
model.add(Conv2D(64, (3, 3), input_shape=(150,150,3)))
model.add(Activation('relu'))
model.add(MaxPooling2D(pool_size=(2, 2)))

model.add(Conv2D(64, (3, 3)))
model.add(Activation('relu'))
model.add(MaxPooling2D(pool_size=(2, 2)))

model.add(Conv2D(64, (3, 3)))
model.add(Activation('relu'))
model.add(MaxPooling2D(pool_size=(2, 2)))
```

Figure 6.61: Feature extraction block

As seen here, there are three pairs of convolutions and Maxpooling layers. This is followed by a single dense layer of 64 neurons:

```
#fully connected layers
model.add(Flatten())
model.add(Dense(64))
model.add(Activation('relu'))
model.add(Dropout(0.2))
```

Figure 6.62: Dense layers

Then the last layer is a Softmax layer consisting of three neurons:

```
#Last Layer - Softmax Layer with 3 neurons
model.add(Dense(3))
model.add(Activation('softmax'))
```

Figure 6.63: Softmax layer

This is the main difference between this model and the model used in the previous example of a binary classifier. Note that, in the previous example, for the binary classifier, the last layer had one neuron with Sigmoid **activation** function. And in this example, the last layer has three neurons with Softmax **activation** function. Later if you need to build a model for 100 classes, you have to just increase the number of neurons to 100- or if for a 1000-class classifier, this last layer will have 1000 neurons with the Softmax **activation** function.

The next step is to call compile method in order to specify the loss function and the optimizer:

```
model.compile(loss='categorical_crossentropy',
              optimizer='adam',
              metrics=['accuracy'])
```

Figure 6.64: Compile

Let us check the configuration of the model using the **summary** method:

```
model.summary()

Model: "sequential"

_____
Layer (type)                 Output Shape              Param #
=================================================================
conv2d (Conv2D)              (None, 148, 148, 64)      1792
_____
max_pooling2d (MaxPooling2D) (None, 74, 74, 64)        0
_____
conv2d_1 (Conv2D)            (None, 72, 72, 64)        36928
_____
max_pooling2d_1 (MaxPooling2 (None, 36, 36, 64)        0
_____
conv2d_2 (Conv2D)            (None, 34, 34, 64)        36928
_____
max_pooling2d_2 (MaxPooling2 (None, 17, 17, 64)        0
_____
flatten (Flatten)            (None, 18496)             0
_____
dense (Dense)                (None, 64)                1183808
_____
dense_1 (Dense)              (None, 3)                 195
=================================================================
Total params: 1,259,651
Trainable params: 1,259,651
Non-trainable params: 0
```

Figure 6.65: Model summary

Our model has a little over 1 million trainable parameters. Now that the model is ready let us prepare the data. Create two instances of **ImageDataGenerator**, one each for **Train** and **Test**:

```
train_datagen = ImageDataGenerator(rescale=1./255)

test_datagen = ImageDataGenerator(rescale=1./255)
```

Figure 6.66: ImageDataGenerator instances

Image Recognition ■ 193

Load the train and test data using these instances:

```
train_set = train_datagen.flow_from_directory('data/train',target_size=(150, 150),class_mode='categorical')
Found 1050 images belonging to 3 classes.

test_set = test_datagen.flow_from_directory('data/test',target_size=(150, 150), class_mode='categorical')
Found 105 images belonging to 3 classes.
```

Figure 6.67: Train and test data

Now that the model is ready and the data is ready, it is time to train the model. We will train it for five epochs:

```
model.fit(train_set,epochs=5,validation_data=test_set)

Epoch 1/5
33/33 [==============================] - 28s 840ms/step - loss: 0.5306 - accuracy: 0.7800 - val_loss: 0.8155 - val_accuracy: 0.6667
Epoch 2/5
33/33 [==============================] - 28s 842ms/step - loss: 0.4031 - accuracy: 0.8543 - val_loss: 0.7123 - val_accuracy: 0.7143
Epoch 3/5
33/33 [==============================] - 29s 888ms/step - loss: 0.3570 - accuracy: 0.8657 - val_loss: 0.8159 - val_accuracy: 0.7619
Epoch 4/5
33/33 [==============================] - 29s 874ms/step - loss: 0.2794 - accuracy: 0.8952 - val_loss: 0.8437 - val_accuracy: 0.7238
Epoch 5/5
33/33 [==============================] - 30s 905ms/step - loss: 0.2037 - accuracy: 0.9305 - val_loss: 0.8824 - val_accuracy: 0.7143
```

Figure 6.68: Model training

The model achieved more than 70% accuracy, which is good enough to run some inferences and see whether it is predicting correctly or not. You run the training for more epochs if you need more accuracy. The images for inference are available in the folder called inference, and these are not seen by the model before **ie**. These images are not available either in the **train** folder or the **test** folder.

Let us start with the image of a car:

```
test_image= image.load_img('data/inference/car007.jpg' ,target_size =(150,150))

test_image
```

Figure 6.69: Load test image

As explained earlier, before we run inference using the **predict** method, the image has to be converted into a NumPy array and reshaped:

```
## Convert image to array
test_image = image.img_to_array(test_image)
```

```
test_image=test_image.reshape(1,150, 150, 3)
```

Figure 6.70: Data preparation

Now, we run the inference by calling the **predict** method:

```
result = model.predict(test_image)
```

```
result
array([[0., 1., 0.]], dtype=float32)
```

Figure 6.71: Inference

Observe that the output is the one-hot encoded output of the Softmax classifier. It is an array with three values with the second position set to 1. This means the model predicted that the image belongs to the second class.

Keras allocates the class numbers in alphabetical order based on the names of the classes, which in turn is the same as the names of the folders. For example, in this case, the folder names in the test and train folders are **airplane**, **car**, and **motorbike,** as shown here:

- airplane
- car
- motorbike

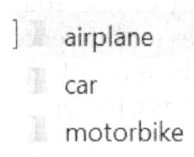

Figure 6.72: folder names

Therefore, the class **airplane** is assigned Number 0, **car** is 1, and **motorbike** is 2. And this information is stored by Keras in the property **class_indices,** and we can check this by running the following command:

```
train_set.class_indices
```

```
{'airplane': 0, 'car': 1, 'motorbike': 2}
```

Figure 6.73: class indices

The Softmax output will correspond to this. If the result is [1,0,0] it means the model has predicted the image as **airplane**. If the result is [0,1,0], it means the model has predicted the image as a car and if the result is [0,0,1] means it has predicted the image as **motorbike**.

With car image as input, the model returned [0,1,0] as we see earlier, which is for a car. That means our model predicted correctly. Let us try with a couple of more images.

First with the image of a bike:

```
test_image= image.load_img('data/inference/bike34.jpg' ,target_size =(150,150))
```

```
test_image
```

Figure 6.74: Test image

Now, let us see the code here:

```
## Convert image to array
test_image = image.img_to_array(test_image)

test_image=test_image.reshape(1,150, 150, 3)

## For single prediction change the dimension using axis. To remove problem of batch

result = model.predict(test_image)

result

array([[0., 0., 1.]], dtype=float32)
```

Figure 6.75: Inference result

The result of [0,0,1] indicates the model has correctly predicted it to be a motorbike. Now the last image:

```
test_image= image.load_img('data/inference/air.jpg' ,target_size =(150,150))
```

test_image

Figure 6.76: Test image of Aeroplan

Now the code is as follows:

```
## Convert image to array
test_image = image.img_to_array(test_image)

test_image=test_image.reshape(1,150, 150, 3)

## For single prediction change the dimension using axis. To remove problem of batch
result = model.predict(test_image)

result
array([[1., 0., 0.]], dtype=float32)
```

Figure 6.77: Second inference result

The result of [1,0,0] indicates the model has correctly predicted this image as an airplane. It is usually a good idea to write a small code to convert these numeric results into the human-readable text, as we did in the binary classification example above. There are many ways of doing it, and one of the simplest ways is given as follows:

```
result

array([[1., 0., 0.]], dtype=float32)

result=result.argmax()

result

0

## Class Label of dog and cat

if result == 0:
    prediction = 'airplane'
elif result == 1:
    prediction = 'car'
else:
    prediction = 'motorbike'

prediction

'airplane'
```

Figure 6.78: text label

Recall the function of argmax that was explained in *Chapter 3: TensorFlow*. It returns the index of the maximum value in an array, and in this case, which happens to be 1. In other words, running argmax on the result directly gives us the class index. In this example, it is 0 for airplane.

We use this new result value to map it to the text of the class label in the **if-else** condition block as shown in the preceding code.

It's that simple!

Load from data frame—binary

In the preceding example, the data was neatly arranged in subfolders. All the cat images were made available in the **cats** subfolder and all the dog images in the **dogs** subfolder. And Keras has the ability to recognize the subfolders as labels. Therefore, there was no need for additional labeling of the data.

However, very often, data does not come so neatly organized. Usually, all the images are dumped into one single folder. And an **xl** or **csv** file is provided with the labels. In such a case, we do not have to separate the images into different folders. Fortunately, Keras has a provision for handling this. There is a method called **flow_from_dataframe** in the **ImageDataGenerator** class that we use instead of the **flow_from_directory** method. In this section, we will see a couple of examples: one with binary classification and the other with multiclass classification. And to make it easy to understand, we will use the same examples of **Cat/Dog** for binary and **Airplane/Car/Motorbike** for multiclass.

Before we begin with the code, let us take a look at how the data is organized. There are three folders with data:

- inference
- test
- train

Figure 6.79: Folder structure

And there are two `.csv` files, one each for training data and test data:

- test-files-labels
- train-files-labels

Figure 6.80: Two .csv files

Let us take a look at the **train** subfolder:

Figure 6.81: Images in train folder

There is a mix of images of both cats and dogs. And the same with the test subfolder as well. The labels of these images are provided in the CSV files. Let us take a look at the CSV file. It has two columns. In this example, the names are of the columns are label and id where **id** contains the name of the image file and label contains the corresponding label in text format:

label	id
dog	dog.1.jpg
dog	dog.10.jpg
dog	dog.11.jpg
dog	dog.12.jpg
dog	dog.13.jpg
dog	dog.14.jpg
dog	dog.15.jpg
dog	dog.16.jpg
dog	dog.17.jpg

Figure 6.82: CSV file

The names of the columns can be different, but the same names have to be given in the code, as we will see soon. Let us get started with the code:

```
import tensorflow as tf
import pandas as pd

##Import Libraries
from tensorflow.keras.models import Sequential
from tensorflow.keras.layers import Conv2D,MaxPooling2D, Flatten,Dense, Dropout

from tensorflow.keras.preprocessing.image import ImageDataGenerator
```

Figure 6.83: Import libraries and packages

After loading the required libraries and packages, we load the **.csv** files into the corresponding **pandas** data frames:

```
df=pd.read_csv("train-files-labels.csv")

df1=pd.read_csv("test-files-labels.csv")
```

Figure 6.84: Label information

These will be used as parameters while preparing the data. Create an instance of **ImageDataGenerator**:

```
datagen=ImageDataGenerator(rescale=1./255)
```

Figure 6.85: Instance of ImageDataGenerator

Next, we call the **flow_from_dataframe** method for training and test data:

```
train_set=datagen.flow_from_dataframe(dataframe=df, directory="train",
                            x_col="id", y_col="label",
                            class_mode="binary",
                            target_size=(64,64))
```

Found 98 validated image filenames belonging to 2 classes.

```
test_set=datagen.flow_from_dataframe(dataframe=df1, directory="test",
                            x_col="id", y_col="label",
                            class_mode="binary",
                            target_size=(64,64))
```

Found 38 validated image filenames belonging to 2 classes.

Figure 6.86: Train and test data

Let us take a look at the parameters that are passed.

- **dataframe = df**: This is the data frame of the training labels CSV file that was loaded earlier. In the case of test data, it is **df1**.
- **directory = "train"**: This is the path of the subfolder where the training data is available. It can be an absolute path or a relative path. In this, it is the relative path.
- **x_col = "id"**: This is the column name of the CSV file where the image file names are stored. In this case, the column name is **"id"** as we have seen above. If the column name in the CSV file is different, then we have the mention the corresponding name here.
- **y_col = "label"**: This is the column name of the CSV file where the labels are stored. In this case, it is **"label"**. If the column name is different, then the corresponding column name has to be given here.
- **class_mode = "binary"**: This specifies that the classifier is a binary classifier. If it is a multiclass classifier, the value will be **categorical** as we will see in the next example.
- **target_size = (64,64)**: We have already used this parameter earlier—this specifies the size of the image.

Next, we build the CNN model like before:

```
classifier = Sequential()
## Convolution(64 feature detector of dimension 3 by 3), input shape 3 Layer for color image)
classifier.add(Conv2D(64,(3,3),input_shape = (64,64,3), activation = 'relu'))
## MaxPooling
classifier.add(MaxPooling2D(pool_size = (2,2)))

## Add another Layer
classifier.add(Conv2D(64,(3,3), activation = 'relu'))
classifier.add(MaxPooling2D(pool_size = (2,2)))

## Add another Layer
classifier.add(Conv2D(64,(3,3), activation = 'relu'))
classifier.add(MaxPooling2D(pool_size = (2,2)))


classifier.add(Flatten())
classifier.add(Dense(128,activation = 'relu'))


classifier.add(Dense(1, activation='sigmoid'))
```

Figure 6.87: Model creation

Run summary to check the configuration of the model and the number of parameters:

```
classifier.summary()
Model: "sequential"
_____
Layer (type)                 Output Shape              Param #
=================================================================
conv2d (Conv2D)              (None, 62, 62, 64)        1792
_____
max_pooling2d (MaxPooling2D) (None, 31, 31, 64)        0
_____
conv2d_1 (Conv2D)            (None, 29, 29, 64)        36928
_____
max_pooling2d_1 (MaxPooling2 (None, 14, 14, 64)        0
_____
conv2d_2 (Conv2D)            (None, 12, 12, 64)        36928
_____
max_pooling2d_2 (MaxPooling2 (None, 6, 6, 64)          0
_____
flatten (Flatten)            (None, 2304)              0
_____
dense (Dense)                (None, 128)               295040
_____
dense_1 (Dense)              (None, 1)                 129
=================================================================
Total params: 370,817
Trainable params: 370,817
Non-trainable params: 0
```

Figure 6.88: Model summary

Assign the optimizer and loss function before training:

```
classifier.compile(optimizer='adam',loss='binary_crossentropy', metrics=["accuracy"])
```

Figure 6.89: Compile

Then, we run the training with 100 epochs:

```
classifier.fit(train_set,epochs=100,validation_data=test_set)
Epoch 1/100
4/4 [==============================] - 1s 274ms/step - loss: 0.6912 - accuracy: 0.5000 - val_loss: 0.6973 - val_accuracy: 0.5000
Epoch 2/100
4/4 [==============================] - 1s 230ms/step - loss: 0.6936 - accuracy: 0.5000 - val_loss: 0.6935 - val_accuracy: 0.5000
Epoch 3/100
4/4 [==============================] - 1s 174ms/step - loss: 0.6901 - accuracy: 0.5000 - val_loss: 0.6921 - val_accuracy: 0.5263
Epoch 4/100
```

Figure 6.90: Model training

At the end of 100 epochs, the model achieves an accuracy of 60%:

```
Epoch 98/100
4/4 [==============================] - 1s 182ms/step - loss: 7.4060e-04 - accuracy: 1.0000 - val_loss: 3.0781 - val_accuracy: 0.6053
Epoch 99/100
4/4 [==============================] - 1s 172ms/step - loss: 7.2719e-04 - accuracy: 1.0000 - val_loss: 3.0893 - val_accuracy: 0.6053
Epoch 100/100
4/4 [==============================] - 1s 212ms/step - loss: 7.0532e-04 - accuracy: 1.0000 - val_loss: 3.0955 - val_accuracy: 0.6053
```

Figure 6.91: Accuracy after 100 epochs

Now let us run the inference to see if it predicts the images correctly. Let us start with the image of a dog first:

```
test_image= image.load_img('inference\\dog1.jpg' ,target_size =(64,64))

test_image

## Convert image to array
test_image = image.img_to_array(test_image)

## For single prediction change the dimension using axis. To remove problem of batch

test_image = test_image.reshape(1,64,64,3)

result = classifier.predict(test_image)

result

array([[1.]], dtype=float32)

## Class Label of dog and cat

if result == 1:
    prediction = 'dog'
else:
    prediction = 'cat'


prediction

'dog'
```

Figure 6.92: Inference

The model correctly predicts the input image as a dog. Now let us try with the image of a cat:

```python
test_image= image.load_img('inference\\cat1.jpg' ,target_size =(64,64))

test_image
```

```python
## Convert image to array
test_image = image.img_to_array(test_image)

## For single prediction change the dimension using axis. To remove problem of batch

test_image = test_image.reshape(1,64,64,3)

result = classifier.predict(test_image)
result

array([[0.]], dtype=float32)

## Class label of dog and cat

if result == 1:
    prediction = 'dog'
else:
    prediction = 'cat'

prediction

'cat'
```

Figure 6.93: *Second inference*

Once again, the model correctly predicts the image as cat. In the next section, we will see the example of a multiclass classifier.

Load from data frame—multiclass

In this example, we will build a multiclass classifier. There are a few differences that will be highlighted as we go along. First, let us take a look at the data. The top-level folder structure pretty remains the same as the binary classifier example:

- inference
- test
- train
- multi-test-label1
- multi-train-label1

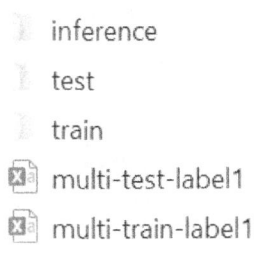

Figure 6.94: *Folder structure*

If we look into the train subfolder, there is a mix of all images that belong to all three classes:

Figure 6.95: Images in "train" folder

The .csv file has the same structure:

label	id
airplane	plane_001.jpeg
airplane	plane_002.jpeg
airplane	plane_003.png
airplane	plane_004.jpeg
airplane	plane_005.jpeg
airplane	plane_006.jpeg
airplane	plane_007.jpeg
airplane	plane_008.jpeg

Figure 6.96: CSV file structure

Let us get started with the code. The first part is similar to the binary classifier:

```python
import tensorflow as tf
import pandas as pd

##Import Libraries
from tensorflow.keras.models import Sequential
from tensorflow.keras.layers import Conv2D,MaxPooling2D, Flatten,Dense, Dropout

from tensorflow.keras.preprocessing.image import ImageDataGenerator

import numpy as np
from tensorflow.keras.preprocessing import image

df=pd.read_csv("multi-train-label.csv")

df1=pd.read_csv("multi-test-label.csv")
```

Figure 6.97: Import libraries and load CSV files

There is a small difference in the parameters of the method **flow_from_dataframe**:

```python
datagen=ImageDataGenerator(rescale=1./255)


train_generator=datagen.flow_from_dataframe(dataframe=df,
                                directory='data/train',
                                x_col="id", y_col="label",
                                class_mode="categorical",
                                target_size=(150,150))


Found 1050 validated image filenames belonging to 3 classes.
```

Figure 6.98: Training data

`class_mode= "categorical"` instead of "`binary`". Same for the test data as well:

```
valid_generator=datagen.flow_from_dataframe(dataframe=df1,
                                  directory='data/test',
                                  x_col="id", y_col="label",
                                  class_mode="categorical",
                                  target_size=(150,150))

Found 104 validated image filenames belonging to 3 classes.
```

Figure 6.99: Test data

The rest of the code remains pretty much the same as the binary classifier. Shown here for quick reference, but the entire code will also be available on the GitHub repository of this book. The link will be provided at the end:

```
#conv layers
model = Sequential()
#model.add(Conv2D(64, (3, 3), input_shape=(150,150,3)))
model.add(Conv2D(64,(3,3),input_shape = (150,150,3), activation = 'relu'))

model.add(MaxPooling2D(pool_size=(2, 2)))
model.add(Dropout(.2))

model.add(Conv2D(64,(3,3), activation = 'relu'))

model.add(MaxPooling2D(pool_size=(2, 2)))

model.add(Conv2D(64,(3,3), activation = 'relu'))
model.add(MaxPooling2D(pool_size=(2, 2)))

#fully connected layers
model.add(Flatten())

model.add(Dense( activation = 'relu', units=64))
model.add(Dropout(.2))
model.add(Dense( activation = 'softmax', units=3))

model.compile(loss='categorical_crossentropy',
              optimizer='adam',
              metrics=['accuracy'])
```

Figure 6.100: Create and compile the model

Now let us run the `summary()` as follows:

```
model.summary()

Model: "sequential_1"
_____
Layer (type)                 Output Shape              Param #
=================================================================
conv2d_3 (Conv2D)            (None, 148, 148, 64)      1792

max_pooling2d_3 (MaxPooling2 (None, 74, 74, 64)        0

dropout_2 (Dropout)          (None, 74, 74, 64)        0

conv2d_4 (Conv2D)            (None, 72, 72, 64)        36928

max_pooling2d_4 (MaxPooling2 (None, 36, 36, 64)        0

conv2d_5 (Conv2D)            (None, 34, 34, 64)        36928

max_pooling2d_5 (MaxPooling2 (None, 17, 17, 64)        0

flatten_1 (Flatten)          (None, 18496)             0

dense_2 (Dense)              (None, 64)                1183808

dropout_3 (Dropout)          (None, 64)                0

dense_3 (Dense)              (None, 3)                 195
=================================================================
Total params: 1,259,651
Trainable params: 1,259,651
Non-trainable params: 0
```

Figure 6.101: Model summary

We train the model with five epochs:

```
model.fit(train_generator,validation_data=valid_generator, epochs=5)

Epoch 1/5
33/33 [==============================] - 38s 1s/step - loss: 0.7009 - accuracy: 0.6857 - val_loss: 0.7737 - val_accuracy: 0.6250
Epoch 2/5
33/33 [==============================] - 43s 1s/step - loss: 0.5985 - accuracy: 0.7505 - val_loss: 0.8331 - val_accuracy: 0.5673
Epoch 3/5
33/33 [==============================] - 49s 1s/step - loss: 0.5042 - accuracy: 0.7838 - val_loss: 0.9346 - val_accuracy: 0.6923
Epoch 4/5
33/33 [==============================] - 45s 1s/step - loss: 0.5133 - accuracy: 0.7952 - val_loss: 0.9386 - val_accuracy: 0.6923
Epoch 5/5
33/33 [==============================] - 43s 1s/step - loss: 0.4053 - accuracy: 0.8486 - val_loss: 0.8526 - val_accuracy: 0.7019
```

Figure 6.102: Model training

Let us try with the image **airplane** in the **inference** folder:

```
## Inference
test_image= image.load_img('data/inference/car007.jpg',target_size =(150,150))
```

test_image

Figure 6.103: Test image

Hence, the code is as follows:

```
## Convert image to array
test_image = image.img_to_array(test_image)

test_image=test_image.reshape(1,150, 150, 3)

result = model.predict(test_image)

np.around(result)

array([[1., 0., 0.]], dtype=float32)

result=result.argmax()

result

0

if result == 0:
    prediction = 'airplane'
elif result == 1:
    prediction = 'car'
else:
    prediction = 'bike'

prediction

'airplane'
```

Figure 6.104: Inference

And the model predicts **airplane** correctly. You can try with the other images in the inference folder.

Save and restore models

The purpose of training a model is to later use it for inference. In general, the training of the model happens as a part of the development process, and the trained model is then deployed into a production system for real-time application. Keras offers an easy way to save a trained model so that it can be used later on for inference. In this section, we will see how to save a model after training and then restore that model to run inference. As we saw in the earlier chapter on Neural Networks, the process of training involves changing the weights and biases of the various neurons in the different layers of the neural network. Hence, saving the model means saving the values of these weights and biases along with the configuration of the model–the number of layers, the activation functions and the number of neurons per layer, and so on. All this is saved into a model file that can then be reloaded for running the inference. In order to save the model, we use the same method. Let us say in the above example you are satisfied with the performance of the model, and you would like to save it to run inference later on. All you need to do is add one line of code as below:

```
#save the Model for later use
model.save('multi-bpb.h5')
```

Figure 6.105: *Model save*

This will save the model in the local drive:

- model-restore.ipynb
- multi-bpb.h5

Figure 6.106: *File on a local drive*

This file contains the values of all the trainable parameters of the trained model. This file can be transferred to a location of choice from where it can be used by the application that runs the inference. In this case, let us assume it remains in the same location, and we want to use it to run inference on a couple of test images. We can create a new Jupyter notebook. Import some of the libraries and some basic packages:

```
import tensorflow as tf
from tensorflow import keras

import numpy as np
from tensorflow.keras.preprocessing import image
```

Figure 6.107: *Import libraries*

Load the trained model using the **load_model** method and passing the save mode file name as the parameter:

```
#Load model
model = keras.models.load_model('multi-bpb.h5')
```

Figure 6.108: Load model

We can run the summary method to check the configuration of the model:

```
model.summary()
```

```
Model: "sequential"
_____
Layer (type)                 Output Shape              Param #
=================================================================
conv2d (Conv2D)              (None, 148, 148, 64)      1792
_____
max_pooling2d (MaxPooling2D) (None, 74, 74, 64)        0
_____
conv2d_1 (Conv2D)            (None, 72, 72, 64)        36928
_____
max_pooling2d_1 (MaxPooling2 (None, 36, 36, 64)        0
_____
conv2d_2 (Conv2D)            (None, 34, 34, 64)        36928
_____
max_pooling2d_2 (MaxPooling2 (None, 17, 17, 64)        0
_____
flatten (Flatten)            (None, 18496)             0
_____
dense (Dense)                (None, 64)                1183808
_____
dense_1 (Dense)              (None, 3)                 195
=================================================================
Total params: 1,259,651
Trainable params: 1,259,651
Non-trainable params: 0
```

Figure 6.109: Model summary

Since this is a trained model, you can run the inference straight away on it. We begin by loading the image:

```
## prediction of new image
test_image= image.load_img('data/inference/air.jpg' ,target_size =(150,150))
```

```
test_image
```

Figure 6.110: Test image

Pre-processing of the image:

```
## Convert image to array
test_image = image.img_to_array(test_image)
```

```
##reshape
test_image=test_image.reshape(1,150, 150, 3)
```

Figure 6.111: Data preparation

And then prediction:

```
result=model.predict(test_image)
```

```
result
```

```
array([[1., 0., 0.]], dtype=float32)
```

```
result=result.argmax()
result
```

```
0
```

```
## Map to the class label
if result == 0:
    prediction = 'airplane'
elif result == 1:
    prediction = 'car'
else:
    prediction = 'motorbike'
```

```
prediction
```

```
'airplane'
```

Figure 6.112: Inference

This image has been predicted correctly. Another use of saving and restoring models is that you can retrain the model with additional training data. For example, while working on the model, let us say there were only 5000 images available for training. And the model is trained to 80% accuracy. Over a period of time, maybe after a year, you have gone more training data available, maybe 5000. You can restore this model and retrain from where it left off, and accuracy increases from 80% to 90% or higher.

Pre-trained models

Training a CNN model, in general, is a tedious and time-consuming activity. In the preceding examples, the data was relatively small, and even the number of classes was small. In real life, the models need to be trained for hundreds of classes with thousands of images, if not millions of them. This needs a lot of computing power which is very expensive. The good news is that we do not have to train a new model to solve each and every problem. There are several pre-trained models available for free which can be used to build applications to solve some of the common problems.

These pre-trained models are trained on millions of images by some of the large organizations that can afford the huge computation power. This is also done as a part of an annual competition by ImageNet, which hosts millions of labeled images.

Some of the pre-trained models are VGGNet, ResNet, ZFNet, GoogLeNet, and so on. These models are tightly integrated with Keras API. Let us see how to use them.

Start by importing the required libraries and packages:

```
from keras.preprocessing.image import load_img
from keras.preprocessing.image import img_to_array
from keras.applications.vgg16 import preprocess_input
from keras.applications.vgg16 import decode_predictions
from keras.applications.vgg16 import VGG16
from keras.applications.resnet50 import ResNet50
from keras.preprocessing import image
from keras.applications.resnet50 import preprocess_input
```

Figure 6.113: Import libraries

VGG16 and ResNet are tightly integrated into Keras. Let us start with VGG16 by creating an instance of the model:

```
# Load the model
model = VGG16()
```

Figure 6.114: pre-trained model

This pre-trained model has been trained to classify 1000 different classes of some of the very common days to objects. Let us check by running inference on some sample images.

Load the image:

```
# Load an image from file
image = load_img('plane.jpg', target_size=(224, 224))

image
```

Figure 6.115: Test image

Next, pre-process the image file:

```
# convert the image pixels to a numpy array
image = img_to_array(image)
# reshape data for the model
image = image.reshape((1,image.shape[0] , image.shape[1],image.shape[2]))
# prepare the image for the VGG model
image = preprocess_input(image)
```

Figure 6.116: Image pre-process

Next, call the predict method, which returns the Softmax output of the last layer, which has 1000 neurons, and hence, there are 1000 values that are not one hot encoded:

```
# predict the probability across all output classes
result = model.predict(image)
result
```

```
array([[2.05304439e-15, 2.82675494e-14, 1.46225718e-12, 9.12206291e-13,
        6.15273728e-13, 4.66305402e-15, 4.69088381e-16, 1.14722549e-14,
        5.89498975e-15, 9.68206900e-17, 1.05756277e-15, 5.73922166e-15,
        1.03579153e-14, 3.04403418e-15, 2.56727745e-15, 2.72820551e-16,
        1.29120845e-15, 8.70149747e-16, 5.85109286e-14, 3.63692739e-15,
        2.68956000e-15, 5.18520719e-13, 1.82418540e-14, 3.67102534e-13,
        5.70318612e-16, 2.72127254e-16, 1.67646523e-14, 1.41184839e-15,
        2.77465918e-16, 2.81147218e-15, 1.09544050e-17, 1.12464824e-17,
        1.10524151e-17, 2.35789790e-15, 1.11095816e-14, 3.69224070e-16,
        3.93692708e-16, 7.00513784e-18, 1.38020470e-17, 1.25629822e-16,
        4.18872549e-17, 2.43281743e-17, 1.06005426e-16, 4.78144639e-18,
```

Figure 6.117: Inference

There is a built-in function that helps in decoding this:

```
# convert the probabilities to class labels
label = decode_predictions(result)
label

[[('n02690373', 'airliner', 0.98752207),
  ('n04592741', 'wing', 0.011765054),
  ('n04266014', 'space_shuttle', 0.00061397295),
  ('n04552348', 'warplane', 8.872779e-05),
  ('n02692877', 'airship', 9.056787e-06)]]
```

Figure 6.118: Result

This function returns the top five probabilities. We can then get the label of the class with the highest probability:

```
# retrieve the most likely result, e.g. highest probability
label = label[0][0]
# print the label
print(label[1])

airliner
```

Figure 6.119: Final result

And as we can see in this case, it is Airliner, which is the correct prediction. Let us try another image:

```
# load an image from file
image = load_img('bird.jpeg', target_size=(224, 224))
image
```

```
# convert the image pixels to a numpy array
image = img_to_array(image)
# reshape data for the model
image = image.reshape((1,image.shape[0] , image.shape[1],image.shape[2]))
# prepare the image for the VGG model
image = preprocess_input(image)

# convert the image pixels to a numpy array
image = img_to_array(image)
# reshape data for the model
image = image.reshape((1,image.shape[0] , image.shape[1],image.shape[2]))
# prepare the image for the VGG model
image = preprocess_input(image)

# convert the probabilities to class labels
label = decode_predictions(result)
label

[[('n01560419', 'bulbul', 0.27711904),
  ('n01806567', 'quail', 0.18150388),
  ('n01807496', 'partridge', 0.112342924),
  ('n01828970', 'bee_eater', 0.09756893),
  ('n01797886', 'ruffed_grouse', 0.056491535)]]

# retrieve the most likely result, e.g. highest probability
label = label[0][0]
# print the label
print(label[1])

bulbul
```

Figure 6.120: Second inference

And in this case, it predicted it as **bulbul** which is fairly accurate. As seen above, the other predictions are quail, partridge, and so on, which are birds. Instead of VGG16, we can use ResNet as the pre-trained model. All we need to do is change one line of code:

```
# Load the model
model = ResNet50()
```

Figure 6.121: Pre-trained model

The rest of the code remains the same.

Transfer learning

Transfer learning is a mechanism by which you take a pre-trained model which was trained for certain classes of images and then retrain for a different set of classes. For example, we can take VGG16, which is trained to classify 1000 different classes of day-to-day objects and retrain it classifies very specific types of objects, maybe motor parts or computer hardware, and so on. The main advantage of this mechanism is that it works when the training data is very less. The reason is, we do not train all the layers of the model since that would take very long. Only the last layer of the last few layers dense layers is trained. The convolution layers are not trained, but the trained values of their parameters are reused. That is the reason this is called transfer learning.

Refer to the following diagram:

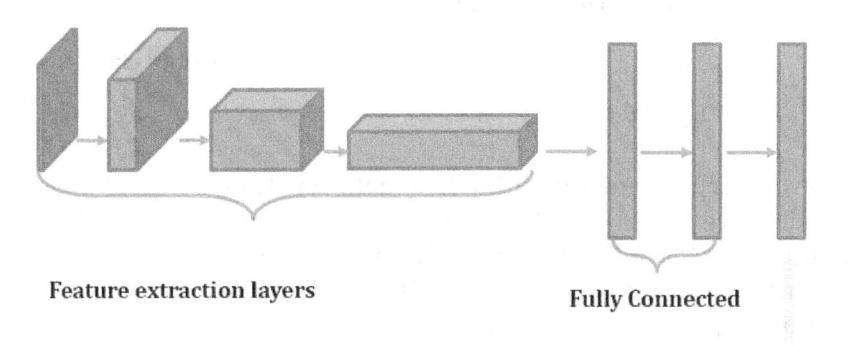

Figure 6.122: Pre-trained model

During transfer learning, we load the entire pre-trained model and then remove the full connected layers:

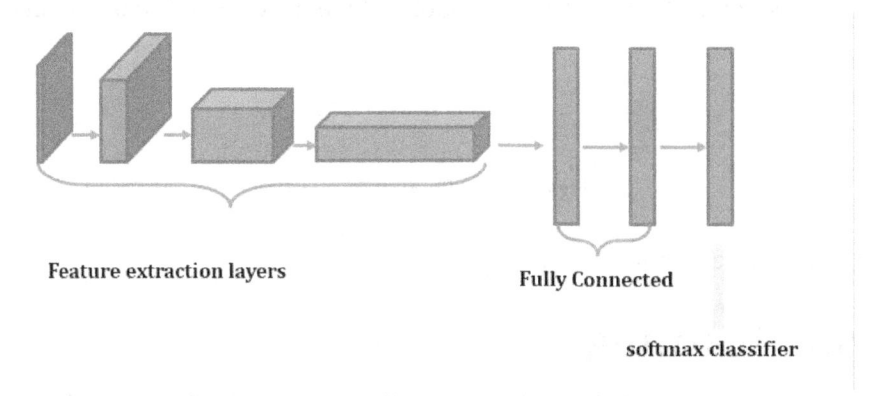

Figure 6.123: Feature extraction layers

These layers retain the values of their trainable parameters. Then we add our own dense layer/layers:

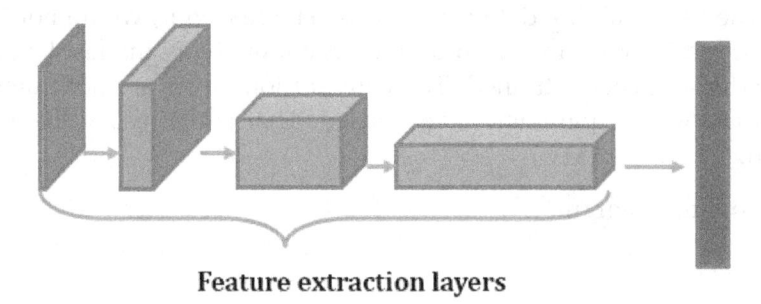

Figure 6.124: Feature extraction layers + Softmax layer

Only this new layer is trained with the new data set. Thereby the time it takes to train the model is very less, and the amount of data required is also relatively less. Let us see this with the following example. We will create a three-class classifier using transfer learning and using the VGG16 pre-trained model. The data for this exercise is shown as follows. These are subfolders in the training folder:

- Earphones
- Keychain
- Marker

Figure 6.125: Folder structure

Each of these folders contains images of **Earphones**, **Keychain,** and **Marker**, respectively, which is shown as follows. Earphones' images in the **Earphones** folder:

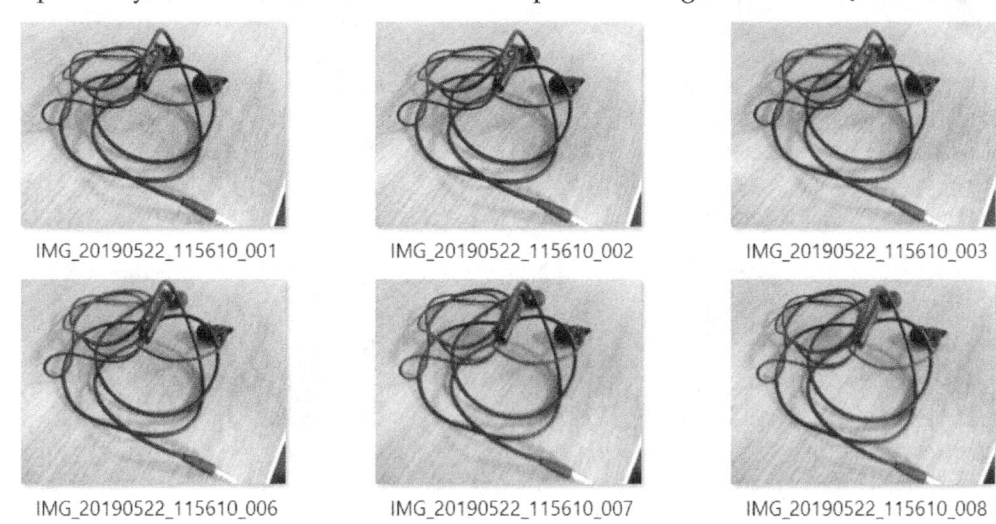

Figure 6.126: Images in "Earphones" subfolder

Keychains' images in **Keychain** folder:

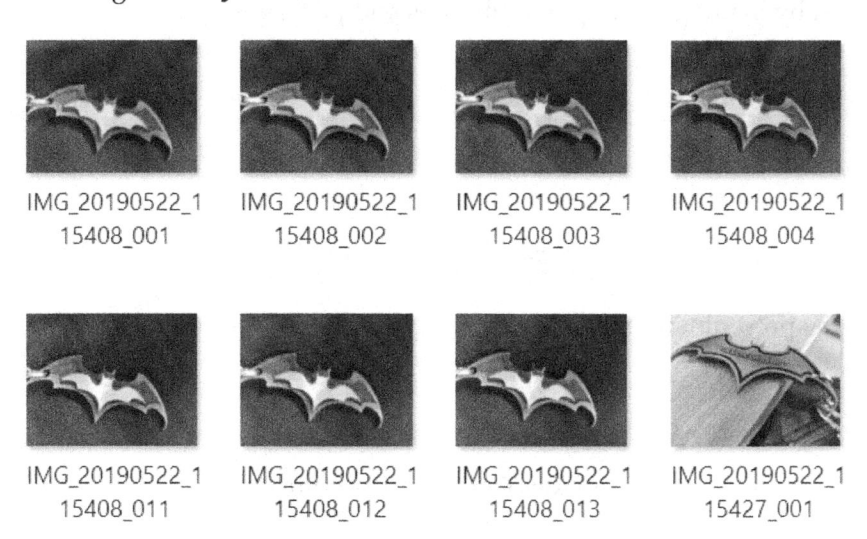

Figure 6.127: Images in "Keychain" subfolder

218 ■ *Beginning with Deep Learning Using TensorFlow*

Markers' images in `Marker` folder:

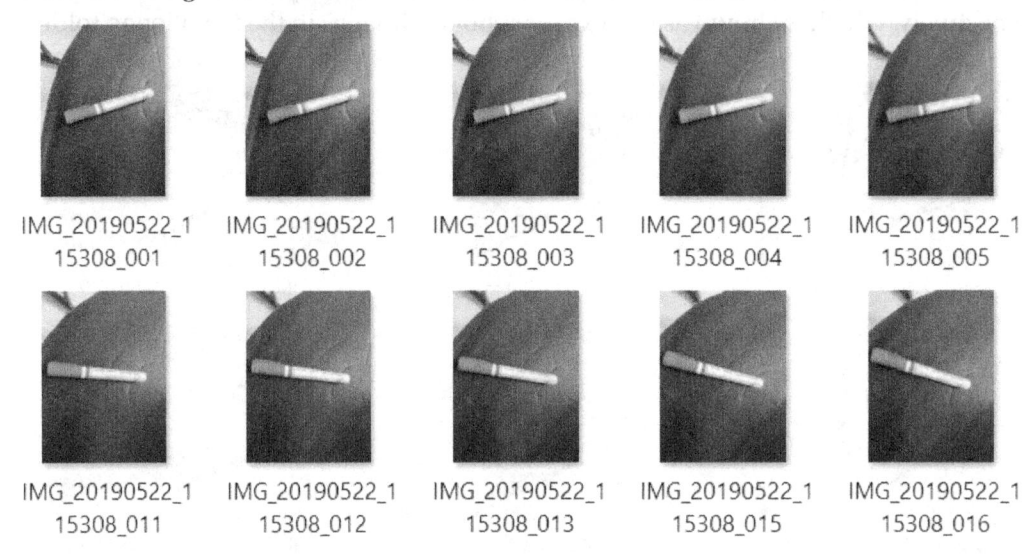

IMG_20190522_1	IMG_20190522_1	IMG_20190522_1	IMG_20190522_1	IMG_20190522_1
15308_001	15308_002	15308_003	15308_004	15308_005
IMG_20190522_1	IMG_20190522_1	IMG_20190522_1	IMG_20190522_1	IMG_20190522_1
15308_011	15308_012	15308_013	15308_015	15308_016

Figure 6.128: Images in "Marker" subfolder

The aim is to build a three-class classifier to classify these items. This is how the code looks. Start by loading the required libraries and packages:

```
##Import libraries
from tensorflow.keras.models import Sequential
from tensorflow.keras.layers import Convolution2D
from tensorflow.keras.layers import MaxPooling2D
from tensorflow.keras.layers import Flatten
from tensorflow.keras.layers import Dense

import tensorflow.keras as keras
```

Figure 6.129: Load libraries

We load the pre-trained model:

```
IMG_SHAPE = (64, 64, 3)

base_model = keras.applications.VGG16(input_shape=IMG_SHAPE, include_top=False, weights='imagenet')
```

Figure 6.130: Pretrained model

The parameters are as follows:

- **input_shape** is the input size of the images to be considered. In this case, it is 64×64×3.
- **include_top** is set to false so that the dense layers are excluded.

Weights are set to **imagenet** to indicate that they correspond to the weights the model got by training on the ImageNet data set:

```
base_model.trainable = False
```

Figure 6.131: Disable training

We do not want to change the parameters (**weights**) of this part of the model; hence, the attribute trainable is set to **False**. Now when we execute the summary to check the configuration of the model, we see that the dense layers are not there:

```
Model: "vgg16"
_____
Layer (type)                 Output Shape              Param #
=================================================================
input_2 (InputLayer)         [(None, 64, 64, 3)]       0
_____
block1_conv1 (Conv2D)        (None, 64, 64, 64)        1792
_____
block1_conv2 (Conv2D)        (None, 64, 64, 64)        36928
_____
block1_pool (MaxPooling2D)   (None, 32, 32, 64)        0
_____
block2_conv1 (Conv2D)        (None, 32, 32, 128)       73856
_____
block2_conv2 (Conv2D)        (None, 32, 32, 128)       147584
_____
block2_pool (MaxPooling2D)   (None, 16, 16, 128)       0
_____
block3_conv1 (Conv2D)        (None, 16, 16, 256)       295168
_____
block3_conv2 (Conv2D)        (None, 16, 16, 256)       590080
_____
block3_conv3 (Conv2D)        (None, 16, 16, 256)       590080
_____
block3_pool (MaxPooling2D)   (None, 8, 8, 256)         0
_____
block4_conv1 (Conv2D)        (None, 8, 8, 512)         1180160
_____
block4_conv2 (Conv2D)        (None, 8, 8, 512)         2359808
_____
block4_conv3 (Conv2D)        (None, 8, 8, 512)         2359808
_____
block4_pool (MaxPooling2D)   (None, 4, 4, 512)         0
_____
block5_conv1 (Conv2D)        (None, 4, 4, 512)         2359808
_____
block5_conv2 (Conv2D)        (None, 4, 4, 512)         2359808
_____
block5_conv3 (Conv2D)        (None, 4, 4, 512)         2359808
_____
block5_pool (MaxPooling2D)   (None, 2, 2, 512)         0
=================================================================
Total params: 14,714,688
```

Figure 6.132: Model summary

Now, we create the Softmax layer consisting of three neurons that need to be added as the last layer. However, before we feed the output of the Maxpool layer to this **Dense** layer, the output has to be flattened. Hence, we create a flatten layer:

```
# Create additional layers
flatten_layer=keras.layers.Flatten()

prediction_layer = keras.layers.Dense(3, activation='softmax')
```

Figure 6.133: Softmax layer

Next, we create a sequential model consisting of the base model and these two layers:

```
classifier = keras.Sequential([
    base_model,
    flatten_layer,
    prediction_layer
])
```

Figure 6.134: Final model

We provide the optimizer and loss details as a part of the **compile** method:

```
classifier.compile(optimizer='adam',loss='categorical_crossentropy', metrics=['accuracy'])
```

Figure 6.135: Compile

Now we can see the final configuration of the model by running the **summary** method:

```
classifier.summary()
```

Model: "sequential_1"

Layer (type)	Output Shape	Param #
vgg16 (Functional)	(None, 2, 2, 512)	14714688
flatten_1 (Flatten)	(None, 2048)	0
dense_1 (Dense)	(None, 3)	6147

Total params: 14,720,835
Trainable params: 6,147
Non-trainable params: 14,714,688

Figure 6.136: Summary

Observe that this model now has 14,714,688 non-trainable parameters and only 6147 trainable parameters.

Then we prepare the data to train the model. Since the amount of data is small, we use the Keras functionality of data enhancement. The parameters **shear_range**, `zoom_range`, `horizontal_flip` in the `ImageDataGenerator` is used for data enhancement:

```
## data importing and transforming and scaling
from tensorflow.keras.preprocessing.image import ImageDataGenerator
train_datagen = ImageDataGenerator(
        rescale=1./255,
        shear_range=0.2,
        zoom_range=0.2,
        horizontal_flip=True)
```

Figure 6.137: Train ImageDataGenerator

This is a special Keras feature. In this example, the data has been enhanced three times. For every single image, there will be three additional images in the training data set, and they will be slightly different—based on the three additional parameters—`shear_range`, `zoom_range`, and `horizonal_flip`—provided in the `ImageDataGenerator` method. Therefore, we have four times the original size of the training data set. If we had originally 50 images now, we will have 200 images without actually creating new data; this is a very powerful function of Keras and particularly used when the training data set is small, and in this case, since the training data set is small, we are making use of this data enhancement feature of Keras.

Next, we create the `ImageDataGenerator` instance for the test data. Remember we do not need data enhancement for testing—hence, the additional parameters are not needed:

```
## Scaling test data
test_datagen = ImageDataGenerator(rescale=1./255)
```

Figure 6.138: Test ImageDataGenerator

Then we prepare the data, both training data and test data, before we run the fit method to train the model:

```
## Importing training data
train_set = train_datagen.flow_from_directory('train',target_size=(64,64),class_mode='categorical')

Found 132 images belonging to 3 classes.

## Importng test data
test_set = test_datagen.flow_from_directory('test',target_size=(64, 64),class_mode='categorical')

Found 47 images belonging to 3 classes.
```

Figure 6.139: Train and test data

As seen above, there are only 132 total training images across the three classes, and these are the original images. Since we used data enhancement for the training data set, during training, four times (4*132 images), the number of images will be created in memory and fed to the model as a part of the training process.

We can check the class labels by printing the **class_indices** property:

```
train_set.class_indices

{'Earphones': 0, 'Keychain': 1, 'Marker': 2}
```

Figure 6.140: Class indices

Now it is time to train the model. We start with five epochs:

```
## training the model
classifier.fit(train_set,epochs=5,validation_data=test_set)

Epoch 1/5
5/5 [==============================] - 26s 5s/step - loss: 1.1472 - accuracy: 0.3333 - val_loss: 0.9038 - val_accuracy: 0.5532
Epoch 2/5
5/5 [==============================] - 19s 4s/step - loss: 0.6958 - accuracy: 0.7273 - val_loss: 0.6800 - val_accuracy: 0.7021
Epoch 3/5
5/5 [==============================] - 20s 4s/step - loss: 0.4799 - accuracy: 0.9318 - val_loss: 0.4372 - val_accuracy: 1.0000
Epoch 4/5
5/5 [==============================] - 19s 4s/step - loss: 0.3123 - accuracy: 0.9924 - val_loss: 0.2754 - val_accuracy: 0.9787
Epoch 5/5
5/5 [==============================] - 21s 4s/step - loss: 0.2357 - accuracy: 1.0000 - val_loss: 0.2031 - val_accuracy: 1.0000
```

Figure 6.141: Model training

Note how quickly the accuracy increases and the loss decreases. Time to check how well our trained model is performing:

```
## Load a single image to run inference
test_image= image.load_img('inference/k1.jpg',target_size =(64,64))
```

test_image

Figure 6.142: Test image

We load a sample image of a keychain. Perform data preparation before running the inference:

```
## Convert image to array
test_image = image.img_to_array(test_image)

## For single prediction change the dimension using axis. To remove problem of batch
test_image=test_image.reshape(1,64,64,3)
```

Figure 6.143: Data preparation

Finally, run the **predict** method for inference:

```
result = classifier.predict(test_image)

result=result.argmax()

## print label

if result == 0:
    prediction = 'Earphones'
elif result == 1:
    prediction = 'Keychain'
else:
    prediction = 'Marker'


prediction

'Keychain'
```

Figure 6.144: Inference

The model predicted this correctly. Let us try another image from a different class.

```
## load a single image to run inference
test_image= image.load_img('inference/m1.jpg',target_size =(64,64))

test_image


## Convert image to array
test_image = image.img_to_array(test_image)

## reshape
test_image=test_image.reshape(1,64,64,3)

result = classifier.predict(test_image)

result=result.argmax()

## print label

if result == 0:
    prediction = 'Earphones'
elif result == 1:
    prediction = 'Keychain'
else:
    prediction = 'Marker'


prediction

'Marker'
```

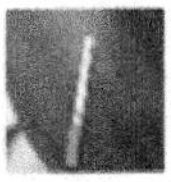

Figure 6.145: Second inference

And this also gets predicted correctly. This concludes this demo.

We have seen how with minimum effort and very little data; we were able to create a classifier of very high accuracy using the transfer learning technique.

Inference with Webcam images

So far, we have been using images already saved on the local drive for running the inference. It is also possible to run inference on a live image captured through a Webcam. This will help you understand the working of OpenCV. This example will also help when we learn about object detection in video. In this example, we will use a pre-trained model, VGG16. In an earlier example, we have seen how to use a pre-trained model for inference. However, in this case, instead of loading an image from the local folder, we will capture the image from the Webcam. We capture a single frame from the Webcam, which is one image.

Let us get started with the code. As always, we begin by importing all the required libraries and packages:

```
from tensorflow.keras.preprocessing.image import img_to_array
from tensorflow.keras.applications.vgg16 import preprocess_input,decode_predictions,VGG16
from tensorflow.keras.models import load_model
from PIL import Image

import cv2

import matplotlib.pyplot as plt
%matplotlib inline

import numpy as np
```

Figure 6.146: Load libraries

Next, we load the pre-trained model VGG16:

```
# Load the model
model = VGG16()
```

Figure 6.147: Pre-trained model

The next piece of code starts the Webcam and waits for the *Esc* key from the keyboard, which triggers the capture of the current frame from the video stream:

```
webcam = cv2.VideoCapture(0) #Use camera 0

while True:
    (rval, im) = webcam.read()

    # Show the image
    cv2.imshow('LIVE',    im)
    key = cv2.waitKey(10)
    # if Esc key is press then break out of the loop
    if key == 27: #The Esc key
        break

    frame = cv2.cvtColor(im, cv2.COLOR_BGR2RGB)

        # Stop video
webcam.release()

# Close all started windows
cv2.destroyAllWindows()
```

Figure 6.148: Webcam capture

This code starts capturing the video steam from Webcam and displays it on a new window titled **LIVE** as shown here:

Figure 6.149: Video display

226 ■ *Beginning with Deep Learning Using TensorFlow*

On pressing the *Esc* key, this window gets closed, and the current frame gets captured as an image. This is then displayed in the Jupyter notebook to make sure the image has been captured properly, and we also see what has been captured as the image:

```
image1 = Image.fromarray(np.uint8(frame))
plt.imshow(image1)
plt.show()
```

Figure 6.150: Image display

There is some pre-processing needed, like we have seen in the earlier examples before running the inference.

```
image = Image.fromarray(np.uint8(frame))
image = image.resize((224, 224))
resize_frame = np.asarray(image)


resize_frame=resize_frame.reshape(1,224,224,3)
```

Figure 6.151: Data preparation

Now we run the inference and get the label and print:

```
# predict the probability across all output classes
result = model.predict(resize_frame)
# convert the probabilities to class labels
label = decode_predictions(result)
# retrieve the most likely result, e.g. highest probability
label = label[0][0]
```

```
# print the label
print(label[1])
```

```
moped
```

Figure 6.152: Inference

The model predicted it like a moped, which is not a very exact description of the image, but it is the closest to Mobike.

When we try with another example with the airplane as in the following image, the model predicted it as **warplane,** which is fairly accurate as shown here:

Figure 6.153: Warplane image

And let us run the inference to get the label and print:

```
image = Image.fromarray(np.uint8(frame))
image = image.resize((224, 224))
resize_frame = np.asarray(image)


resize_frame=resize_frame.reshape(1,224,224,3)

# predict the probability across all output classes
result = model.predict(resize_frame)
# convert the probabilities to class labels
label = decode_predictions(result)
# retrieve the most likely result, e.g. highest probability
label = label[0][0]

# print the label
print(label[1])

warplane
```

Figure 6.154: Second inference

Now that you have got a good idea about image classification, in the next section, we will talk about object detection.

Object detection

While image classification is one of the foundational capabilities of Image recognition of AI, it has limited application by itself. For example, in real life, a single image can have several objects belonging to different classes. Let us perform a simple experiment and use the pre-trained VGG model to classify this image:

Figure 6.155: Sample image

When we run inference on this image, the result is **banana** even though there are apples in this image:

```
# retrieve the most likely result, e.g. highest probability
label = label[0][0]
# print the label
print(label[1])

banana
```

Figure 6.156: Inference

Let us try one more image, which has two dogs and a cat:

Figure 6.157: Sample image

The result is **Great_Pyrenees** which is a breed of dogs:

```
# retrieve the most likely result, e.g. highest probability
label = label[0][0]
# print the label
print(label[1])

Great_Pyrenees
```

Figure 6.158: Inference

This is where object detection can help. When we apply object detection on these images, it will detect objects of different classes in the same image, and this has more real-life applications. Object detection algorithm identifies objects of different classes in the same image and marks them with bounding boxes as shown in the following image:

Figure 6.159: Object detection (Image source: TensorFlow GitHub https://github.com/tensorflow/models/tree/master/research/object_detection)

While the whole working of object detection is out the scope of this book, we will discuss how we can use pre-trained object detection models to develop object detection applications.

In order to run object detection API, you need a bunch of additional libraries and packages. It is a good idea to create a new anaconda environment. You can refer to the following links to get the latest information on setting up the environments. To

230 ■ *Beginning with Deep Learning Using TensorFlow*

help you get started, we will provide you with some quick installation steps on our GitHub link. Once you set up the new environment, run the Jupyter notebooks from the **research** folder.

There is a standard template provided for running object detection on video streaming from Webcam. You can run the notebook named **object_detection_ video_webcam**. If the environment is set up properly, you will see the object detection output on a display window like this:

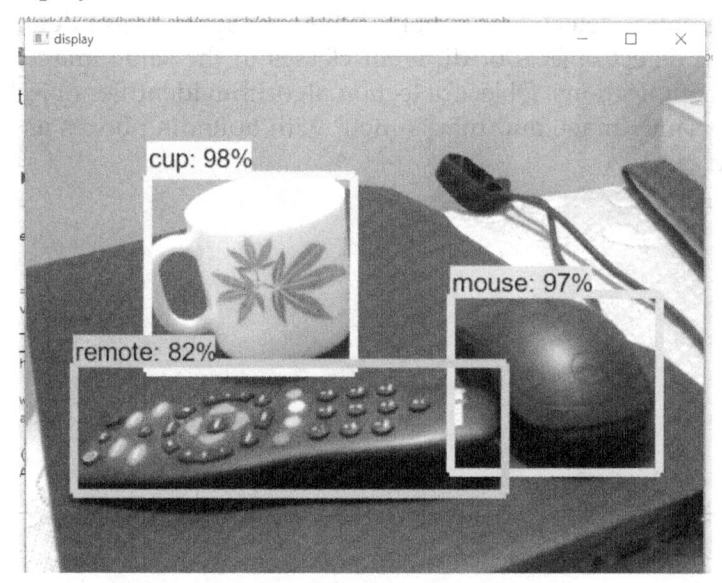

Figure 6.160: *Object detection*

There are other variations of this in the same folder. To run object detection on a pre-recorded video or even an image. You can try them. This example used the pre-trained model—**ssd_mobilenet_v1_coco_2017_11_17**:

Figure 6.161: *Pre-trained model*

There are several pre-trained models that are available on the TensorFlow Model Zoo page:

https://github.com/tensorflow/models/blob/master/research/object_detection/g3doc/tf2_detection_zoo.md

Conclusion

This brings us to the end of this chapter. Image recognition is an important component of artificial intelligence and deep learning, and in this chapter, we discussed how Image recognition works using **Convolution Neural Networks (CNN)**, and we went through a variety of code demos and examples.

In the upcoming chapter, we will discuss another important component of AI, that is, speech recognition.

Points to remember

- Convolutional Neural Networks are used for image recognition.
- Pre-trained models like VGG16 and ResNet are available for free for image classification.
- Transfer learning can be used to create classification models when training data is small.
- Object detection has many practical applications as it identifies multiple objects in an image.

CHAPTER 7
Speech Recognition

Introduction

Image recognition and speech recognition are the two main sub-domains within artificial intelligence and deep learning today. In the previous chapter, we have seen how image recognition works. In this chapter, we will see how speech recognition works and what are some of its applications. For many years there was very slow progress in the area of speech recognition. But over the past few years, there have been a lot of significant developments, particularly with the advent of transformers. Part of the reason for the slow progress is the complexity of speech recognition. Before we begin, let us clarify the terminology. "*Speech recognition*" was originally coined to mean interpretation of speech, which is just one part of the entire process, but today speech recognition refers to the entire end to end process of recognizing human speech, converting it to text for **Natural Language Processing** (**NLP**) and converting back the result to speech (*synthesis*). In this chapter, we will discuss the entire end-to-end process.

Structure

In this chapter, the following topics will be covered:

- What is speech recognition?—Historical perspective
- How speech recognition works?

- Natural language processing (NLP)
- Language models
- Word Embedding—Word2Vec
- Recurrent Neural Networks (RNN)
- Text classification with RNN
- Transformers
- Text classification with BERT
- Q&A with BERT—SQUAD

Objective

After reading this chapter, you will be able to understand the concepts of speech recognition and NLP using deep learning. Some of the latest techniques, like transformers, are covered here with hands-on code demos to help you try them out and grasp the concepts faster.

What is speech recognition?—Historical perspective

We human beings have been fascinated by the concept of talking to machines or computers, and this is well depicted in several science fiction movies like Star Wars.

The first non-voice recognition device was developed by the scientists at bell laboratories in 1952; this was known as Audrey or audio digit recognition; this is similar to the handwriting recognition that we saw in the image recognition chapter; this device could recognize the spoken numbers or digits from zero to nine and was considered to be a breakthrough innovation. This was only able to recognize the discrete spoken numbers. In the early sixties, IBM developed Shoebox, which was able to take simple mathematical operation commands. It was able to recognize 16 spoken words, including the numbers 0–9 (refer to *figure 7.1*):

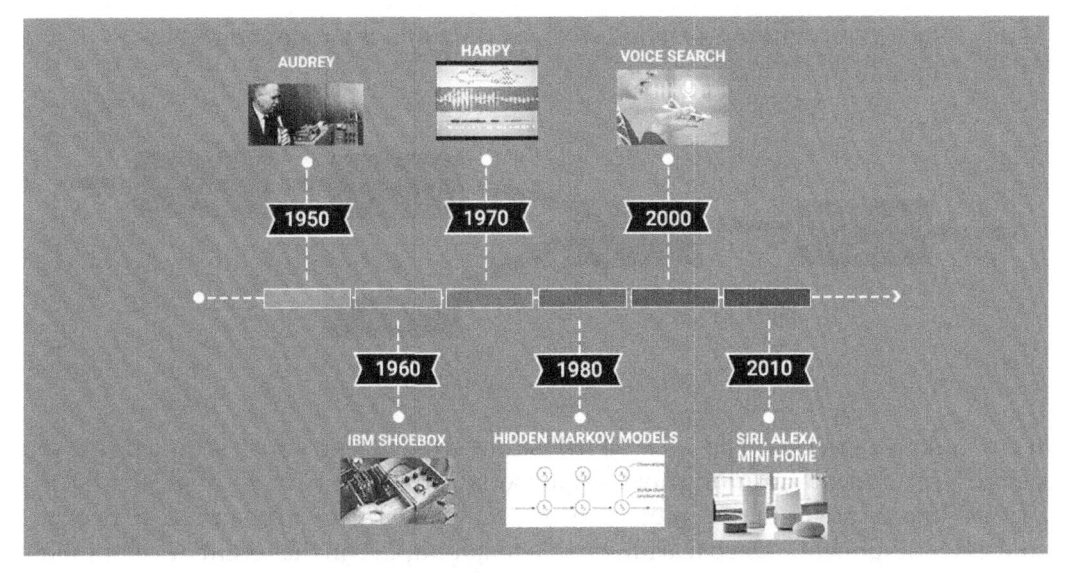

Figure 7.1: Early trends of speech recognition

Speech recognition has come a long way since then. Today's speech recognition systems can work with a vocabulary of thousands of words with a high level of accuracy.

Application of speech recognition

Speech recognition is very prevalent today; almost everyone uses speech recognition on day-to-day basis applications, such as Siri, okay Google, and speech-enabled chatbots are good examples of speech recognition applications. Speech recognition makes it very easy to interact with machines, and therefore, there is a lot of interest in this space.

Speech recognition, unlike image recognition, is a much more complicated process as it involves multiple steps. In image recognition, the input is an image, and the neural network classifier test result there is no conversion of an image into skills about technicians for completed because the neural network cannot process the raw audio. Therefore, the raw audio needs to be converted to text which can be processed by the neural network using natural language processing or anything; this further results in text, and this text is further converted voice, much known as synthesis process much more complicated as compared with image recognition.

Today's speech recognition systems work as shown in the following figure:

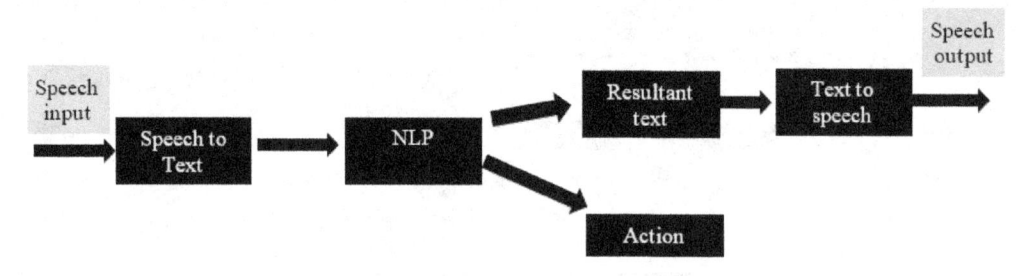

Figure 7.2: Speech recognition process

It is a multistep process. The voice signal is converted to text, which is then processed using NLP, and the resulting text response is converted back to a speech by the process known as synthesis. In this process, NLP plays a key role, and it, in turn, has multiple components. Deep learning had a major impact on the recent developments in the NLP space, and this will be our focus in this chapter. There is already a lot of literature around speech to text and text to speech as they have existed for a long time. Hence, we will focus on NLP in this chapter.

NLP has the following components:

- Word embedding
- Language models
- Sequence to sequence models—RNN, LSTM, and GRU
- Transformers

Before we begin, let us first take a quick look at a very simple demo of speech to text and text to speech.

The Jupyter notebook, **speechrecog.ipynb** is available in the GitHub link which is provided in the Appendix. This has two parts. One is speech to text, in which an audio file is transcribed to text using the free speech recognition library, which in turn uses Google's free cloud-based text to speech service. This also means that you should be connected to the internet for this demo to work. Before running the code, there is a one-time installation of the following libraries:

- speech recognition
- gTTS

You can install them with pip install either through the Jupyter notebook or through the command prompt. In the code provided, these lines are commented. Uncomment these two lines in the first cell and run the cell only once and make sure they are successfully installed:

```
#run the following installs before using this code
#pip install speechrecognition
#pip install gTTS
```

Figure 7.3: Pip install

Install these libraries the first time you are running this code. For the subsequent runs, keep these lines commented:

```
#run the following installs before using this code
#pip install speechrecognition
#pip install gTTS

import os
import speech_recognition as sr
from gtts import gTTS
```

Figure 7.4: Importing libraries

Then import the required libraries:

```
os.system("bangalore.wav")

0
```

Figure 7.5: Demo audio file

There is a demo audio file made available. Play the audio file to listen to the audio content:

```
r=sr.Recognizer()

input1=sr.AudioFile('bangalore.wav')

with input1 as source:
    audio=r.record(source)


mytext=r.recognize_google(audio)
```

Figure 7.6: Playing an audio file

The function **recognize_google** is the Google function that takes the audio input and returns the corresponding text. This is stored in the variable **mytext**:

```
mytext=r.recognize_google(audio)
```

```
mytext
```

'I would like to take a topic as Bangalore Bangalore is a capital city of Karnataka Bangalore is sometimes referred as Silicon Valley of India because it was roller National leading Information Technology expert expert the Indian Technology organisations like ISRO Infosys Wipro and HAL at Quest headquarter in the city of Bangalore in a culture in the bank Bangalore known as a garden city in India many public Park like Lalbagh Cubbon Park and sometime it called as pub city in India the Bangalore Karega or the'

```
file1 =open("obama1.txt","r")
mytext=file1.read()
```

Figure 7.7: Storing audio input using recognize_google function

Upon printing the contents of **mytext**, it is seen that the audio has been transcribed fairly accurately. Now you can do the other way round, that is, pass some text and get the corresponding audio file.

```
mytext=r.recognize_google(audio)
```

```
mytext
```

'I would like to take a topic as Bangalore Bangalore is a capital city of Karnataka Bangalore is sometimes referred as Silicon Valley of India because it was roller National leading Information Technology expert expert the Indian Technology organisations like ISRO Infosys Wipro and HAL at Quest headquarter in the city of Bangalore in a culture in the bank Bangalore known as a garden city in India many public Park like Lalbagh Cubbon Park and sometime it called as pub city in India the Bangalore Karega or the'

```
file1 =open("obama1.txt","r")
mytext=file1.read()
```

Figure 7.8: Storing some text in "mytext"

There is a sample text file of President Obama's speech provided along with the code. You can also replace it with any other text file. Open the text file and read the contents into the variable '**mytext**':

```
mytext
```

'When my staff told me that I was to deliver a lecture, I thought back to the stuffy old professors in bow ties and tweed, and I wondered if this was one more sign of the stage of life that I'm entering, along with gray hair and slightly failing eyesight. I thought about the fact that my daughters think anything I tell them is a lecture. I thought about the American press and how they often got frustrated at my long-winded answers at press conferences, when my responses didn't conform to two-minute soundbites.'

```
# Language in which you want to convert
language = 'en'

# Passing the text and language to the engine,
# here we have marked slow=False. Which tells
# the module that the converted audio should
# have a high speed
myobj = gTTS(text=mytext, lang=language, slow=False)
```

Figure 7.9: Open/read the variable "mytext"

Display the content:

```
#instantiate gTTS
myobj = gTTS(text=mytext, lang='en')
```

Figure 7.10: Set language

Instantiate gTTS and pass the text, and set the language to English:

```
# Save the converted audio file

myobj.save("obama.wav")
```

Figure 7.11: Save the audio file

Save the audio as a wav file named **Obama.wav**:

```
#play the audio file
os.system("obama.wav")

0
```

Figure 7.12: Play the saved file

Play the audio file to check the accuracy. Observer that, while content accuracy will be good, but some of the nuances of the human speech will be missing. However, this is really good, considering that there were very few lines of code that were needed for this whole process.

The process of converting speech to text and text to speech has been there for quite some time, and it is commoditized. Hence, in this chapter, we will not spend delve into these areas. However, in this whole process, the machine did not need to understand the meaning of the voice or the text. It just blindly converted the audio to text and text to audio. But to build an intelligent system like Alexa, the machine needs to also understand the meaning of the text, and this is where Natural Language Processing or NLP comes in. There have been a lot of advances in the NLP space, and in this chapter, we will see some of the latest advances in NLP like Transformers and their applications in NLP.

Natural Language Processing (NLP)

The core of speech recognition is Natural Language Processing or NLP. The speech to text converts the spoken words to text, but the system does not understand what it means. NLP is the process that makes sense of what is said and then initiates the corresponding response. Hence, NLP is further broken down into two parts—**Natural Language Understanding** (NLU) and **Natural Language Generation** (NLG).

Before we begin, let us quickly go over some of the commonly used NLP terminologies:

- **Text corpus**: A large text document or several text documents that are used for training the NLP model.
- **Document**: A set of words or tokens. This could be a single sentence, a tweet, or a text file.
- **Tokens**: Individual words in a sentence or a document.
- **Embedding**: Mechanism of converting text to numbers.

For a better understanding of NLP, we will consider the various NLP tasks listed below and run a code demo for each of them.

- Sentiment analysis or text classification
- Question and answer—like in chatbot
- Text summarization
- Language translation

One of the first steps in an NLP process is Word Embedding.

Word Embedding

Machines do not understand the text. So, the first step is to convert the text to numbers. There are several traditional ways in which this was done, such as Bag of words, **Term Document Frequency (TDF)**, and so on. But in deep learning, we use a mechanism called Word Embeddings.

The simplest way of converting text to numbers is by assigning a number to every unique token in our text corpus. However, just the individual words are not of much use in a language. They are used along with each other to communicate meaning. In addition, a lot of the words are related to each other in some form. For example, Man and King are similar in the sense they have the same gender. And Man and woman are related as they are antonyms and so on. With word embedding, each word is converted into a multi-dimensional vector in such a way that this similarity or relationship is maintained. Word2vec is one such technique. GloVe (short for Global Vectors) is another.

In order to understand the concept of word embedding, let us go through a demo. In this demo, we will use pre-trained Word2vec model. It is also possible to train your own model, but it is time-consuming and very often not required. Let us get started with the code.

The code explained below is a part of the Jupyter notebook, word2vec-demo, available in the corresponding folder in the GitHub link that will be provided. We will be using the genism library for this. As a first step, install this library using **pip install**. This needs to be only once:

```
#!pip install gensim

#original path
#https://s3.amazonaws.com/dl4j-distribution/GoogleNews-vectors-negative300.bin.gz
```

Figure 7.13: *Installing okyo*

The pre-trained word2vec model we will be using is called **GoogleNews-vectors-negative300.bin**. A link to the location of the compressed file is provided. This is a large file (1.6 GB in compressed format), and hence, is it already downloaded and provided for you along with the code. In case you want to download it yourself, you need to download the above-compressed file and extract it. The extracted file size is about 3.5 GB. If you are interested in a more detailed working of this model, visit their web page:

https://code.google.com/archive/p/word2vec/

The next step is to load this model. It will take a few seconds since it is a large file:

```
from gensim.models import KeyedVectors
# Load the google word2vec model
filename = 'GoogleNews-vectors-negative300.bin'
model = KeyedVectors.load_word2vec_format(filename, binary=True)
```

Figure 7.14: *Loading okyo model*

This pre-trained model has been trained on a very large corpus, and hence, it includes almost the entire English vocabulary. So let us see the vectors created for some of the words:

```
vector_rich=model.get_vector('rich')
```

```
vector_rich.shape
```

```
(300,)
```

Figure 7.15: *Get vector of the word*

We use the method **get_vector** to fetch the vector for a given the word. As you can see, this is a 300-dimension vector. We can check the values:

```
vector_rich

array([ 2.08984375e-01,   9.32617188e-02,  -1.21093750e-01,   1.47460938e-01,
       -1.36718750e-01,   1.00585938e-01,   1.19628906e-01,  -3.30078125e-01,
       -2.08007812e-01,   2.83203125e-01,  -9.66796875e-02,   8.59375000e-02,
        8.44726562e-02,   4.10156250e-02,  -6.68945312e-02,   2.09960938e-02,
       -1.22070312e-01,   2.27539062e-01,  -6.68334961e-03,  -1.43554688e-01,
       -1.25000000e-01,  -1.19628906e-01,  -3.96728516e-03,   1.04492188e-01,
        3.08593750e-01,  -1.33789062e-01,  -2.01416016e-02,   7.37304688e-02,
        1.25976562e-01,  -2.14843750e-01,  -9.52148438e-02,   3.78906250e-01,
        1.69921875e-01,  -2.58789062e-02,  -3.12500000e-01,   2.44140625e-01,
       -1.69921875e-01,  -2.09960938e-01,   8.39843750e-02,   3.88671875e-01,
        3.84765625e-01,   2.67578125e-01,   2.63671875e-01,  -5.05371094e-02,
        3.33984375e-01,  -1.34765625e-01,  -2.98828125e-01,   2.51953125e-01,
       -1.25000000e-01,  -2.73437500e-02,   9.76562500e-02,  -1.04003906e-01,
        9.32617188e-02,  -1.38671875e-01,  -1.45507812e-01,   1.80664062e-01,
       -3.55468750e-01,  -2.75390625e-01,   1.27929688e-01,  -1.09375000e-01,
        1.52343750e-01,   3.88183594e-02,  -2.75390625e-01,   8.64257812e-02,
       -1.85546875e-02,  -7.32421875e-02,  -8.39843750e-02,  -1.03149414e-02,
        2.91015625e-01,  -1.23046875e-01,   7.91015625e-02,  -1.67968750e-01,
```

Figure 7.16: Vector representation of "rich"

Let us take a look at one more word, poor:

```
model.get_vector('poor')

array([ 2.14843750e-01,   2.63671875e-01,  -4.07714844e-02,   1.11328125e-01,
        4.45556641e-03,   2.73437500e-01,  -7.03125000e-02,   4.05273438e-02,
       -3.12500000e-02,   1.21093750e-01,  -7.81250000e-02,   4.29687500e-02,
        1.16210938e-01,   4.61425781e-02,   1.92260742e-03,   6.00585938e-02,
        1.12304688e-01,   4.46777344e-02,  -3.18359375e-01,  -2.64892578e-02,
        1.75781250e-02,   1.33056641e-02,   1.45507812e-01,  -1.57470703e-02,
        4.04296875e-01,  -1.84570312e-01,  -3.00781250e-01,   3.68652344e-02,
        8.78906250e-02,  -7.42187500e-02,  -2.59765625e-01,  -3.49121094e-02,
        2.46093750e-01,  -9.81445312e-02,   1.37329102e-02,   2.79296875e-01,
       -7.91015625e-02,  -1.29882812e-01,  -2.31933594e-02,   4.61425781e-02,
        1.94335938e-01,   8.20312500e-02,   3.02734375e-01,  -7.12890625e-02,
        3.20312500e-01,  -7.47070312e-02,  -1.40380859e-02,   1.14257812e-01,
       -1.10839844e-01,  -2.80761719e-03,   7.86132812e-02,   5.76171875e-02,
```

Figure 7.17: Vector representation of "poor"

One of the major advantages of word2vec is its ability to understand the relation between the words. And this is done by calculating the cosine distance between them. And we can check for similar words using the similarity functions. Let us take a look at some examples.

If we want to check for the **top3** words similar to **poor**, we can call the method **most_similar**.

```
#similarity
model.most_similar("poor",topn=3)

[('poorer', 0.6462290287017822),
 ('abysmal', 0.5980105400085449),
 ('poorest', 0.5948267579078674)]
```

Figure 7.18: Check for words similar to "poor"

In the result, the number on the right-hand side is the measure of similarity. The higher the value, the more similar the words are. We can take one more example for the word **fast**:

```
model.most_similar("fast",topn=3)

[('quick', 0.5701605677604675),
 ('rapidly', 0.5525554418563843),
 ('Fast', 0.5490223169326782)]
```

Figure 7.19: Check for words similar to "fast"

We can also measure the similarity between two words by calling the method similarity and passing the two words:

```
model.similarity(w1="rich", w2="richer")

0.6159481
```

Figure 7.20: Similarity index between "rich" and "richer"

This may appear like a very trivial example, but keep in mind that, whereas it is very easy for humans to recognize that rich and richer are pretty much the same word, as far as the machine is concerned, these are completely different words. However, through word2vec it understands that there is a good amount of similarity.

We can take one more example:

```
model.similarity(w1="good", w2="fantastic")

0.6407778
```

Figure 7.21: Similarity index between "good" and "fantastic"

It recognizes that **good** and **fantastic** are closely related.

Finally, let us take two antonyms and check:

```
model.similarity(w1="poor", w2="rich")

0.37228
```

Figure 7.22: Similarity index between "rich" and "poor"

Observer that in this case, the value is low, which means the words are dissimilar. One more very interesting aspect of word2vec is the ability to do Math. The most famous example is this.

King - man + woman = queen

This is known as word analogies. Other examples are as follows:

man -> woman :: prince -> princess

okyo -> okyoh :: spain -> okyoh

india -> delhi :: okyo -> okyo

man -> woman :: boy -> girl

small -> smaller :: large -> larger

Let us take a couple of examples of these looks in the code. We will start with the king, queen example:

```
# calculate: (king - man) + woman = ?
result = model.most_similar(positive=['woman', 'king'], negative=['man'], topn=1)
print(result)

[('queen', 0.7118193507194519)]
```

Figure 7.23: Math operation with word2vec

We use the **most_similar** method like before but use the parameters named positive and negative. This is a very powerful capability of word2vec.

Let us take one more example to further illustrate this:

```
# calculate: (moscow - russia) + france = ?
result = model.most_similar(positive=['moscow', 'france'], negative=['russia'], topn=1)
print(result)

[('italy', 0.4832305908203125)]
```

Figure 7.24: One more Math operation with word2vec

As you can see, the model understands the relations between the countries and their capitals. And one last example:

```
# calculate: (kitten - cat) + dog = ?
result = model.most_similar(positive=['kitten', 'dog'], negative=['cat'], topn=1)
print(result)

[('puppy', 0.7699725031852722)]
```

Figure 7.25: One more Math operation with word2vec

This example shows that the model understands the relation between the animals and their young ones. Hope this gives a good understanding of word embeddings and pre-trained models of word embeddings. Although these models like word2vec and GloVe are a great improvement compared with the earlier techniques like Bag of words, but there is still one problem. The models still do not understand the context.

A classic example is the use of the word bank. This word can have two different meanings: one is the bank where we keep money, and the other could be a riverbank. We understand the meaning based on the context:

`Rajesh is going to the bank to withdraw cash.`

In this sentence, it is clear the meaning of the word is the place where we keep the money. And we have another sentence like:

`Ramesh is sitting on the bank and enjoying the breeze.`

In this case, the meaning of the word is a riverbank. ELMO was one of the early models for context-based embedding. This uses Bidirectional LSTM. LSTM is a variation of RNN. However, the latest in Embeddings is the transformer-based language models like BERT. We will understand them in the next section on language models.

Language model

The language model is a system that predicts the next word of a sentence based on the previous words. This is implemented using a sequence-to-sequence model. In the past few years, there has been tremendous development in this space. In the past language, models were implemented using **Recurrent Neural Networks** (**RNN**). The regular DNN or CNN could not be used as they are not time-dependent. However, there are drawbacks in regular RNN, like vanishing gradient and exploding gradient. The improved versions of RNN are LSTM and GRU. LSTMs are very popular with language models, but they are slow and take a lot of time to train. Now we have transformer-based models like BERT, which are much more accurate and faster. The progress is depicted in the following diagram:

RNN → LSTM → ELMO → BERT

Figure 7.26: Progress in the language model

Recurrent Neural Networks (RNN)

An RNN unit (*figure 7.27*) looks like a regular neuron, except that the output is fed back along with the other inputs; thus, making it time-dependent:

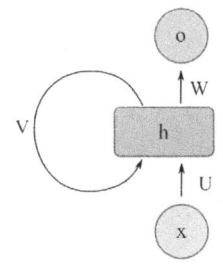

Figure 7.27: RNN unit

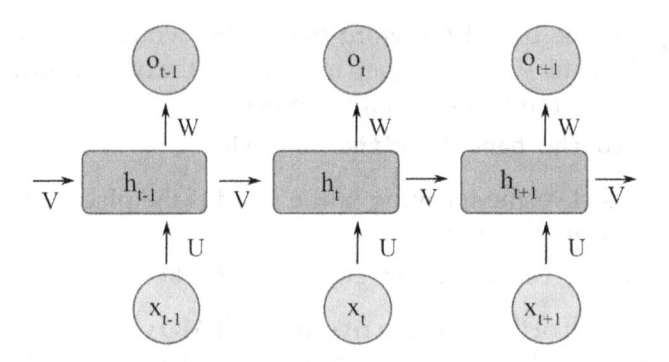

Figure 7.28: Unrolled RNN

The unrolled RNN (*figure 7.28*) is a single unit of RNN taking multiple inputs over certain time steps. For example, at time step *t*, the input is $Xt + V$ which is the output from the previous time step *t*–1. At time step *t*+1, the input is $Xt+1 + V$ which is the output of time step *t*, and so on.

Hence, this is better suited for time-dependent data than a regular DNN or CNN. The RNN-based language model can be represented in the following diagram:

What would be the next possible word in the following sequence:

What is your ………..

There are, of course, several possibilities like … "plan", "question", "designation", and so on. However, the probability of the next word is "name" is the highest.

And this prediction can be done with greater accuracy if we had more context or knowledge of some more previous words:

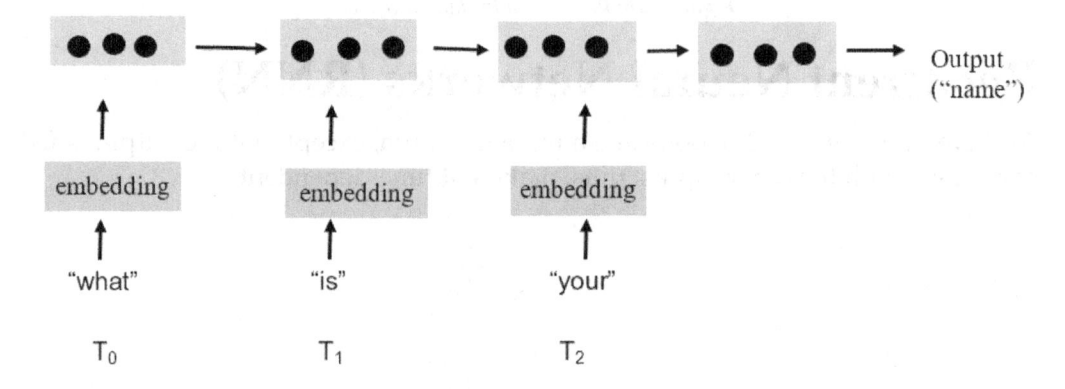

Figure 7.29: RNN-based language model

Text classification

Text classification is one of the NLP tasks. Let us go through a code demo to see how RNN's can be used for text classification. The process is broadly depicted in this diagram:

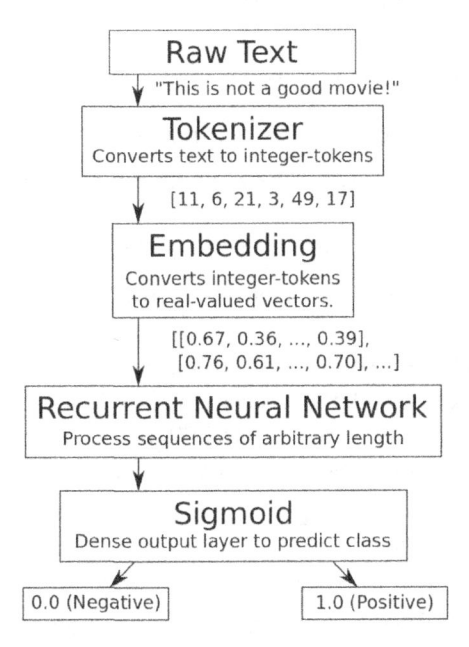

Figure 7.30: Text classification

We will use Keras to build the RNN model and the inbuilt imdb text data set. Please refer to the file RNN.ipynb. As the first step, let us import all the necessary libraries:

```
from tensorflow.keras.datasets import imdb
from tensorflow.keras import preprocessing
from tensorflow.keras.models import Sequential
from tensorflow.keras.layers import SimpleRNN,Flatten,Dense,Embedding,SpatialDropout1D,Dropout
from sklearn.metrics import accuracy_score
```

Figure 7.31: Importing necessary libraries

Next, the **imdb** data set is loaded. This data set is inbuilt in Keras and consists of movie review comments. There are a total of 5000 reviews split between training and test. And the reviews are labeled 0 or 1 based on whether the review is positive or negative. They are encoded as follows:

```
(train_text,train_label),(test_text,test_label) =imdb.load_data(num_words=5000)
```

Figure 7.32: load data

The method **load_data** takes parameter **num_words,** which in this case is passed a value of 5000. This will load all the 5000 most frequently used words. The method **load_data** returns two tuples, one each for training and test:

```
Train_text -> training  data (25000 reviews)
train_label-> the corresponding labels
test_text  ->  test data
test_label -> corresponding labels
```

This needs some pre-processing before feeding to our model for training:

```
train_text = preprocessing.sequence.pad_sequences(train_text,maxlen=200)

test_text = preprocessing.sequence.pad_sequences(test_text,maxlen=200)
```

Figure 7.33: Pre-processing before training

Since the sentences can be of different lengths, this step will prepare them with equal lengths of sequences, that is, 200 in this case. In case the original sequence is less than 200, then it is padded, and if it is more than 200, then it is truncated. Now the data is ready. Next, a Sequential model is created by adding the various layers:

```
model_rnn=Sequential()
model_rnn.add(Embedding(5000,output_dim=32))
model_rnn.add(SimpleRNN(32))
model_rnn.add(Dropout(0.4))
model_rnn.add(Dense(1,activation='sigmoid'))
```

Figure 7.34: Sequential model creation

The Embedding layer converts the sequence to word embeddings. The first parameter is the size of the vocabulary, and the second is the dimension of the embedding, in this case, 32. This is followed by an RNN layer of 32 units, followed by a dropout layer.

Finally, there is a dense layer consisting of one neuron with Sigmoid activation function in order to achieve binary classification. Next, we provide the loss function and the optimizer in compile:

```
model_rnn.compile(loss='binary_crossentropy',optimizer='rmsprop',metrics=['accuracy'])
```

Figure 7.35: Loss function and the optimizer

A quick look at the summary of the model:

```
model_rnn.summary()

Model: "sequential"
_____
Layer (type)                 Output Shape              Param #
=================================================================
embedding (Embedding)        (None, None, 32)          160000

simple_rnn (SimpleRNN)       (None, 32)                2080

dropout (Dropout)            (None, 32)                0

dense (Dense)                (None, 1)                 33
=================================================================
Total params: 162,113
Trainable params: 162,113
Non-trainable params: 0
_____
```

Figure 7.36: Summary of the sequential model

Now the model is ready to be trained. Let us run the training for 10 epochs:

```
history_run=model_rnn.fit(train_text,train_label,batch_size=128,validation_split=0.2,epochs=10)
Epoch 1/10
157/157 [==============================] - 7s 46ms/step - loss: 0.6536 - accuracy: 0.6030 - val_loss: 0.5287 - val_accuracy: 0.7584
Epoch 2/10
157/157 [==============================] - 7s 45ms/step - loss: 0.4591 - accuracy: 0.8041 - val_loss: 0.4531 - val_accuracy: 0.7932
Epoch 3/10
157/157 [==============================] - 7s 43ms/step - loss: 0.3474 - accuracy: 0.8598 - val_loss: 0.3874 - val_accuracy: 0.8410
Epoch 4/10
157/157 [==============================] - 7s 43ms/step - loss: 0.2896 - accuracy: 0.8853 - val_loss: 0.4031 - val_accuracy: 0.8310
Epoch 5/10
157/157 [==============================] - 7s 44ms/step - loss: 0.2396 - accuracy: 0.9081 - val_loss: 0.5590 - val_accuracy: 0.8086
Epoch 6/10
157/157 [==============================] - 7s 43ms/step - loss: 0.1969 - accuracy: 0.9258 - val_loss: 0.4427 - val_accuracy: 0.8270
Epoch 7/10
157/157 [==============================] - 7s 43ms/step - loss: 0.1538 - accuracy: 0.9449 - val_loss: 0.4472 - val_accuracy: 0.8306
Epoch 8/10
157/157 [==============================] - 7s 43ms/step - loss: 0.1314 - accuracy: 0.9536 - val_loss: 0.5003 - val_accuracy: 0.8148
Epoch 9/10
157/157 [==============================] - 7s 44ms/step - loss: 0.0977 - accuracy: 0.9680 - val_loss: 0.5957 - val_accuracy: 0.7976
Epoch 10/10
157/157 [==============================] - 7s 43ms/step - loss: 0.0786 - accuracy: 0.9752 - val_loss: 0.5549 - val_accuracy: 0.8330
```

Figure 7.37: Training for 10 epochs

The model achieves a training accuracy of 83%. Let us evaluate the model with test data:

```
y_test_pred=model_rnn.evaluate(test_text,test_label)
782/782 [==============================] - 4s 5ms/step - loss: 0.5641 - accuracy: 0.8326
```

Figure 7.38: Testing the model

This also shows 83% accuracy. We can run an inference with some samples of the test data and check:

```
result=model_rnn.predict(test_text[[40]])
result.round()
array([[1.]], dtype=float32)
```

Figure 7.39: Round off the output

We try with the review in location 40. The prediction is 1. Let us check the corresponding label:

```
test_label[[40]]
array([1], dtype=int64)
```

Figure 7.40: Checking the label

The label is also 1, which indicates the prediction is correct. You can try with a few more samples.

The RNN's used in this demo is known as vanilla RNNs. There are a few problems with RNNs like the Vanishing gradient and the Exploding gradient, due to which their usage is limited. There are variations of these vanilla RNN's like LSTM (**long short-term memory**) and **GRU** (**gated recurrent unit**), which help in overcoming some of these problems.

In spite of these variants, RNN's are very difficult to train. They are very time-consuming. And this is where transformer-based pre-trained models like BERT are extremely useful.

Transformers

Transformers were first introduced through a paper titled "*Attention is all you need*" in 2017, and since then, transformers have become a rage and have accelerated major developments in the area of NLP and speech recognition. We have seen that for NLP, sequence matters, and hence, RNN's and their variations like LSTM and GRU were used. However, since the processing happens sequentially, they are very slow.

In transformers, the processing happens in parallel. Let us take a look at the transformer architecture:

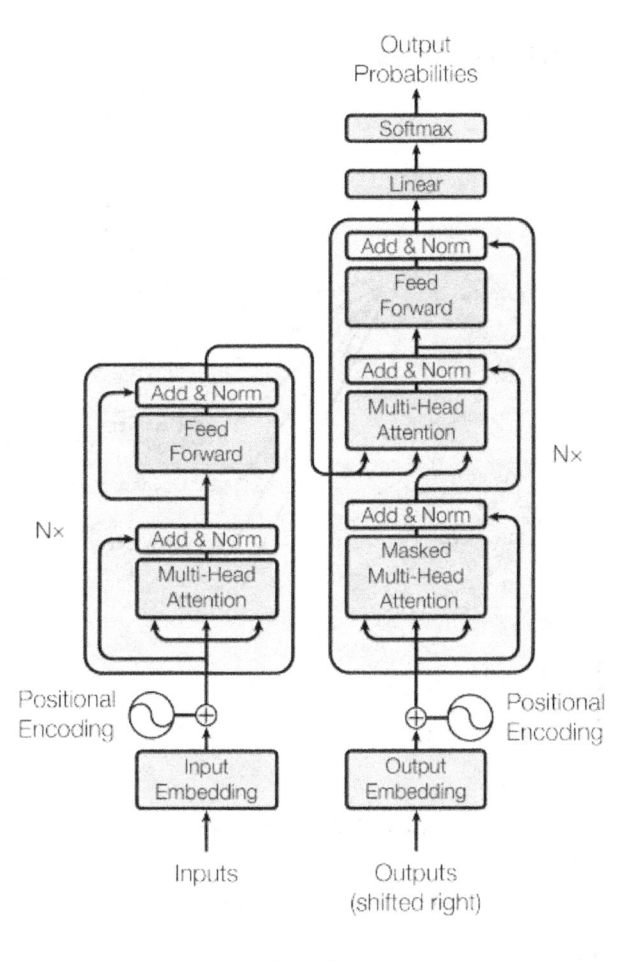

Figure 7.41: Transformer architecture

It has two parts: encoder and decoder. The encoder, in turn, consists of the following:

- Input embedding
- Positional encoding
- Encoding layers

The original design of the transformer had six encoding layers.

And the decoder, in turn, consists of the following:

- Output embedding

- Positional encoding
- Decoding layers

And the original design had six decoding layers:

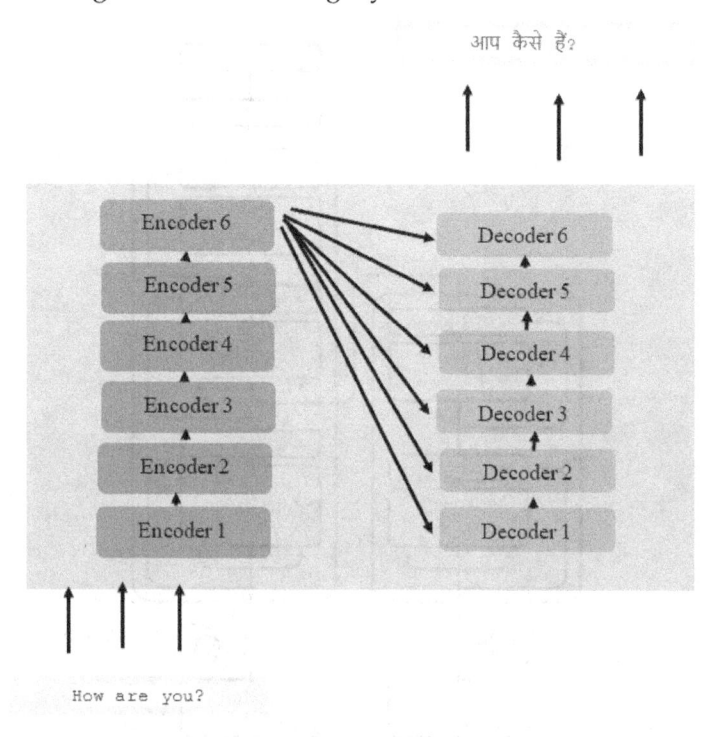

Figure 7.42: Encoder–Decoder

Each encoding layer, in turn, consists of two parts:

- Self-attention
- Feedforward neural network

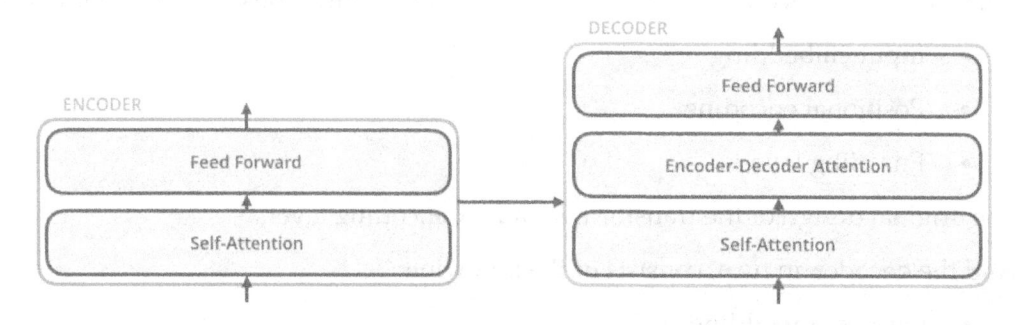

Figure 7.43: Encoder

And each decoder, in turn, consists of three parts:

- Self-attention
- Encoder decoder attention
- Feed forward neural network

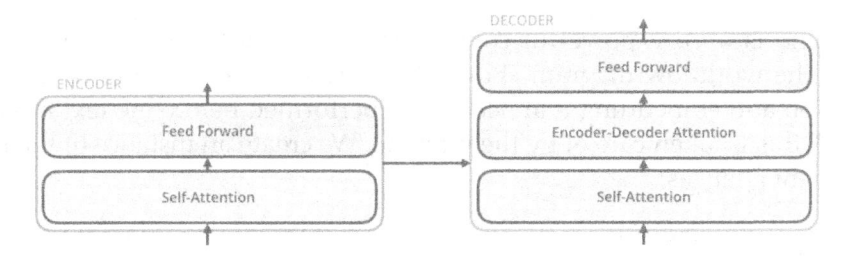

Figure 7.44: *Decoder*

The major advantage of using Transformers for NLP tasks compared to RNN's or their variations like LSTM and GRU is the parallelization while training.

Now that you got a basic understanding of Transformers, let us look at how they are used for NLP tasks. In the last code demo, we saw how text classification is done using RNNs. Let us do a similar exercise with BERT, which is a language model based on Transformers.

Pre-trained transformer models

There are several pre-trained models that are freely available to perform various NLP tasks. Hugging face offers some such models, which we will use and demonstrate how easy it is to use them to perform various NLP tasks. You can get more details by visiting their website:

https://huggingface.co/

This, however, needs **pytorch** environment, and since we are working with TensorFlow local environment, we will use Google Colab for these demos. In case you are keen on setting up your local PyTorch environment, you can check this link:

https://huggingface.co/course/chapter0

We need to just write a couple of lines of code to use these pre-trained models, as shown below. The code is available in the Jupyter notebook, **Transformer_Classification.ipynb**. First, we have to install transformers:

```
!pip install transformers
```

Figure 7.45: *Transformer installation*

Next import pipeline:

```
from transformers import pipeline
```

Figure 7.46: Pipeline import

The pipeline is a very powerful concept that simplifies the code drastically. As shown in the workflow diagram above, there are several pre-processing steps like tokenization and embedding that need to be performed before the text is fed to the model. All this is taken care of by the pipeline. We create an instance of the pipeline for sentiment analysis:

```
classifier = pipeline("sentiment-analysis")
```

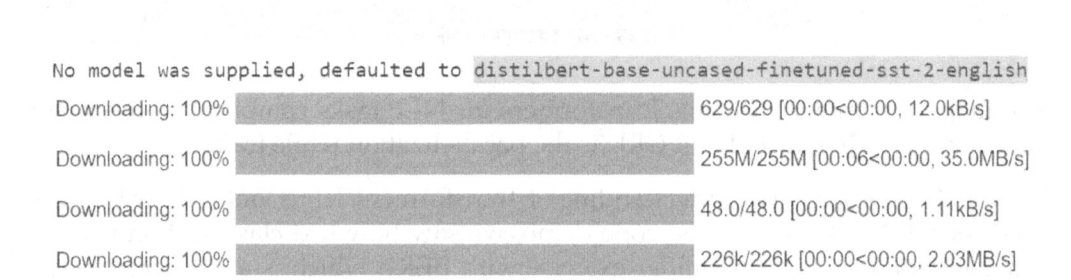

```
No model was supplied, defaulted to distilbert-base-uncased-finetuned-sst-2-english
Downloading: 100%  629/629 [00:00<00:00, 12.0kB/s]
Downloading: 100%  255M/255M [00:06<00:00, 35.0MB/s]
Downloading: 100%  48.0/48.0 [00:00<00:00, 1.11kB/s]
Downloading: 100%  226k/226k [00:00<00:00, 2.03MB/s]
```

Figure 7.47: Pipeline for sentiment analysis

When we execute this line of code, it downloads the pre-trained model and the corresponding tokenizer. In this case, we did not specify the model, so it will pick up a default model:

`distilbert-base-uncased-finetuned-sst-2-english`

Now, all we need is to use an instance of the pipeline, named classifier in this case, and pass sentence. As simple as that:

```
classifier("Huggingface is awesome!")

[{'label': 'POSITIVE', 'score': 0.9998612403869629}]

classifier("This movie is terrible")

[{'label': 'NEGATIVE', 'score': 0.9997201561927795}]
```

Figure 7.48: Classifier method

It returns the label as POSITIVE or NEGATIVE along with a score that is a measure of positivity or negativity. If the sentence has a neutral sentiment, it will still give either a positive or negative label, but the score will be much lower. You can also pass multiple sentences:

```
classifier([
    "Transformers are revolutionary for NLP",
    "RNN's have problems like vanishing gradients"
])

/usr/local/lib/python3.7/dist-packages/torch/utils/data/dataloader
  cpuset_checked))
[{'label': 'POSITIVE', 'score': 0.9971047043800354},
 {'label': 'NEGATIVE', 'score': 0.9979013204574585}]
```

Figure 7.49: Classifying two sentences

Usually, we just need the label in order to further process the results, for example, to calculate the percentage and so on. In such cases, a preferred option would be to capture the results as a list of dictionaries and process them in a loop:

```
results= classifier([
    "I love this car.",
    "I feel tired this morning.",
"I feel great this morning.",
"I do not like this car.",
"This view is horrible.",
"This view is amazing."
])
```

Figure 7.50: Classifying multiple sentences

Now we can use results for further processing:

```
positive=0
negative=0
for result in results:
    if result['label'] =='POSITIVE':
        positive=positive+1
    else:
        negative=negative+1

total=positive+negative
total

6

percentages_positive=(positive/total)*100
percentages_positive

50.0

percentages_negative=(negative/total)*100
percentages_positive

50.0
```

Figure 7.51: Overall sentiment of a passage

This demo shows how easy it is to use pre-trained models to perform NLP tasks. However, if you need to build your own classifier without using the pipeline, that is also possible. In the next demo, we will do exactly that, and it will also help us see what is going in on under the hood. We will do this using the BERT model.

BERT

BERT stands for bidirectional encoder representations from transformers. It is pre-trained on a large corpus of unlabeled text that includes the entire Wikipedia and Book Corpus (800 million words). The pre-trained BERT model just needs one additional output layer for fine-tuning to perform a variety of NLP tasks.

BERT's architecture consists of only encoders of the transformer. There are two variants of BERT models—BERT base and BERT large. BERT base has 12 layers of encoders, and BERT large has 24 layers:

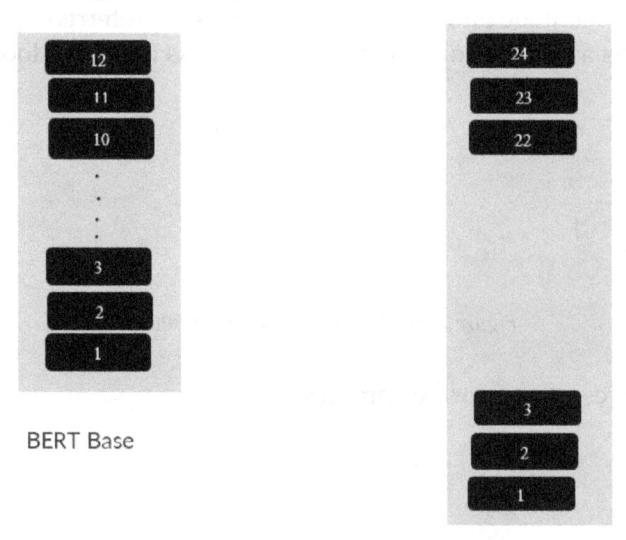

Figure 7.52: *BERT layers*

Both variants can take 512 words as input. One of the NLP tasks that BERT is used for is sentence classification. The flow is shown as follows:

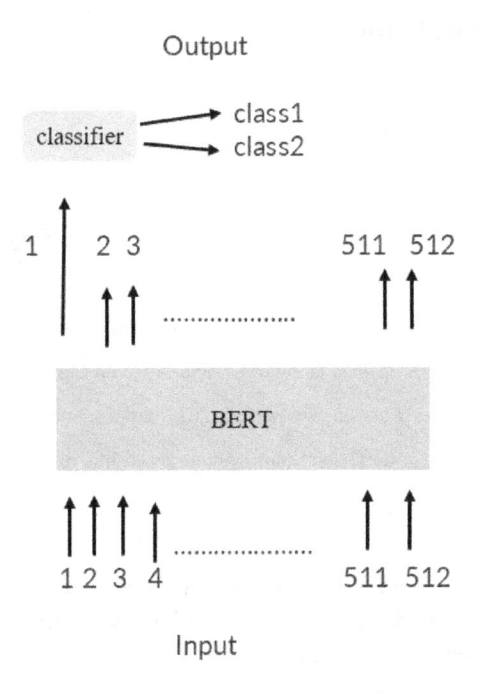

Figure 7.53: BERT for sentence classification

Let us take a look at a code demo of text classification with BERT. In this example, we will build a spam classifier for e-mails. The e-mails are exported and available in CSV format, and based on the text; they are labeled. A 1 in label indicates the e-mail is spam, and 0 indicates it is not. Use the Jupyter notebook, **BERT_email_classification.ipynb** for this demo:

```
#!pip install tensorflow-text
#!pip install tensorflow-hub
```

Figure 7.54: pip install

We will use TensorFlow-text and TensorFlow-hub. Perform a **pip install** of these libraries the first time:

```
import tensorflow as tf
import tensorflow_hub as hub
import tensorflow_text as text
import pandas as pd
```

Figure 7.55: importing TensorFlow libraries

Import all the necessary libraries:

```
#Load the data

df = pd.read_csv("spam.csv")
df.head(5)
```

	Category	Message
0	0	Go until jurong point, crazy.. Available only ...
1	0	Ok lar... Joking wif u oni...
2	1	Free entry in 2 a wkly comp to win FA Cup fina...
3	0	U dun say so early hor... U c already then say...
4	0	Nah I don't think he goes to usf, he lives aro...

Figure 7.56: Read data from CSV file

Then load the data from CSV file and inspect. As seen here, the CSV file has just two columns, Message, and Category. The Message column contains the body of the e-mail, and the category is the label, where 1 indicates this e-mail is spam and 0 means it is not.

```
from sklearn.model_selection import train_test_split

X_train, X_test, y_train, y_test = train_test_split(df['Message'],df['Category'], stratify=df['Category'])

X_train.head()
3862    Free Msg: Ringtone!From: http://tms. widelive....
4196    Double mins and txts 4 6months FREE Bluetooth ...
5353    Guai... U shd haf seen him when he's naughty.....
4537    Never blame a day in ur life. Good days give u...
3883    Short But Cute: "Be a good person, but dont tr...
Name: Message, dtype: object
```

Figure 7.57: Load data from CSV file

The CSV file has over 5500 e-mails which we split into train and test data and also separate the labels:

```
bert_preprocess = hub.KerasLayer("https://tfhub.dev/tensorflow/bert_en_uncased_preprocess/3")
bert_encoder = hub.KerasLayer("https://tfhub.dev/tensorflow/bert_en_uncased_L-12_H-768_A-12/4", trainable=True)
```

Figure 7.58: Load preprocessor and encoder

Next, we download and load the BERT models.

Before feeding the data to the model, the text needs to be processed. We have seen this in the case of RNN as well. The BERT pre-trained models above can be used for this. They both together perform pre-processing and embedding:

```
# Bert Layers
text_input = tf.keras.layers.Input(shape=(), dtype=tf.string, name='text')
preprocessed_text = bert_preprocess(text_input)
outputs = bert_encoder(preprocessed_text)
```

Figure 7.59: Download and load the BERT models

The model has two parts. The first part consists of the BERT layers, and the rest is the regular neural network layers. The output of this section is the word embeddings corresponding to the text:

```
# Regular NN Layers
l = tf.keras.layers.Dropout(0.1, name="dropout")(outputs['pooled_output'])
l = tf.keras.layers.Dense(1, activation='sigmoid', name="output")(l)


# final model
model = tf.keras.Model(inputs=[text_input], outputs = [l])
```

Figure 7.60: Build the model

This output is fed to a single neuron with a Sigmoid activation function for performing the binary classification. There is a dropout layer added to overcome overfitting:

```
model.summary()
Model: "model_1"
```

Layer (type)	Output Shape	Param #	Connected to
text (InputLayer)	[(None,)]	0	
keras_layer (KerasLayer)	{'input_word_ids': (	0	text[0][0]
keras_layer_1 (KerasLayer)	{'pooled_output': (N	109482241	keras_layer[0][0] keras_layer[0][1] keras_layer[0][2]
dropout (Dropout)	(None, 768)	0	keras_layer_1[0][13]
output (Dense)	(None, 1)	769	dropout[0][0]

```
Total params: 109,483,010
Trainable params: 109,483,009
Non-trainable params: 1
```

Figure 7.61: Model summary

From the summary of the model, it is observed that there are more than 100 million parameters:

```
model.compile(optimizer='adam',
              loss='binary_crossentropy',
              metrics=['accuracy'])
```

Figure 7.62: mode compile

The optimizer and loss function are provided as **adam** and **binary_crossentropy** in compile. With this, the model is ready for training:

```
model.fit(X_train, y_train, epochs=5)

Epoch 1/5
131/131 [==============================] - 25s 181ms/step - loss: 0.3450 - accuracy: 0.8615
Epoch 2/5
131/131 [==============================] - 24s 182ms/step - loss: 0.2509 - accuracy: 0.8894
Epoch 3/5
131/131 [==============================] - 24s 181ms/step - loss: 0.2136 - accuracy: 0.9172
Epoch 4/5
131/131 [==============================] - 24s 180ms/step - loss: 0.1872 - accuracy: 0.9296
Epoch 5/5
131/131 [==============================] - 24s 181ms/step - loss: 0.1736 - accuracy: 0.9373

<tensorflow.python.keras.callbacks.History at 0x25a2ef372e0>
```

Figure 7.63: Training

We train the model for 5 epochs. The training does take some time on a regular machine, and at the end of 5 epochs, the model achieves 93% accuracy:

```
model.evaluate(X_test, y_test)

44/44 [==============================] - 9s 182ms/step - loss: 0.1475 - accuracy: 0.9548

[0.14750021696090698, 0.9547738432884216]
```

Figure 7.64: Training 5 epochs

The model is then evaluated with test data:

```
#inference with new data

mails = [
    'You won a lottery',
    'Become a millionaire',
    'Machine learnin conference',
    'Artificial intelligence is good',
    "Why don't you wait 'til at least wednesday to see if you get your ."
]
```

```
model.predict(reviews)

array([[0.6472808 ],
       [0.7122627 ],
       [0.5710311 ],
       [0.06721176],
       [0.02479185]], dtype=float32)
```

Figure 7.65: Test data

And the last step is to run inference on the model with some completely new data using the predict method.

Machine language translation

Language translation is another important NLP task, and once again, Transformers make translation much easier. There are several pre-trained models that are available that can be used for translation. In fact, transformers were originally designed for machine translation.

Let us once again use the hugging face pipeline for translation and see how it works. As a first step, install transformers:

```
!pip install transformers[sentencepiece]
```

Figure 7.66: transformer installation

For this demo, we also need a sentence piece. Next, we import pipeline:

```
from transformers import pipeline
```

Figure 7.67: import pipeline

We can use an instance of the pipeline for translation. We can do this without specifying any model, but just by mentioning the source and target languages. It will automatically determine the module and download and load it.

For example, we can mention the translation is from English to German:

```
translator = pipeline("translation_en_to_de" )

No model was supplied, defaulted to t5-base (https://huggingface.co/t5-base)
```

Figure 7.68: Model loaded

As seen here, it automatically picked the t5-base pre-trained model. This is Google's multilanguage pre-trained transformer model:

```
translator("Have a wonderful day" )

[{'translation_text': 'Haben Sie einen wunderbaren Tag'}]
```

Figure 7.69: Translation from English to German

To cross-check this is correct, we can use Google translate:

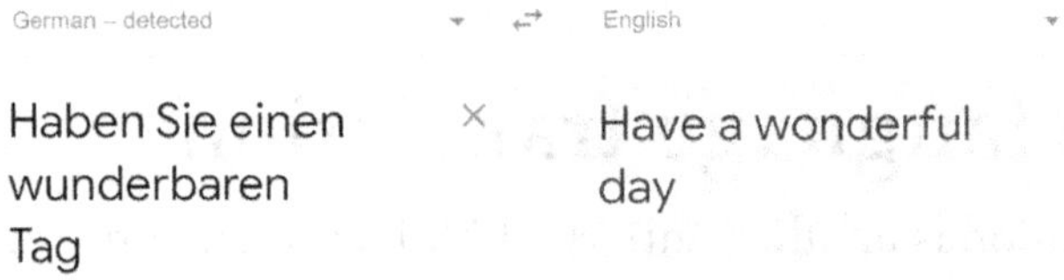

German – detected		English
Haben Sie einen wunderbaren Tag	×	Have a wonderful day

Figure 7.70: Verifying in Google translate

Alternatively, we can create a pipeline for German to English and test it:

```
translator12 = pipeline("translation", model="Helsinki-NLP/opus-mt-de-en")

translator12("Haben Sie einen wunderbaren Tag")

[{'translation_text': 'Have a wonderful day'}]
```

Figure 7.71: Pipeline for German to English

We can also try English to Hindi:

```
translator55 = pipeline("translation", model="Helsinki-NLP/opus-mt-en-hi")

translator55("How are you?")

[{'translation_text': 'आप कैसे हैं?'}]
```

Figure 7.72: Pipeline to translate English to Hindi

And Hindi to English:

```
translator56 = pipeline("translation", model="Helsinki-NLP/opus-mt-hi-en")

translator56("आप कैसे हैं?")

[{'translation_text': 'How are you?'}]
```

Figure 7.73: Pipeline to translate Hindi to English

Q&A—SQUAD

Q&A or question and answer is another common NLP task, and in this code demo, we will see how easy it is to build one using a trained BERT model. The name **SQUAD** comes from Stanford Question and Answering data set on which this model was trained. We will then fine-tune it with some additional text, and the model will be able to answer any questions related to this new text. This requires PyTorch, and to avoid the complexity of installing PyTorch; we will run this code on Google Colab.

The file name is **Bert-squad-demo.ipynb**. After uploading the notebook, make sure you also upload the text file used for a demo. To start with, a text file by the name **mohan.txt** has been provided, but you can create your own text file. Upload this text file to Google Colab before executing the code as shown in *figure 7.73*:

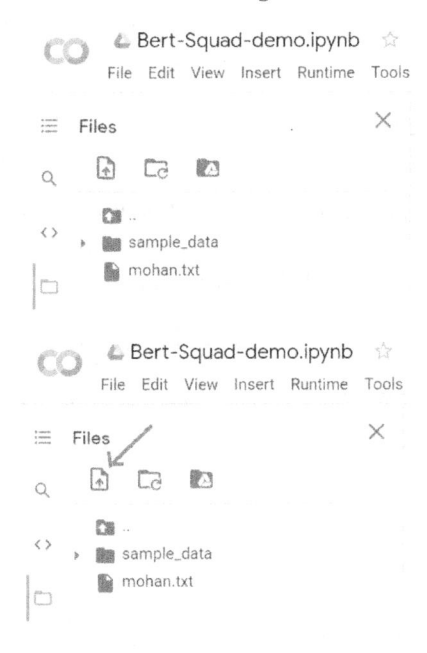

Figure 7.74: *Uploading mohan.txt in Google Colab*

As a first step, install transformers by running `pip install`:

```
!pip install transformers
Collecting transformers
  Downloading transformers-4.11.3-py3-none-any.whl (2.9 MB)
     |████████████████████████████████| 2.9 MB 5.4 MB/s
Requirement already satisfied: numpy>=1.17 in /usr/local/lib/python3.7/dist-packages (from transformers) (1.19.5)
Collecting huggingface-hub>=0.0.17
  Downloading huggingface_hub-0.0.19-py3-none-any.whl (56 kB)
     |████████████████████████████████| 56 kB 4.6 MB/s
```

Figure 7.75: *Install transformers by pip*

Import the required libraries:

```python
from transformers import BertForQuestionAnswering, AutoTokenizer
from transformers import pipeline
import textwrap
```

Figure 7.76: Import libraries

There are a couple of different pre-trained models, but we will use:
Bert-large-uncased-whole-word-masking-finetuned-squad

```python
modelname='bert-large-uncased-whole-word-masking-finetuned-squad'
model = BertForQuestionAnswering.from_pretrained(modelname)
tokenizer = AutoTokenizer.from_pretrained(modelname)
```

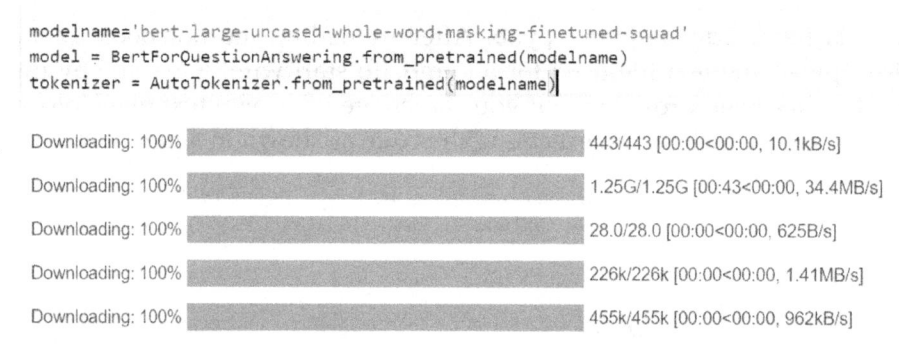

Downloading: 100%	443/443 [00:00<00:00, 10.1kB/s]
Downloading: 100%	1.25G/1.25G [00:43<00:00, 34.4MB/s]
Downloading: 100%	28.0/28.0 [00:00<00:00, 625B/s]
Downloading: 100%	226k/226k [00:00<00:00, 1.41MB/s]
Downloading: 100%	455k/455k [00:00<00:00, 962kB/s]

Figure 7.77: "Bert-large-uncased-whole-word-masking-finetuned-squad" pre-trained model

Download and load the model and the tokenizer:

```python
nlp = pipeline('question-answering', model=model, tokenizer=tokenizer)
```

Figure 7.78: Download and load of model and tokenizer

Prepare the pipeline:

```python
def QandA(question, context):
    response=nlp({
    'question': question,
    'context': context })
    print(list(response.values())[3])
```

Figure 7.79: Preparing pipeline

Create a function named Q&A, which takes the context and the question and returns the answer:

```python
# Wrap text to 80 characters.
wrapper = textwrap.TextWrapper(width=80)
strPath = "mohan.txt"
f = open(strPath)
mycontext=f.read()
```

Figure 7.80: Creating a function Q&A

Prepare the context. In this case, it is read from a text file, **mohan.txt,** which is a brief profile of a person. Let us display the context:

```
print(wrapper.fill(mycontext))
```

```
Mohan is A recognized thought leader, Mohan has been in the IT industry for
more than 30 years working for Multi-nationals like SAP and IBM . Mohan is
currently Head - Technology Programs at the Times Group.  Mohan is an organizer
of Bangalore Artificial Intelligence Meetup group consisting of more than 3500
members.   He is a Trainer / Speaker / Author in the areas of AI, Machine
Learning,Deep Learning, Tensorflow, Python, R,  Big Data, Hadoop
```

Figure 7.81: Displaying context

Now let us construct some relevant questions with reference to this context and call the function to check the response:

```
question = "how many years of experience does Mohan have?"

QandA(question, mycontext)

more than 30
```

Figure 7.82: Constructing Question 1

One more:

```
question = "which companies did Mohan work for?"

QandA(question, mycontext)

SAP and IBM
```

Figure 7.83: Constructing Question 2

And the last one:

```
question = "what are the areas of Mohan's technical expertise?"

QandA(question, mycontext)

AI, Machine Learning,Deep Learning, Tensorflow, Python, R
```

Figure 7.84: Constructing the last question

All the responses are spot on.

Conclusion

With this, we come to the end of this chapter and the book. Speech recognition and NLP will see tremendous growth in the upcoming years, and this will lead to the overall development of artificial intelligence. Voice will be used more and more in our interaction with machines and will become the main mode of the interface rather than a mouse, keyboard, or remote control.

Further reading

- Paper on transformers. Attention is all you need.

  https://proceedings.neurips.cc/paper/2017/file/3f5ee243547dee91fbd053c1c4a845aa-Paper.pdf

- Jay Alammar's blog

  https://jalammar.github.io/illustrated-transformer/

Index

A

AlphaGo 5
Anaconda command prompt
    used, for installing
        TensorFlow 2 145-148
Anaconda Navigator
    used, for installing
        TensorFlow 2 140-145
Artificial General Intelligence (AGI) 7
artificial intelligence (AI)
    about 2-4, 6
    classification 7-9
artificial intelligence (AI) industries
    automotive 15, 16
    health care 12, 13
    manufacturing 17
    retail 16, 17
    robotic surgery 14
Artificial Narrow Intelligence (ANI) 7
Artificial Neural Networks (ANN) 96
artificial neuron
    about 98
    versus biological neuron 97
Artificial Super Intelligence (ASI) 7

B

bidirectional encoder
        representations from
        transformers (BERT) 256-260
Big Data 11
binary image classification
    data, loading from data frame 197-200
    parameters 200
    with Keras 181-188

biological neuron
  components 97
  versus artificial neuron 97

C
clustering 24
CNN model
  creating 201
  summary, running 201
  training 202
constant
  about 63
  working 65, 66
Convolutional Neural Networks (CNN)
  about 152, 164, 166
  working 165
convolution layer 166-173

D
data science 9, 10
decision tree 46-48
decoder 251
Deep Blue 5
Deep Mind 5
Deep Neural Network 130
Dense Neural Network 131

E
elbow technique 50, 51
ELIZA 4
encoder 251
environment set up
  about 24
  Google Colab, using 24, 25
  local environment, setting up in Python 26

F
features 108
feature selection 42
fully connected neural network 131

G
gated recurrent unit (GRU) 250
Global Vectors (GloVe) 240
Google Colab
  about 148, 149
  using 24, 25

H
Hadoop 11

I
independent variable 34
Iris data set
  classification 158-162

K
Keras API 151-158
Keras
  using, in binary image classification 181-188
k-means clustering 48-50

L
labels 108, 109
language model 245
linear algebra
  with TensorFlow 78-85
logistic regression 44-46
long short-term memory (LSTM) 250
loss function 117

M

machine intelligence 3
machine language translation 261, 262
machine learning (ML)
  components 20
  defining 20, 21
machine learning (ML) types
  supervised learning 21
  unsupervised learning 21
maxpooling 170
model parameters 37
Modified National Institute of Standards and Technology (MNIST)
  about 119, 120, 126
  with CNN 173-180
multiclass image classification
  about 189-197
  data, loading from data frame 203-208
  model, training 208-211
multilayer binary classifier 131-135
multilayer multiclass neural network 135-137
multilayer neural network 130, 131
multilinear regression 41-43

N

Natural Language Generation (NLG) 239
Natural Language Processing (NLP)
  about 239
  components 236
Natural Language Understanding (NLU)
  about 239
  tasks 240

net input function 103-105
Neural Network
  about 96
  activation function (G) 100-102, 110-112, 118, 119
  bias 100
  inputs 99
  MNIST 119-125
  net input function (F) 100
  weights 99, 100
NLP terminologies
  document 240
  embedding 240
  text corpus 240
  token 240

O

object detection 228-230
online analytical processing systems (OLAP) 10
online transaction processing (OLTP) 10
optimizer
  about 86-91
  applying, to solve mathematical problems 92, 93

P

perceptron
  components 98
  training 106
pre-trained transformer models 253-255
placeholder
  about 63
  working 65-78
placeholder for label 102

pooling layer 170
pre-trained models
  about 212-215
  parameters 218
Python ML environment
  prerequisite 26-34
  setting up 26

Q
question and answer (Q&A) 263-265

R
Recurrent Neural Networks (RNN) 245, 246
regression algorithms 34-36
reinforcement learning 6
ReLu activation function 135
reshape 82

S
session 64, 65
shallow neural network 130
sigmoid function 100
simple linear regression
  about 34
  training 37-40
single layer multi-neuron model 126-129
single perceptron 107
Softmax activation function 113-116
Sophia 6
speech recognition
  about 234, 235
  application 235-239
supervised learning 21-23

supervised learning technique
  classification 22
  regression 22
support vector machine (SVM) 48
synthesis 236

T
tensor 61
TensorFlow
  about 59
  challenges 60, 61
  components 61
  features 59
  using, in linear algebra 78-85
TensorFlow 2
  about 149-151
  installing 140
  installing, from Anaconda command prompt 145-148
  installing, with Anaconda Navigator 140-145
TensorFlow development environment
  setting up 54-59
TensorFlow program, elements
  about 62
  constant 63
  placeholder 63
  session 64, 65
  variable 63
Term Document Frequency (TDF) 240
text classification 247-250
training process 21
transfer learning 215-223

transformers
  about 250, 252
  advantage 253

U

unlabeled data
  example 22
unsupervised learning 21, 48
unsupervised learning technique
  clustering 24

V

variable
  about 63
  working 65-68

W

Webcam images
  inference with 224-227
Word2vec 240
word embedding 240-245
World Health Organization (WHO) 13